D1806796

The Market, Happiness, and Solidarity

The past two decades of market operation has generated welfare and economic growth in Western countries, but increasing income inequalities, depletion of the natural environment and the current financial crisis have led to an intense debate about the advantages and disadvantages of the free market. With this book, Professor Graafland makes a valuable contribution to the Christian debate about the market economy. In particular, it aims to clarify the links between ethical values, Christian belief and economics, as well as informing theologians and economists about recent economic insights into market operation.

The book investigates the effect of free market operation on welfare and well-being, calling into question why one would favour more market competition as a means of increasing happiness. As well as this, Professor Graafland examines how free market competition relates to principles of justice and looks at whether it enforces or crowds out Christian virtues like love, humility and temperance.

Books that systematically link biblical teaching about the economy to recent theoretical and empirical research in economics on free market operation are rare. Most Christian books on the market system are theologically oriented, lacking a sound basis in the extensive knowledge of the recent economic literature on market operation. This book confronts Christian ethical standards with current economic literature on the effects of market operation on welfare, happiness, human rights, inequality and virtues in order to develop a well-based and balanced view of the pros and cons of market operation. This book will be of interest to both undergraduate and postgraduate students of economics, philosophy and theology.

Johan J. Graafland is Professor of Economics, Business and Ethics and director of the Center for Corporate Social Responsibility at the Faculty of Economics and Business Administration of Tilburg University, the Netherlands.

Routledge frontiers of political economy

The Market, Happiness, and Solidarity

A Christian perspective

Johan J. Graafland

Routledge
Taylor & Francis Group

LONDON AND NEW YORK

First published 2010
by Routledge
2 Park Square, Milton Park, Abingdon, Oxon OX14 4RN

Simultaneously published in the USA and Canada
by Routledge
270 Madison Avenue, New York, NY 10016

Routledge is an imprint of the Taylor & Francis Group, an informa business

© 2010 Johan J. Graafland

Typeset in Times by Wearset Ltd, Boldon, Tyne and Wear
Printed and bound in Great Britain by TJI Digital, Padstow, Cornwall

All rights reserved. No part of this book may be reprinted or reproduced or utilized in any form or by any electronic, mechanical, or other means, now known or hereafter invented, including photocopying and recording, or in any information storage or retrieval system, without permission in writing from the publishers.

British Library Cataloguing in Publication Data
A catalogue record for this book is available from the British Library

Library of Congress Cataloging in Publication Data
Graafland, J.J.
The market, happiness, and solidarity: a Christmas perspective/Johan J. Graafland.
p. cm.
Includes bibliographical references and index.
1. Economics–Religious aspects–Christianity. 2. Free enterprise–Religious aspects–Christianity. I. Title.
BR115.E3G68 2010
241'6426–dc22

2009037423

ISBN10: 0-415-56127-2 (hbk)
ISBN10: 0-203-85553-1 (ebk)

ISBN13: 978-0-415-56127-3 (hbk)
ISBN13: 978-0-203-85553-9 (ebk)

Contents

Figures

Tables

Preface

The past two decades of market operation have generated welfare and economic growth in Western countries. But increasing income inequalities, depletion of the natural environment, and the current financial crisis have caused an intense debate about the advantages and disadvantages of the free market. This calls into question why one would favor more market competition as a mean to increase well-being.

The primary aim of this book is to contribute to the Christian debate about the market economy. In particular, it aims to clarify the links between ethical values, Christian belief, and economics, and to present recent economic insights into the market in relation to three core values: welfare (happiness), justice, and virtue. For this purpose, the book researches three main questions:

1   What are the effects of the market on welfare and happiness?
2   Does the market contribute to or harm respect for human rights and distributive justice?
3   Do markets reinforce or exclude Christian virtues like love, humility, and temperance?

The book has been written for various audiences, such as: teachers and (undergraduate) students in theological faculties; teachers and (undergraduate) students in economics faculties, particularly in Christian-based universities; economists interested in the link between Christian faith and economics; policy makers in Western countries with Christian-based political parties; centers that are related to the advancement of Christians in business; global Christian networks that are focused on Business as Mission and members of the general public with an interest in the relationship between Christian faith and the (market) economy.

The book is based on a more extensive book that was published in the Netherlands in 2007 titled *Het oog van de naald. Over de markt, geluk en solidariteit* (The eye of the needle: about the market, happiness, and solidarity). American scholars encouraged me to publish an English version of this book so that a larger international audience could access its content. The themes that are discussed in the Dutch version of the book return in a more comprehensive form in this book. Some parts have been updated and benefit from ongoing research into the various themes discussed in the book.

I want to start by thanking several colleagues who made the effort to comment on some chapters of the book, first, my colleagues at the Department of Philosophy: Mandy Bosma, Wim Dubbink, Corrie Mazereeuw, and Bert van de Ven.

Second, I want to thank Theo van de Klundert for commenting on the economic sections of the book, as well as Lans Bovenberg and Bob Goudzwaard for stimulating book reviews of the Dutch version, *Het oog van de naald*. I thank Gerrit de Kruijf for his willingness to read and comment on the theological sections of the Dutch version of this book.

Third, I want to thank colleagues from Calvin College for their hospitality during my stay in Grand Rapids in December 2006, when I was preparing the Dutch version of this book, and particularly George Monsma and Shirley Roels for their assistance and personal contacts during my visit to Calvin College.

Finally, I want to thank Routledge for publication of the manuscript and two referees for useful suggestions to further improve it.

Gouda
The Netherlands

1 Introduction

1.1 Rejection of the free market: the Accra declaration

In August 2004 in Accra, Ghana, the General Council of the World Alliance of Reformed Churches (WARC) committed itself to a declaration of faith about the world economy. The declaration is a response to growing worldwide economic injustice and environmental destruction.[1] The declaration refers to the huge disparities between rich and poor. To illustrate, the annual income of the richest 1 percent is equal to that of the poorest 57 percent; 24,000 people die each day from poverty and malnutrition; the debt of poor countries continues to increase.

According to the WARC, these problems are directly related to neoliberal globalization stimulated by international finance and trade institutions such as the International Monetary Fund (IMF), World Bank, and World Trade Organization (WTO). According to the declaration, the neoliberal economic system is based on the following beliefs:[2]

- Unrestrained competition, consumerism, and the unlimited growth and accumulation of wealth are best for the whole world.
- Ownership of private property carries no social obligations.
- Capital speculation, liberalization and deregulation of the market, privatization of public utilities and national resources, unrestricted access for foreign investments and imports, lower taxes, and the unrestricted movement of capital will achieve wealth for all.
- Social obligations, protection of the poor and the weak, trade unions, and personal relationships are subordinate to the processes of economic growth and capital accumulation.

The character of the declaration is most visible where the WARC connects its analysis to biblical teaching. The declaration is very clear in its wording. It claims that the worldwide economic system enables the rich to accumulate wealth at the expense of the poor, and it regards this as unfaithfulness to God. The declaration refers to Luke 16:13, where Jesus teaches that we cannot serve both God and Mammon.

The strong condemnation of the free market system is particularly clear in the third part of the declaration that makes a statement of faith, followed by a rejection of one aspect of the free market economy. Specifically, the declaration states in articles 18 and 19:

> We believe that God is sovereign over all creation. "The earth is the Lord's and the fullness thereof" (Ps. 24:1). Therefore, we reject the current economic order imposed by global neo-liberal capitalism and any other economic system, including absolute planned economies, which defy God's covenant by excluding the poor, the vulnerable and the whole of creation from the fullness of life.

And in articles 20 and 21:

> We believe that God has made a covenant with all of creation (Gen. 9:8–12). God has brought into being an earth community based on the vision of justice and peace … Jesus shows that this is an inclusive covenant in which the poor and marginalized are preferential partners. Therefore we reject the culture of rampant consumerism and the competitive greed and selfishness of the neo-liberal global market system, or any other system, which claims there is no alternative.

The WARC states that the integrity of Christian faith can be questioned if the churches refuse to take action against the current economic system of globalization. In this it seems to endorse Duchrow's (1987) claim that the global economy is a confessional issue for the churches. The declaration therefore ends with a commitment that the churches will devote their time and energy to change, renew, and restore the economy. This is considered to be a matter of a choice for life: "so that we and our descendants might live" (Deut. 30:19).

The declaration of Accra appeals to a widespread feeling of uneasiness about the current worldwide economic order and the lack of just income distribution.[3] This feeling is shared by many people outside and inside the church. It raises the question how we can align the free market to the purpose of human life as revealed in the Word of God.

1.2 Traditional defense of the free market

The market economy or capitalism is an economic system combining the private ownership of productive enterprises with competition between them in the pursuit of profit (Chryssides and Kaler, 1993). The market is one of the most important institutions of the current national and international economic order. It is a societal phenomenon where people of flesh and blood interact when trading all kinds of goods and services. The supply of goods and services is geared to the needs and wants of purchasers by price signals. This does not necessarily mean that the market is mechanical, impersonal, or atomistic. But it does mean that the market has an important role in coordinating the demand and supply of goods and services.

The defense of the market is traditionally based on two arguments. First, it serves the value of freedom. This argument goes back to the philosophy of John

Locke (1632–1704). According to Locke, reason teaches that nobody may harm the life, health, freedom, or property of other people. Everybody has a natural right to freedom and the right to private property. The free market is based on this assumption. It assumes that the government secures private property rights and allows private agents maximum freedom in economic transactions.

The second argument is that the market and respect for private property create more wealth than any other institution (such as government planning or non-market household economy) and in this way contributes to human happiness. This argument was developed by Adam Smith (1723–1790) in his well-known book *An inquiry into the nature and causes of the wealth of nations* (1776). The market allows a high degree of labor specialization. In the first chapter of the *Wealth of nations* (*WN*) Adam Smith uses the example of a pin factory to illustrate the remarkable growth in productivity that is possible through the division of labor. If a workman makes pins on his own, he can scarcely make twenty a day. By dividing the work into eight distinct operations, a group of ten workers can make 48,000 pins a day. This division of labor is, however, only possibly if one can efficiently trade the products that specialized industries supply.

The market provides this service very efficiently because competition in the market forces prices down to the lowest level possible, encourages producers to innovate and facilitates an optimal coordination of demand and supply of goods and services. In a highly competitive market any supplier who demands a higher price than his or her competitor will lose market share. There are also dynamic efficiency gains as competition stimulates innovation. Through innovation a company gains temporary advantage over its competitors and can earn extra profit. On the macro level, this creates a dynamic growth path toward more wealth. Market competition also efficiently reallocates the resources of the economy (capital and labor) among the various industries. A decline in consumer interest in a certain product will lower the price of this product and harm the profitability of companies offering it. The companies will be forced to reallocate their means of production into an alternative and more profitable line in response to changing consumer preferences. Price variation thus provides much information about changes in consumer wants and fosters an optimal match between the demand and supply of goods and services.

According to Adam Smith, these favorable outcomes are realized without raising ethical problems. The societal advantages of market operation are possible if all economic agents are motivated only by their own self-interest. As Smith states:

> He [the businessman] generally, indeed, neither intends to promote the public interest, nor knows how much he is promoting it … he intends only his own gain, and he is in this, as in many other cases, led by an *invisible hand* to promote an end which was no part of his intention.… By pursuing his own interest he frequently promotes that of the society more effectually than when he really intends to promote it.
>
> (Smith, 1776: 351–2)

This citation refers to the famous invisible hand. Adam Smith uses this metaphor to convey the idea that if people interact freely, the pursuit of their self-interest is not incompatible with serving the common good (Peil, 1995). Although self-interested market participants seek only their own gain, the consequence of their actions is that the overall welfare increases. This is also illustrated by one of the other rare citations where Adam Smith refers to the invisible hand:

> He [the rich landlord] is led by an *invisible hand* to make nearly the same distribution of the necessaries of life which would have been made had the earth been divided into equal portions among all its inhabitants; and thus, without intending it, without knowing it, advance the interest of the society, and afford means to the multiplication of the species. When providence divided the earth among a few lordly masters, it neither forgot nor abandoned those who seemed to have been left out in the partition. These last, too, enjoy their share of all that it produces. In what constitutes the real happiness of human life, they are in no respect inferior to those who would seem so much above them.
>
> (Smith, 1759: 265)

The incentive that the market provides the rich landlord to produce contributes to an abundant supply of goods. As a result, the price of food declines and, hence, the poor can also acquire the basic goods that they need for a happy life. This is again an example of the unintended consequences of economic behavior motivated by self-interest. Without a thought for the wants of his brethren, the landlord tries to produce as much as possible. But he can consume only little more than the poor. The rest is supplied to other people (through the market mechanism). In spite of his natural selfishness and his intention to serve only his own convenience, he divides with the poor the produce of his land. A current example is the supply of second-hand computers in Western countries. Because of constant innovation, second-hand computers are so cheap that even the lowest-income groups can afford them.

1.3 The disconnection

There is a large gap between the traditional defense of the free market and the WARC declaration. What can explain this divergence?

In order to clarify the underpinnings of diverging views on the market, it is useful to distinguish differences in value orientation from differences in views about the effects of market operation. How one judges the market depends both on one's normative view on the values that the economy should serve and on one's perception of how the economy actually works and, more specifically, whether the market contributes to the realization of the values that one supports. According to Friedman (1953), most disagreements in debates on the economy originate in differences of the second kind. Scientific knowledge of the effects of markets is scarce and allows various different views. This also holds for Christian economists and policy makers. Hill (1994: 101) is not optimistic about the possibility of unifying Christian views on specific economic policies, because "we will discover that Christians have substantial differences about how the world works." For example, economists and politicians often have different expectations of a rise in minimum wages in the fight against poverty. Some believe that this will reduce poverty, because it raises the wages of the unskilled. Others expect it to increase poverty because of adverse effects on the employment of the unskilled, because employers will lay off unskilled workers whose productivity (i.e. the revenue that the employer receives from the worker's effort) is too low to finance the higher minimum wage or because competition from foreign countries means that unskilled jobs are lost if the workers are paid more.

In the debate between the defenders and critics of the free market both positive and normative aspects play a role (see Table 1.1).

1.3.1 Different perceptions of the effects of the market

A major difference between perceptions of the effects of the market concerns the incidence and persistence of market imperfections such as trade barriers and negative externalities. The anti-market approach perceives that market imperfections are highly persistent and a major cause of the main societal problems of our times: the exhaustion of the natural environment and mass poverty in Third World countries. Multinational companies have the economic power to determine the terms of trade. As a result, labor markets in developing countries still exhibit many features of the proletariat in Marxian economics. Because of their poverty, they face much higher interest rates on the capital market and therefore lack the power to acquire the means of production that they need to become

Table 1.1 Differences in views and values in the debate on the market

Differences in views on the effects of the market		Differences in value orientation	
Contra free market	*Pro free market*	*Contra free market*	*Pro free market*
Markets generate inequality	Markets generate equality by open competition	Reducing poverty has top priority	The economy should serve the goal of overall welfare
Markets generate negative externalities	Markets create mechanisms to reduce negative externalities	People have a basic right to subsistence	People have a right to be free from interference by others
Markets yield suboptimal allocation because of lack of rationality of individuals	Markets foster rationality by providing opportunities for learning	Markets should respect community bonds	Markets should respect the individuality of humans

more independent of the multinationals. Critics of the free market also argue that the market is incapable of solving environmental problems. Although innovation allows more eco-efficient production patterns, it is insufficient to counterbalance the pressure on ecological systems caused by the economic growth that markets facilitate. A third criticism concerns the efficiency of the allocation of means. In reality, people are not as rational as economics often assumes. Through manipulation of their wants, individual agents are seduced into transactions that do not serve their welfare and happiness.

Defenders of the free market like Norberg (2002) argue, however, that the free market contributes to equality in the long run, because it protects the private property of all. This is particularly relevant for the poor, because in a non-market economy that does not safeguard private property rights they are much more vulnerable than the rich and powerful. Lack of respect for private property rights limits economic opportunities and forces the poor to restrict their economic activities to the informal sector. Only the rich elite have the power and opportunities to initiate profitable modern economic activities.

Defenders of the free market also have a much more optimistic view of the relevance and persistence of negative externalities. They believe that the economic growth induced by the free market will in time change people's preferences toward a more sustainable and eco-friendly economy. As wealth increases, the market will develop incentives to reduce negative externalities. An example is the reputation mechanism that motivates companies to contribute to corporate social responsibility.

Defenders of the free market also believe that the harm of bounded rationality is limited. Because of the volume of transactions on the market, people have ample opportunity to learn from their mistakes and find out how to increase their happiness. On the supply side, competition guarantees that rationality is rewarded by business success, so that only rational companies can continue their operations in the long run.

1.3.2 Different value orientations

The churches' criticism of the free market is based not only on their critical views on the effects of market operation. They also have moral objections to the values of the market.

As discussed in section 1.2, the free market serves two important values: freedom (in the sense of protection against coercion by others) and welfare (or efficiency). The churches criticize both values. The value of welfare is criticized because fostering societal welfare does not necessarily benefit the poor. One important element in all the main Christian traditions is the "preferential option for the poor" (Santa Ana, 1977). It calls on us to put justice for the least advantaged at the center of community life. Church documents prescribe such special attention to the needs of the world's poor, because God is the defender of the poor. Respect for property rights does not guarantee that the poor receive the means of subsistence that they need to live their life in dignity. This positive right to subsistence imposes a duty on others to assist (through collective arrangements) when the poor lack subsistence. The positive right to subsistence has priority over the negative right to private property.

Another difference in value orientation concerns the relative importance of respect for the individual versus preserving community bonds. In liberal philosophy, the individual person and his or her preferences take priority over communion with other people and communal values (Anderson, 1998). The market will channel self-interest in socially beneficial directions. There is no call for devotion to the community as a whole or for self-sacrifice. One helps others by helping oneself. It is enlightened self-interest, not communitarian solidarity, which produces the best of all possible worlds.

Communitarian philosophers like Alasdair MacIntyre (1985) and Amitai Etzioni (1988) stress the social nature of the human being. The liberal notion of free-standing rational individuals is replaced by the concept of persons as members of communities that to a significant degree shape individual decisions. People define themselves in terms of ancestry, religion, language, history, values, customs, and institutions (Huntington, 1997). Only if communal relationships are good and if individuals can experience membership of the community, can they attain a good life. The community is therefore logically prior to the individual. Policy decisions should therefore be evaluated not in terms of individual preferences, but in terms of the common good. Since a good community is a critical factor, the communitarian theory stresses other values and norms than the liberal theory. In liberalism, personal autonomy, self-command, prudence, and individual development are admired. In contrast, communitarian philosophers are more concerned about values and virtues that enhance communal relationships and relations of care.

Christian ethics combines liberal values and communitarian notions (Graafland, 2007a, 2007b). It respects people's individuality and impartiality. But Christian ethics also features many communitarian characteristics. The agency of individuals, although preeminently personal, is always also understood as relational. The moral agency of individuals is significantly formed through participation in communities (Atherton, 2008). Each individual is called to be part of the Christian community and to sustain it by his or her personal capacities (Loonstra, 2000). Furthermore, stewardship and personal calling are in line with the importance of virtues and care. The character that is formed through participation in communities generates and nurtures virtues that are necessary to connect human life to God's purposes. The focus is not solely on doing Christian deeds, but also on being a Christian.

1.4 Methodology of this book

In this book I want to contribute to the Christian debate on the market economy. For this purpose, I will evaluate the market from three perspectives: welfare, justice, and virtue (see Figure 1.1). This corresponds to the three different value orientations discussed above. Each of these concepts represents a major ethical

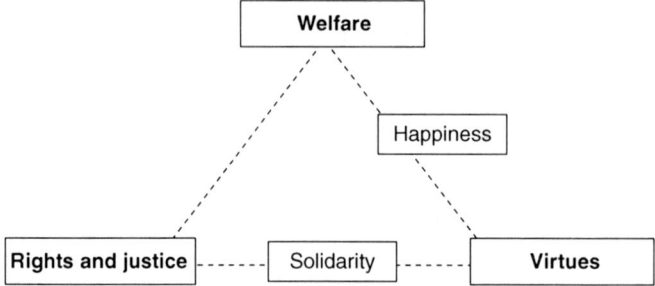

Figure 1.1 Evaluation of the market from three perspectives.

standard, namely utilitarianism, justice ethics, and virtue ethics. The book thus researches three main questions.

The first question concerns the effect of the market on welfare and happiness. One of the main arguments in favor of markets is that they create welfare. That markets foster the welfare of society has not been proven theoretically and should be decided by empirical research. Research shows that wealth has only modest effects on happiness. Since market competition may harm other values that have proven to have a substantial impact on happiness, the overall effect of the market on happiness is unclear.

The second theme is how the market relates to principles of justice. In the Accra declaration the WARC condemns neoliberal globalization on the grounds of injustice. Still, many churches think that the declaration lacks a nuanced view on the causes of worldwide poverty and the role of globalization. To contribute to this debate, I want to investigate two claims underpinning the Accra declaration: the theological statement that poverty is unjust; and the empirical statement that the free market system benefits the rich at the expense of the poor and causes extreme poverty. For this purpose, I first investigate which concepts of (distributive) justice are supported by biblical texts. Next, I turn to empirical evidence that free markets increase poverty and inequality within countries and between countries.

Christian ethics is not only about applying certain principles such as those of distributive justice. It is also very much concerned with character formation or virtue. Market competition is often accused of stimulating vices like greed, envy, and materialism. The third question therefore considers whether a free market strengthens or excludes Christian virtues like love, humility, and temperance. The debate on the influence of markets on virtue has focused on two opposite hypotheses: the doux commerce thesis and the self-destruction thesis. Whereas the doux commerce hypothesis assumes that capitalism polishes human manners, the self-destruction hypothesis holds that capitalism erodes the moral foundation of society. In this book we research for which type of Christian virtues the doux commerce or self-destruction thesis is likely to hold.

In the title of the book – *The Market, Happiness, and Solidarity* – these three perspectives have been incorporated into two concepts: happiness and solidarity.

The concept of happiness is central not only in utilitarianism, but also in virtue ethics. In both ethical approaches, the goal of human life is happiness. Solidarity is chosen as the linking concept between justice and virtue. According to Verstraeten (2005), justice is one of the poles of solidarity because solidarity requires that the positive rights to subsistence be met. Another pole of solidarity is charity, which is connected to the virtue of love.

The method that I apply to connect Christian faith to economics is reflected in Figure 1.2. The link between Christian faith and economics is ethics. Secular ethics has developed all kinds of conceptual distinctions that were not explicitly recognized by the biblical writers, but are still very useful in linking biblical principles to the modern economy. First, I provide a short overview of some of these standards. As already noted, I consider three basic types of ethical standards: aggregate welfare, justice, and virtue. Detailed knowledge of ethical standards not only allows a new perspective on biblical economic ethics, but also contributes to the implementation of biblical economic notions on the current economic order. Authoritative texts in the Bible cannot always be directly implemented in economic reality nowadays. One needs to translate to a higher level of abstraction, the level of ethical principles. Second, each of these standards is confronted with Christian ethical notions. For that purpose, I will investigate which standards are supported by biblical texts. This provides us with a Christian view on welfare, justice, and virtue. Third, I provide an overview of current economic knowledge of the influence of the market on overall welfare, justice, and virtue. As argued by Atherton (2008), such a connection of ethics and theology with economic literature is necessary to prevent economic illiteracy. Books that systematically link biblical teaching on the economy with recent theoretical and empirical research on the free market are rare. Most Christian books on the market system are theologically oriented, lacking a sound basis in the recent economic literature on the market. In this book I confront Christian ethical standards with current economic literature on the effects of the market on welfare, happiness, human rights, inequality, and virtue in order to develop a well-based and balanced view of the pros and cons of the market.

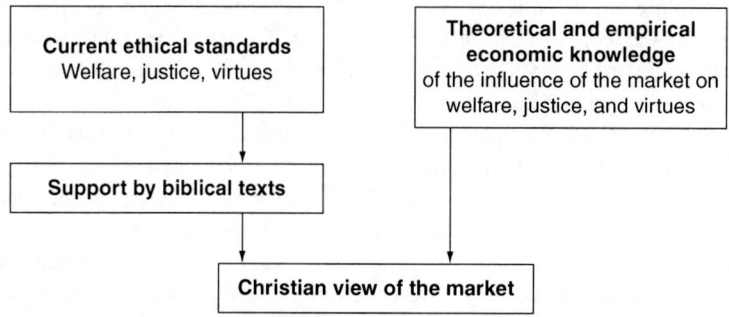

Figure 1.2 Method: ethics, Bible, and economics.

By combining normative Christian standards and economic knowledge of the effects of market operation on these standards I derive a Christian view of the market.

1.4.1 What is Christian ethics?

Ethics is the study of morality. Morality concerns the standards that an individual or a group holds about what is right and what is wrong (Velasquez, 1998: 8). It is a rational reflection on human life from a moral point of view. Moral standards refer to what people should do or ought to do, not to what people actually do.

Christian ethics also reflects on the standards of right and wrong, but does so from the perspective of Jesus Christ's revelation of good and evil (Kruijf, 1999). While the domain is the same as in secular ethics, Christian ethics develops its standards from a commitment to the belief that good and evil are revealed in the Bible. In Christian ethics, Christians seek to understand which principles of behavior are in accordance with the will of God, as expressed in Romans 12:2:

> Do not conform yourselves to the standards of this world, but let God transform you inwardly by a complete change of your mind. Then you will be able to know the will of God – what is good and pleasing to him and is perfect.

One may wonder whether fallible people are really able to know God's will in economic life. Still, Christians should not let go the intention to be guided by the will of God for this earthly reality (Manenschijn, 1982).

1.4.2 Use of the Bible

In this book I will not focus on church traditions but rather derive Christian notions of welfare, justice, and virtue from the biblical texts that have been important to Christian writings on economy.[4] The moral intuitions that underlie Christian analyses often go back to the Bible. Biblical texts are often relevant to daily economic reality and provide inspiration to rethink standard views critically. Biblical texts and stories also often provide Christians with the motivation to change reality. They often have more authority than theories that have been developed in Christian ethics.

Many texts in the Bible deal with economic affairs, such as production, consumption, and distribution of goods and services. The Bible speaks so abundantly about economic affairs that Meeks (1989) uses the term "economist" to describe the character and work of God. Of course, the Bible is not a handbook of economics (Gorringe, 1994) and it does not provide solutions for today's economic problems, which are very different from those of the agricultural economy in the days when the Bible was written. Neither does the Bible present an economic system that could serve as an alternative to the free market. The Bible is about the Word of God, about the revelation of God about Himself and about humans. When using biblical texts to link Christian faith to economics, I will therefore refer not to concrete economic issues, but rather to the more fundamental principles that are relevant for the economic order and provide a justification for modern ethical standards (Wolterstorff, 1987; Solomon, 1997; Monsma, 1999).

1.4.3 Diversity in the Bible

Like church documents on the economy, the Bible presents several traditions with diverging views on economic principles, such as the Tora, the prophetic traditions and the wisdom writings. According to Wolterstorff (1987), different interpretations of the implications of Bible texts for current economic life revert to four types of disagreement as to:

1   what the Bible actually says;
2   what is authoritative for us in what the Bible says;
3   which social ethic is most faithful to what is authoritative for us in what the Bible says;
4   which specific moral imperatives ought to be followed in the light of the economic facts and of the social ethic that is most faithful to what is authoritative for us in what the Bible says.

According to Wolterstorff, the first type of disagreement is not very pressing in Christian debates about markets. Relatively few disagreements among Christians on economic matters are grounded in such disagreements over the interpretation of biblical texts. Although one can differ over the details of the texts or the situational background to which they applied, the general intent of most passages that refer to economic practices is quite clear. Possible exceptions are certain passages about poverty and the discussion as to whether these texts refer to spiritual poverty or economic poverty. More generally, there is room for different interpretations of texts that have a predominantly spiritual focus. In that case, one can question whether the normative principles that are supported by these texts can also be applied to daily economic life. Take, for example, the parable of the three servants, which Jesus uses as an illustration for the Kingdom of Heaven. Can we understand from this parable that the principle of moral deserts also holds for economic affairs here and now? In my approach I assume we can. I cannot think of sufficient reasons why principles of fairness that apply to the Kingdom of God should not apply to our current economic reality. Jesus himself linked daily economic behavior to spiritual life, as in Matthew 6:4.

The second type of disagreement seems more relevant. Take, for instance, the prophecy of Amos. Although the exegesis of Amos' protests against the oppression of the poor by the rich is rather uniform, one can still debate how relevant these protests are compared to other texts in the Bible. Are Old Testament guidelines still valid? In this respect I follow Calvin who considered that the whole

Bible is inspired by the Holy Spirit and that various parts of the Bible are interdependent. Calvin acknowledges that biblical texts sometimes show significant differences. Where that is the case he advises that the most elaborated texts should be chosen. So he uses the Scripture to explain the Scripture. This does not exclude the possibility that people have experienced God in their specific situation in a way that differs from how others have experienced Him. If God speaks to humans, He does so in a context that is understandable and relevant to them. The accents of the revelation can differ at different times and in different places. When interpreting the differences in Bible texts, one should therefore pay sufficient attention to the context so as to discern the elements they have in common.

A certain tension between various traditions in the Bible and the ethical norms that can be derived from them is even desirable, because the reality of life is so complex and varied that only a polar system of ethics can guide us. Wogaman (1993) advises that in cases of conflict, both sides have to be taken into account. He gives several examples. One is the tension between egalitarian traditions and Bible texts that accept a high degree of inequality. Stories of the patriarchs in Genesis treat their relative material wealth with deference. The Bible does not condemn their wealth. Rather, it is portrayed as a blessing of God. And in the New Testament wealthy people like Joseph of Arimathea are portrayed in an altogether favorable light. Yet the prophetic tradition (but also the New Testament) emphasize to a remarkable degree the theme of equality. The Hebrew prophets sharply condemn various forms of oppression of the poor by the rich. Both types of text are relevant in the context in which they were written and must be taken into account when judging the fairness of the present-day economic order.

The third type of disagreement distinguished by Wolterstorff makes us aware that authoritative texts in the Bible cannot always be directly implemented in economic reality nowadays. One needs to translate them to a higher level of abstraction, the level of ethical principles. In this book I take secular ethical standards as a starting point. Secular ethics have developed all kinds of standards that are very useful in linking biblical principles to the modern economy. Secular ethics and Christian ethics more often resemble than contradict each other, partly because secular ethics has been influenced by Christian ethics and vice versa. However, notwithstanding the many similarities between secular and Christian standards, Christian ethics provides a particular combination of ethical principles that differs both in their emphases and their foundation from secular ethics. One therefore needs to test the validity of secular standards by relating them to fundamental Christian values and norms.

Wolterstorff's fourth point stresses that a Christian view on economic order should be informed by knowledge of economic facts as well as Christian values. In the structure of the book this notion is explicitly taken into account, since each chapter elaborates on the economic knowledge of the influence of markets on welfare, justice, and virtue.

1.5 Contents of the book

The contents of this book are summarized in Table 1.2. The structure reflects the methodology of the book.

Chapter 2 evaluates the market from the perspective of aggregate welfare.[5] Section 2.1 starts with the ethical theory of utilitarianism. The standard of evaluation in utilitarianism is total welfare or, in the words of Jeremy Bentham, the greatest happiness of the greatest number. Next, in section 2.2, I investigate Bible texts on welfare. In particular, I focus on the relationship between richness and happiness and between poverty and happiness, and derive a Christian normative view on economic welfare. Section 2.3 researches the recent economic literature about how the market affects economic growth and how economic growth affects happiness. Section 2.4 then derives a Christian view on markets from the perspective of welfare.

Chapter 3 evaluates the market from the perspective of justice. Section 3.1 presents theories of mainstream rights and justice ethics, including utilitarianism which also has distributive implications. I compare these with other distributional ethical (mostly deontological) standards, such as John Rawls' difference principle. Section 3.2 then discusses to what extent the Bible supports the various approaches. Section 3.3 reviews recent economic literature on the relationship between the market and justice. Section 3.4 then derives a Christian view on markets from the perspective of human rights and distributive justice.

Chapter 4 reflects on the market by discussing its contribution to the development of a good personal character. If people are subject to competition, will that make them more virtuous or will it stimulate vices, such as egotism, envy, and materialism? Section 4.1 starts with a description of Aristotle's classical ethics of virtue. Section 4.2 compares classical virtue ethics with virtues in the Bible and takes stock of the similarities and the differences. This provides us with a Christian view on virtue. Section 4.3 gives an overview of recent economic literature on the impact of the market on virtues and vices. Section 4.4 then brings together the Christian view on virtue and economic knowledge of the empirical relationship between the market and virtue and derives a Christian view.

Chapters 2–4 develop a Christian view on the market from three distinct perspectives. But how do these three perspectives relate to each other? Which one

Table 1.2 The structure of the book

Markets and	Chapter 2	Chapter 3	Chapter 4
	Welfare	Justice	Virtues
Ethical standards	2.1	3.1	4.1
Biblical standards	2.2	3.2	4.2
Economic knowledge	2.3	3.3	4.3
Christian view	2.4	3.4	4.4

should have priority if the different perspectives yield different conclusions about the market? This is the subject of the final chapter that integrates the three views into an overall vista on the market operation and illustrates its relevance through an analysis of the credit crisis. I present a practical method of balancing the different values – welfare, justice, and virtue – so as to evaluate concrete proposals of institutional economic reforms. I illustrate this method by a case study of a flat income tax system.

2 The market and welfare

As discussed in Chapter 1, one of the main arguments in favor of markets is the creation of wealth and welfare. Free markets stimulate human beings to exploit their talents and motivate them to economic activities that are favorable to the happiness of all. However, that markets foster the welfare of society has not been proven theoretically. Welfare theory has only proven that perfect markets are efficient in the sense of Pareto optimality (see below). Whether free market operation fosters overall welfare should be decided by empirical research.

The ethical theory that takes overall welfare (or utility or happiness) as its standard is utilitarianism. In this chapter we first describe utilitarianism in section 2.1. The basic principle of utilitarianism is "the greatest happiness of the greatest number." Or, more formally, an act is right if and only if the sum total of utilities produced by that act is greater than the sum total of utilities produced by any other act the agent could have performed in its place (Velasquez 1998: 73). Recent improvements in measuring happiness have increased the popularity of utilitarianism among economists. According to Layard (2003: 50), utilitarianism is the only ethical standard that provides an overarching principle by which to solve conflicts between principles.

Section 2.2 investigates the biblical view on welfare. For the subject of this book, the valuation of material welfare is particularly important. Most attention will therefore be paid to the question of whether economic welfare contributes to human happiness according to the Bible. Finally, we also briefly discuss the concept of stewardship in relationship to environmental sustainability (as a related source of human welfare).

Section 2.3 considers the empirical evidence of the influence of the market operation on wealth, sustainability, and happiness. We evaluate the contribution of markets to welfare in three steps. First, we discuss empirical evidence of the thesis that the market generates wealth by reviewing some economic literature on the impact of various parameters of market operation on economic growth, such as the rule of law index, the index of economic freedom, and the share of trade. Next, we present various reasons why economic growth does not necessarily lead to a reduction in scarcity. This provides a background for the next section that deals with the relationship between wealth and happiness. As in section 2.2, we focus on the impact of economic welfare on overall happiness, but we will also discuss non-material factors that influence human happiness.

Section 2.4 puts the normative and positive perspectives together and formulates a Christian view on the market, economic growth, and welfare.

2.1 Utilitarianism

2.1.1 Introduction

Utilitarianism has great practical value. Economic policy bureaus increasingly use practical applications of utilitarianism (by cost benefit analysis) to evaluate policy options.

Still, utilitarianism is also subject to serious moral criticism, some of which are particularly relevant from a Christian point of view. After the description of the basic characteristics of utilitarianism, we therefore also discuss several criticisms of this ethical standard.

2.1.2 Characteristics of utilitarianism

Utilitarianism essentially combines three elementary requirements: consequentialism, welfarism, and sum ranking (Sen, 1987).

Consequentialism asserts that actions, choices, or policies must be morally judged exclusively in terms of the resulting, or consequent, effects, rather than by any intrinsic features they may have.

Welfarism is the answer to the question: What are good consequences? It requires that the goodness of a state of affairs be a function only of the utility or welfare obtained by individuals in that state. But what is welfare? In this respect, there are different varieties of utilitarianism (Beauchamp, 1982). Some take welfare to be a mental state, like happiness or pleasure. This so-called hedonism is defended by Jeremy Bentham, who claimed that pleasure is a kind of sensation. Since all pleasures and all pains are structurally similar sensations, it should be possible to calculate a net total sum of utility.[1] Thus, Bentham applies a monistic concept of utility by assuming that all values can be measured on the same scale of pleasure (and pain). The other major exponent of utilitarianism, John Stuart Mill (1871), also believed pleasure and prevention of pain to be the only desirable ends, but he distinguished higher and lower pleasures and argued that higher pleasures are qualitatively different from lower pleasures. Economists try to avoid taking a position in this philosophical debate by arguing that any assessment of individual welfare should be based on a person's own judgment, because it is difficult and perhaps impossible to determine objectively the value of an outcome. Utility should instead be equated to the satisfaction of individuals' actual preferences. What is intrinsically valuable for an individual is that which each individual actually prefers to obtain.

The third and most decisive characteristic of utilitarianism is sum ranking. Sum ranking means that the effects of an action on the utilities of all who are affected by it must be aggregated and ranked numerically. Utilitarianism then requires that one should do whatever maximizes the total sum of utilities. For income distribution, this implies that the marginal utility of income should be equal for all individuals.

2.1.3 Utilitarianism and economic welfare theory

In economic welfare theory, economists apply Pareto optimality rather than utilitarianism as a moral standard. Pareto optimality is aligned to utilitarianism, but differs in one crucial aspect. In particular, whereas Pareto optimality endorses consequentialism and welfarism, it rejects sum ranking. Pareto optimality means that a situation is optimal if no further Pareto improvement is possible. A measure generates a Pareto improvement if it makes one person or more in society better off without making anyone worse off. Hence, application of the standard of Pareto optimality does not require comparison of interpersonal utility.

Welfare theory has based an important theorem on the Pareto criterion (Hausman, 1992). This so-called (first) welfare theorem shows that any perfectly competitive market equilibrium is Pareto optimal. This provides a theoretical defense for the market. However, this result is not very useful from an ethical point of view, because Pareto optimality is very biased to the status quo, even if it exhibits huge inequalities. Thus an outcome that has some people in extreme misery and others wallowing in luxury can be Pareto optimal, provided that the miserable cannot be made better off without reducing the luxury of the rich.[2]

In order to solve the limited applicability of the Pareto principle in practical policy decisions, Kaldor and Hicks extended it by the so-called compensation test. This means that any measure is allowed if those who benefit from it still benefit from it even after fully compensating those who are harmed by it. These benefits and harms can be calculated by asking the winners how much they would like to pay for a certain policy and asking the losers how much compensation they would like to receive. This allows cost benefit analysis, whereby all these so-called *willingness to pay* prices can be added together to identify the best policy that yields the highest total net benefits. This test reintroduces a kind of interpersonal utility comparison, however, because it compares the prices different individuals are willing to pay for a certain measure. Cost benefit analysis is therefore often viewed as the practical way to implement utilitarianism. This brings us back to utilitarianism.

2.1.4 Criticisms of utilitarianism

Utilitarianism and cost benefit analysis are vulnerable to several serious criticisms, which can be categorized according to the three characteristics of utilitarianism mentioned above. Table 2.1 presents an overview.

A first criticism of consequentialism is that it does not consider the intentions of a person performing an act, only the consequences of the act. The importance

Table 2.1 Problems of utilitarianism

Consequentialism	Welfarism		Sum ranking
	(all variants)	(Economist variant)	
No consideration of intentions	Well-being is not the only valuable thing; it disregards agency	Immoral preferences	No distributive justice
Disregards retributive justice	Problem of incommensurability	Non-rational preferences	How to discount the utility of future generations or non-human beings?
Consequences are difficult to predict	No intrinsic value of rights	No community valuation	Over-demandingness

Source: adapted version of Graafland (2007a: Table 7.1).

of intentions is expressed in several texts in the Bible (Phil. 2:5). The punishment for harming others depends on the intention of the person who caused the harm (Exod. 22:1; Deut. 19:11–13). The moral value of intention is also stressed in Jesus' condemnation of the Pharisees (Matt. 23:23). Giving money with a wrong intention has no value for God. From this point of view, one can criticize the market because it legitimizes self-interested intentions. Positive effects on total welfare are non-intended and therefore the moral value is questionable. A second problem is that consequentialism is unrelated to considerations of retributive justice; that is, the just imposition of punishments upon those who do wrong. In a utilitarian framework, the entire focus will be on the consequences of punishment. Will it deter the wrongdoer from harming in the future? But the question of whether the wrongdoer deserves to pay compensation for the harm done to others will not be taken into account. A third problem is that the consequences of an action, and hence the costs and benefits it generates, are difficult to predict and are subject to different degrees of uncertainty. This diminishes the value of utilitarianism as an ethical standard compared to other, more deontological ethical standards.

Utilitarianism can also be criticized because of the problems resulting from considering welfare as the only type of good consequence. The first problem with welfarism is that welfare or happiness is not the only relevant factor in an evaluation of an action or policy. Utility is, at best, a reflection of a person's well-being, but personal success cannot be judged exclusively in terms of personal well-being (Sen, 1987). In addition, the Bible shows that suffering is sometimes better than satisfying personal wants (Matt. 10:39). A welfarist calculus that concentrates only on the well-being of a person loses something of real importance. A second fundamental criticism is that welfarism assumes that different values are reducible to one basic value, namely utility. Values are, however, often incommensurable and pluralistic in nature, relating to several generic goods rather than only to a single one (Anderson, 1993). Kant famously proclaimed that rational human beings have dignity and that whatever has dignity is "above all price, and therefore admits of no equivalent" (Kant, 1997: 435). A third criticism is that the utilitarian approach views rights merely as instrumental to achieving utilities. No intrinsic importance is attached to the fulfillment of rights. Utilitarianism can therefore imply that certain actions are morally acceptable when in fact they violate people's rights.

Besides these fundamental criticisms of welfarism in general, some additional types of criticism apply especially to the economist's variant of welfarism that equates welfare with the satisfaction of the actual preferences of individuals. First, individuals may have morally unacceptable preferences (Beauchamp, 1982). This is particularly relevant for Christian ethics, because the Bible acknowledges that human nature is sinful and is therefore often very critical of human preferences. Second, relying on actual preferences assumes that individuals are rational in the sense that satisfaction of their preferences maximizes their well-being. Rationality is a rather strong assumption (Etzioni, 1988; Conlisk, 1996; Rabin, 1998). People may want something that is bad for them through ignorance or false beliefs (Hausman and McPherson, 1996). Some people only want things precisely because they cannot have them (Schwartz, 2004). Moreover, other parties can manipulate people's preferences (for example, by advertisements) (Hausman, 1992). Third, one may doubt whether satisfaction of individual preferences should be the sole base for evaluating social welfare. In Christian ethics communitarian values are equally important. Whether moral rules serve the community well or ill is a critical factor in their acceptability. This may go against individual preferences. Therefore, one cannot take individuals' utility functions as the sole basis of evaluation.

The right-hand column of Table 2.1 lists some moral problems associated with the third characteristic of utilitarianism, sum ranking. A first criticism of sum ranking is that it may result in injustice and override the interests of minorities. In utilitarianism, a distribution is only just if it maximizes total utility. Problems with distribution also emerge if the utility of future generations or non-human beings is affected. Utilitarians often give less weight to the interests of future generations by applying a discount factor, but provide no basis for determining the value of this factor. The interests of non-human beings may also be given a lower weight than the interests of human beings, but again utilitarianism cannot provide a satisfactory answer to the question of what this weight should be. In Christian ethics the life of animals and other parts of creation have an intrinsic value, independent of their value for humans. These issues of fairness cannot be justified in utilitarian terms (Hausman and McPherson, 1996). A final problem of sum ranking is over-demandingness. Utilitarianism requires that, other things being equal, a certain utility should have the same value for me whether it is to be experienced by me, a friend or a relative of mine, or a complete stranger. Because of its impartiality, utilitarianism may become very demanding, especially in the non-ideal situation where most people fail to live up to the moral duties implied by it (Crisp, 1998). In order to reduce the problem of over-demandingness, Scheffler (1994), for example, proposed that each agent should be allowed to give a higher weight to his or her own interests than to those of others. However, utilitarianism provides no procedure for determining the exact level of this weight.

2.1.5 Conclusion

These moral objections show that utilitarianism does not give a fully satisfactory theoretical account of our moral intuitions. Still, as long as one is aware of this criticism, it has several practical advantages. It is consistent with the value of efficiency and is in harmony with the way policy makers often make decisions, by looking at the beneficial and harmful consequences of a particular act. It also stimulates decision makers to conduct a systematic overview of the benefits and costs of an act.

Nevertheless, from a Christian ethical point of view, one should add other ethical standards that put absolute side-constraints on utilitarianism in order to secure fairness. These other ethical standards will be described in Chapters 3 and 4. In Chapter 5 I propose a lexicographic weighting procedure that balances the various ethical standards.

2.2 Wealth, poverty, and welfare in the Bible

The market is often legitimized because of its positive consequences on wealth and, through that, on human happiness. But is wealth creation or human happiness a legitimate or even dominant goal from a Christian point of view? According to John Stuart Mill it is. He defends happiness as a general goal of human life by arguing that according to Christian faith God wants people to be happy. Some texts in the Bible indeed argue in a consequentialist way that obeying the law of God will result in a long and happy life (Deut. 4:40, 5:16).

But to what extent is happiness in the Bible related to economic welfare? Does economic growth contribute to human well-being? In order to answer this question, this section reviews some biblical notions with respect to poverty, wealth, and stewardship. We close this section by developing the thesis that moderate scarcity is consistent with Christian economic ethics.

2.2.1 Scarcity and sin

Genesis 1 sketches a picture of a paradise without scarcity (Carter, 2005). When God looked at everything He made, He was very pleased. He provided man with all kinds of grain and fruit and the wild animals and birds with grass and leafy plants. Notwithstanding the abundance of means, man had to work, to cultivate and guard the garden of Eden. One can therefore characterize paradise as a situation of moderate scarcity.

Scarcity only became tragic and threatening after the disobedience of man. The scarcity in Genesis 3:17–19 expresses the curse that befell the earth after human sin. This type of scarcity therefore has a negative connotation in the Bible. By a deed of consumption sin entered the world and this resulted in a situation of absolute scarcity. Labor became toilsome and frustrating. Humans would have to work all their lives to make the ground produce enough food. Life was barely more than a struggle for survival (Jongeneel, 1996).

2.2.2 Valuation of poverty

That scarcity is negatively valued is also apparent from the way the Bible speaks of poverty. In the Hebrew language various words are used for poverty. The most common (particular in the Psalms and prophets) is *ani*, derived from *anah* that originally means "bent," "depressed," or "humiliated." Although this word is also used to describe sick people, the sorrow of the *ani* mostly concerns economic poverty.

Stott (1990) classifies the various terms for poverty into three categories. The first group comprises the economically deprived. They lack food or clothing or shelter or all three. The second group comprises the socially or politically oppressed. Often, the two groups coincide because lack of power goes together with lack of economic means. The third group comprises the spiritually meek. They are dependent on God. They look to Him for mercy. Oppressed by men and helpless to liberate themselves, they put their trust in God. This group is also known as the pious. Again, there is often a correlation with the other concepts of poverty. Because of this, the various meanings of poverty often refer to the same group of people.

In the Old Testament economic poverty is considered woeful. There is no sign that ascetism is a pious ideal. There should be no poverty in Israel (Deut. 15:4). Poverty leads to great material and social misery. Poor people are not respected by others, no one pays any attention to what they say or think (Eccl. 9:16). They are despised and often lack the support of friends. Even their neighbors do not like the poor. No matter how hard they try, they cannot make friends (Prov. 14:20, 19:7). The poor become socially isolated (Prov. 19:4). They have little rest and continuously have to put all their energy into their and their family's survival. They have to fear the loss of their children because at any time creditors could come and take them away as slaves. The poor man himself could be sold into slavery, even if he is unable to pay back a pair of sandals (Amos 2:6). Because of this deplorable state, Ecclesiastes considered the dead to be better off than those who are poor and still living (Eccl. 4:2).

In the New Testament poverty is again presented as a deplorable state that should be avoided. Jesus teaches his disciples to pray for their daily bread (Matt. 6:11). The bread symbolizes all we need for the sustenance of family life, such as food, clothing, and shelter. Another example is the beatitude "Happy are you who are hungry now; you will be filled" (Luke 6:21). We already see this come true in the care of the first Christian congregation in Jerusalem:"There was no one in the group who was in need ... the money was distributed to each one according to his need" (Acts 4:34–5).

2.2.3 *Wealth and happiness*

The Bible leaves no doubt that the reduction of absolute poverty increases human happiness. But does this mean that the constant accumulation of wealth will also contribute to happiness? How does the Bible value wealth?

Here the biblical valuation is more mixed. On the one hand, wealth is valued positively. An example is Abraham, who was very rich (partly because of the gifts he received from the Pharaoh after presenting his wife Sarah as his sister, although this was not the major cause of his wealth). Abraham is not criticized for his wealth. Rather, his property of flocks of sheep and goats, cattle, silver, gold, slaves, camels, and donkeys is described as a blessing from God (Gen. 24:34). This wealth shows the overflowing beneficence of election by God (Haan, 1985) and is a sign of the richness of the heavenly kingdom.

The wisdom writers also appreciate wealth. Entrepreneurship is approved. Ecclesiastes advises that money should be invested in foreign trade. In order to minimize the risk, investments should be made in several places, because you never know what kind of bad luck you may have (Eccl. 11:1–6). The enjoyment of riches is likewise encouraged. Ecclesiastes invites its readers to consciously enjoy the goods that God gives:"So I realized then that the best thing we can do is to enjoy what we have worked for" (Eccl. 3:22). The author is so convinced of the importance of enjoying life that he repeats this message several times:

> This is what I have found out: the best thing anyone can do is to eat and drink and enjoy what he has worked for during the short life that God has given him. If God gives a man wealth and property and lets him enjoy them, he should be grateful and enjoy what he has worked for. It is a gift from God. Since God has allowed him to be happy, he will not worry too much about how short life is.
>
> (Eccl. 5:18–20; see also Eccl. 8:15, 9:7vv.)

The New Testament also gives a positive value to the enjoyment that wealth gives. In the parable of the good shepherd Jesus says that he has come in order that the people may have life in all its fullness (John 10:10). Already, during his first public appearance at the wedding at Cana Jesus satisfies the needs of the partygoers by changing water into wine. He eat with the rich and is apparently so fond of feasting that his enemies accuse him of being a glutton and drinker (Matt. 11:19). And when he talks about the Kingdom of God, he often uses the metaphor of a feast, where enjoyment and abundance will rule (Luke 14:16–24, 15:11–24). The miraculous feeding of the five thousand also expresses the abundance that will be present in the Kingdom of God: "Everyone ate and had enough. Then the disciples took up twelve baskets full of what was left over" (Matt. 14:20). The apostle Paul does not preach ascetics either. He fights those who want to forbid marriage and the enjoyment of food. And he encourages Timothy to drink a glass of wine because "everything that God has created is good, nothing is to be rejected but everything is to be received with a prayer of thanks" (1 Tim. 4:4).

On the other hand, the happiness that riches allows is also very relative in the Bible. It is not so very important. People tend to take wealth much too seriously. Ecclesiastes notes that riches do not necessarily mean that one will enjoy life. Many rich people let their lives be dominated by sorrow and longing for more money without really enjoying what they already have. Their fear of losing their wealth keeps them from sleeping well (Eccl. 5:11). This restless search for riches is strongly criticized. It obstructs the enjoyment of life, because it is insatiable. "If you love money, you will never be satisfied. If you long to be rich, you will never get all you want. It is useless" (Eccl. 5:10). If someone has worked all his life in order to become rich, death can suddenly cut his down and someone else, who has not had to work for it, will enjoy it (Eccl. 2:21).

The low value of wealth is also apparent in Proverbs 30:8–9 where Agur states:

> let me be neither rich nor poor. So give me only as much food as I need. If I have more, I might say that I do not need you. But if I am poor, I might steal and bring disgrace on my God.

Agur's words point to a real danger of wealth, namely that it produces spiritual blindness. The rich person puts his trust in his property and feels independent of God: "Rich people, however, imagine that their wealth protects them like high, strong walls round a city" (Prov. 18:11). This idea is also present in the Torah, for example in Deuteronomy 8:11–18:

> Make certain that you do not forget the Lord your God ... when you have all you want to eat and have built good houses to live in and when your cattle and sheep, your silver and gold have increased, make sure that you do not become proud and forget the Lord your God who rescued you from Egypt, where you were slaves.

The contrast between riches and piety is also highlighted in other texts:"Better to be poor and fear the Lord than to be rich and in trouble" (Prov. 15:16). Trust in God is more valuable than material wealth.

The New Testament confirms that wealth may easily seduce people into a life independent of God. Jesus' critical attitude is expressed in Luke 6:24–5 by the woes that he prophesies for the rich, who are not aware that their wealth is a gift from God which they can and should use to serve others. Their wealth and self-indulgent pleasures make their lives unfruitful (Luke 8:14). A clear example is the parable of the rich fool in Luke 12. His wealth makes him think that he does not need God. But just when he stops working and wants to start enjoying the fruits of his labor, God says: "You fool. This very night you will have to give up your life." And Jesus concludes: "This is how it is with those who pile up riches for themselves but are not rich in God's sight." The rich fool believed that his wealth provided security for his happiness. Any awareness that all gifts come from God was absent. That kind of wisdom is expressed in Jesus' advice not to worry about the food we need for our bodies. Instead, we should be more concerned about the Kingdom of God, sell all our belongings, and give the money to the poor (Luke 12:22–34).

Paul also urged people not to worry too much about money. He was convinced that God takes care of His children and provides for all their needs (Phil. 4:19). He exhorted believers not to commit themselves to a material life. "(Let those) who deal in material goods, as though they were not fully occupied with them. For this world, as it is now, will not last much longer" (1 Cor. 7:30–1). Wealth is only temporary and induces arrogance and complacency. Instead of pursuing riches, Paul advises believers to be generous with their wealth. This would provide them with a much more solid foundation for the future (1 Tim. 6:17–19). Paul is particularly merciless when he considers avarice:

> But those who want to get rich fall into temptation and are caught in the trap of many foolish and harmful desires, which pull them down to ruin and destruction. For the love of money is a source of all kinds of evil. Some have been so eager to have it that they have wandered away from the faith and have broken their hearts with many sorrows.
>
> (1 Tim. 6:9–10)

Such people invest all their energy in material improvement. There is no time left for the service of God. Avarice is an expression of the rejection of God (Rom. 1:28–9) and of idolatry: "You may be sure that no one who is immoral, indecent or greedy (for greed is a form of idolatry) will ever receive a share in the Kingdom of Christ and of God" (Eph. 5:5; see also Col. 3:5). This is similar to Jesus' statement that avarice is equal to serving Mammon. Paul was so convinced of the harm of avarice that he called on believers not to associate with greedy people (1 Cor. 5:11). Paul exhorted believers to be satisfied if their basic needs are fulfilled instead of striving for wealth: "So then, if we have food and clothes, that should be enough for us" (1 Tim. 6:8). He himself had learned to be satisfied with the varying circumstances in which he lived:

> I know what it is to be in need and what it is to have more than enough. I have learnt this secret, so whether I am full or hungry, whether I have too much or too little. I have the strength to face all conditions by the power that Christ gives me.
>
> (Phil. 4:12)

2.2.4 Stewardship and the environment

Temperance is particularly important nowadays in relation to the environment. If we want to promote human well-being in the long run, we must produce in an environmentally sustainable way. In biblical times environmental pollution was not an issue. Nevertheless, biblical texts have important implications for our dealings with nature. Responsibility for the sustainability of the environment can be argued from the central theme that God created the earth.

In Christian ethics the responsibility of mankind for the creation is often expressed by the metaphor of stewardship. Although the concept of steward or stewardship is only mentioned a few times in the Bible, it very well characterizes the relationship between man and God. A steward is a person who manages someone else's household. He is responsible to the owner of the household. This is a metaphor for the responsibility of mankind toward God, creator of the earth, who owns all things: "The world and all that is in it belong to the lord, the earth and all who live on it are his" (Ps. 24:1–2). He has commanded mankind to safeguard the earth (Gen. 2:15). Although this text originally concerns the garden of Eden, we can broaden its scope to the whole world if we realize that this commandment requires humans to take care of that piece of the earth where they live (Manenschijn, 1988). The Hebrew conveys the concept of safeguarding or caring with the word *shamar*, which is also used in the blessing of Aaron in Numbers 6:24: "May the Lord bless you and take care of you" (DeWitt, 1998). Just as God takes care of man, man should take active and interested care of the creation. Calvin writes in his commentary on Genesis 2:15 that Adam was entrusted with the case of the garden of Eden on condition of his being content with the frugal and moderate use of it. Human beings should use the fruits of the land, neither dissipating them by luxury not permitting them to be marred or ruined by neglect. Calvin also refers to the metaphor of the steward: "Let everyone regard himself as the steward of God in all things which he possesses. Then he will neither conduct himself dissolutely, nor corrupt by abuse those things which God requires to be preserved" (DeWitt, 1998: 31). Stewardship implies that the natural environment is not only used to serve the happiness and quality of life of humankind, it has an intrinsic value of its own as the creation of God and this should be sustained.

A significant example of care for the natural environment is the story of Noah in Genesis 6–8. God's command to build an ark to protect animals of every kind is the first example of human behavior to safeguard endangered species. If Noah had saved only himself and his family, the effort of building the ark would have been much less time-consuming and less expensive. Time, material, and money should now be devoted to rescuing animals.[3]

It should be noted, however, that stewardship does not give an easy answer to how we should balance the needs of current generations against the sustainability of creation. The story of Noah's ark does not imply that humans may not threaten the various species al all. According to Skillen (1998), evidence suggests that 99 percent of all extinct species disappeared before humans inhabited the earth. Apparently God allowed this. The extinction of species is to a certain extent unavoidable. The creation is not godly.[4] But that does not imply that humans can arbitrarily use the earth to increase economic welfare.

2.2.5 The ideal of moderate scarcity

The preceding analysis of the ambiguous valuation of wealth in the Bible puts the importance of economic growth for human happiness into perspective and consequently the institution of the market. On the face of it, one would expect that in an ideal world no scarcity would exist. Scarcity is a defect and an ideal world has no defects. Carter (2005) believes that the heavenly economy is one without scarcity. He points to the miraculous catching of fish and the feeding of the five thousand. Abundance will abolish thievery. Greed will be pointless. The resurrection to life under the kingship of God is comparable to such beauty that it is worth everything. Carter refers to the parable of the hidden treasure and the pearl beyond price (Matt. 13:44–6). The pearl is so perfect in its beauty that its value cannot be quantified. To purchase it the merchant parts with all that he has and this removes any possibility that he can continue to trade as a merchant. Carter concludes that life on the new earth will consist of priceless beauty. Any striving for the maximization of utility on which the economy is based will be redundant. Instead, there will be a situation of rest and satisfaction.

Still, one may wonder whether no defect necessarily implies no restriction on meeting human needs. Complete abolition of scarcity could be the gateway to hell. C.S. Lewis's book *The great divorce* is illustrative here. The problem of hell, Lewis has a passer-by remark, is that you can get all you wish just by imagining it. As a result, the economic basis for community life disappears. People do not need each other any more. With no scarcity, the need to live in the neighborhood of others and deal with them disappears

In the Bible heaven is often depicted as a feast where food and drink are abundant (Matt. 22:1–14). And abundance also exists in the heavenly vision in Revelation 21 and 22, not only in necessary goods, like food, drink, clothing, and health, but also in the luxury goods of beauty and quality. The heavenly city is built of all kinds of precious stones. The trees of life will bear fruit twelve times a year. Nothing will be cursed any more.

That does not imply that labor will no longer be needed to sustain life. If we take the situation in paradise as a point of reference, I tend to believe that the heavenly kingdom will be a place of moderate scarcity. Although humans will have sufficient means, they will still face the task of maintaining the new earth, just like the garden of Eden. They will need to use their talents, creativity, and power to meet this responsibility. Working is not a result of the fall. On the contrary, it is an aspect of the image of God, who Himself maintains heaven and earth.

If we consider some eschatological texts, we find more traces of the continuing relevance of human labor. An example is Isaiah 65:21–2: "People will build houses and live in them themselves ... they will plant vineyards and enjoy the wine ... they will fully enjoy the things that they have worked for." On the other hand, the Bible also speaks of rest, as God rested on the seventh day (Hebr. 4:10). The abundance on the new earth will lessen the necessity of labor for the sustenance of human life.

Hence, neither the abundance in paradise nor heavenly abundance excludes some form of moderate scarcity. Moderate scarcity therefore seems consistent with an ideal world in Christian eschatology. Values like love and justice require some kind of scarcity. It is only possible to show love by offering something the lack of which somehow hurts. This is only possible if there is some kind of scarcity.[5] Moderate scarcity is also a necessary condition for fairness.[6] If there is no scarcity, then there will be no conflict of interests between different people and so people cannot do injustice to one another.

Even the idea of a market with trade and a division of labor is imaginable in an ideal world.[7] McCloskey (2006) refers to the Quakers as a historical example of a community that approximates to a faithful and holy Christian community. It gives much satisfaction to make something that other people need and are prepared to pay for. There is no reason to assume that trading will disappear in an ideal society.

2.3 The influence of markets on welfare: outcomes of economic research

In this section I discuss the relationship between market operation, economic growth, scarcity, and happiness in economic literature. First, I present three theoretical perspectives on the causes of economic growth and an overview of some empirical literature on the influence of markets on economic growth as well as on the relationship between economic equality and economic growth. Then I deal with the question of whether economic growth reduces scarcity and present an overview of the empirical literature on the relationship between wealth and happiness. The final question that I analyze in this section concerns the effect of markets on the natural environment. Will the market succeed in reducing its negative externalities on the ecological system?

2.3.1 Does market operation generate more economic growth?

The causes of economic growth are manifold. Landes (1998) describes in his historical study *The wealth and poverty of nations: Why some are so rich and some so poor* the multiple causes of economic growth. First, natural circumstances have a great impact on wealth. A warm, damp climate discourages hard work and produces parasites which threaten human health. Drought and desertification prevent agriculture. Disasters (floods, earthquakes, cyclones, etc.) may cause many casualties and destroy infrastructure. Still, geographic circumstances are not decisive. Their role can be diminished by science and technology. The major conditions for the development of science and technology are good political structures and stable and honest governance. Other factors have also proven to be of great importance, such as culture (entrepreneurial spirit and the Jewish--Christian respect for labor, Calvinistic frugality and industry, a linear time perspective), the absence of destructive wars, the separation of church and state, the institutionalization of science and research, and military power.

The basis of economic growth is an increase in labor productivity; that is, the output that a human being can produce within a certain time period. Labor productivity rises with investments in the stock of physical capital and knowledge (human capital) through research and innovation that increase the productivity of capital.[8] The growth of productivity through all kinds of innovations had already started in the Middle Ages. An example is the invention of spectacles in 1306, allowing more productive employment of people with bad eyes.

Causes of economic growth: three perspectives

CPB (1992) distinguishes three theoretical perspectives on the causes of economic growth: the neoclassical equilibrium perspective, the Keynesian coordination perspective, and the neo-Austrian free market perspective.

In the neoclassical market equilibrium perspective the basis of economic growth is a well-functioning price mechanism that coordinates the decisions of various economic subjects. The price mechanism leads to equilibrium between supply and demand in the various markets. The level of prosperity depends on the production factors available (natural resources, quantity and quality of labor supply and size of capital stock) and the state of technology. The level of saving

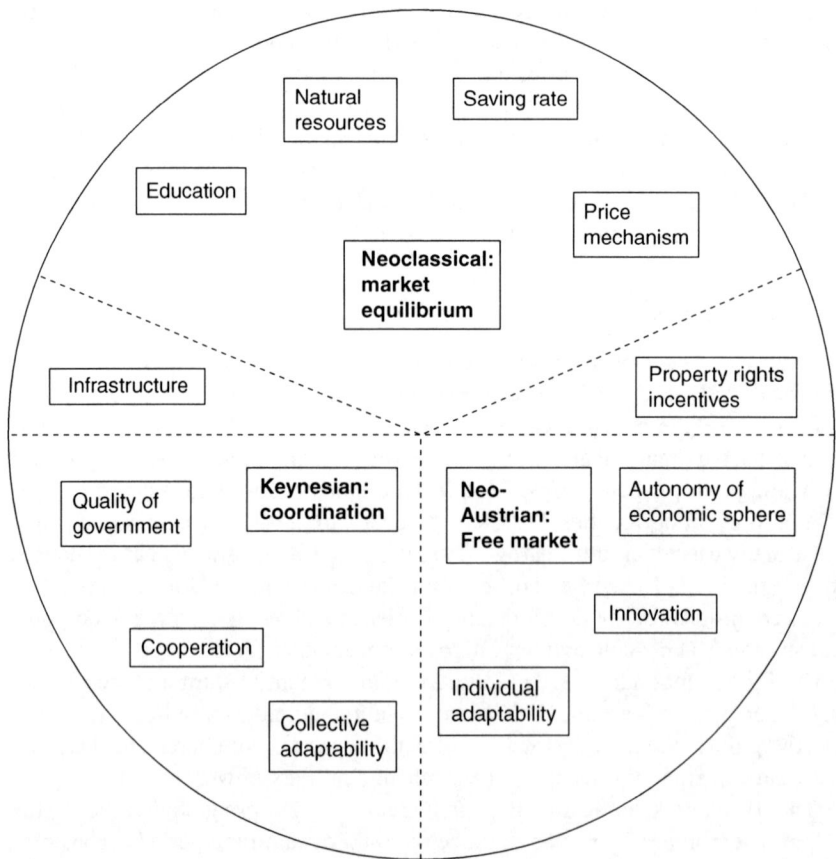

Figure 2.1 Causes of economic growth in three perspectives (source: CPB (1992: 47)).

determines the growth of the capital stock. Research and development (R&D) and investments in human capital are also major growth-determining factors and result from optimal choices by companies and households. In the neoclassical approach it is assumed that economic subjects are rational and well informed. Because of free trade, countries specialize in producing goods in which they have a comparative advantage. International trade provides opportunities to exploit economies of scale. The role of the government is modest and limited to the production of purely public goods (such as for defense, infrastructure, and justice) and fighting market imperfections (see Table 2.2) by antitrust policies, taxation, and subsidies. Strictly speaking, there is no place for collective social insurance in this perspective, because people are rational and able to make their own choices. Nevertheless, the government may correct the income distribution that results in the market equilibrium in order to assist those who are unable to earn a sufficient income. This is a political decision that depends on the trade-off between efficiency and equity.

In the free market perspective of the neo-Austrian School of economic thought (Schumpeter, Hayek), economic growth results not from price competition but rather from competition in introducing new consumer goods, new technologies, new sources of supply, and new types of organizational structure. This kind of competition commands a decisive cost or quality advantage that strikes not at the margins of the profits and output of existing firms – as price competition does – but at their formation and their very survival. Entrepreneurs play a dominant role as inspirers and organizers of technological innovation. According to Schumpeter (1976: 83), the fundamental impulse that sets and keeps the capitalist engine in motion comes from new consumer goods, new methods of production or trans- portation, new markets, and the new forms of industrial organization that capital- ist enterprise creates – not from competition in the sense of offering the lowest price at each moment in time. There is a constant process of renewal that revolu- tionizes the economic structure from within. Schumpeter uses the term "creative destruction" to describe this process and considers it the core of capitalism. This competition (monopolistic and oligopolistic) is not only more common than perfect competition, but also much more effective in expanding output in the long run and bringing prices down. Perfect competition only yields short-term wealth

Table 2.2 Conditions of perfect market operation and market imperfections[a]

Conditions for perfect markets	Market imperfections
Many independent traders on demand and supply side	Trade barriers
Homogeneous goods that are perfectly substitutable	Heterogeneous goods
Perfect knowledge about price, quantity, and quality	Imperfect knowledge
Traders are rational	Traders are not rational
No external effects	External effects
No external parties regulate price, quantity, or quality	External regulation

Note
a For an extensive discussion, see Graafland (2007a: Chapters 2, 3).

creation (because of lower prices), but is inferior in the longer run because it limits the possibilities for a long-term strategy of product and process development by companies. The high profits that oligopolistic structures allow provide a strong incentive to a small group of market leaders that introduce new and successful products which replace other products. This type of competition disciplines before it attacks, because the businessman feels he is in a competitive situation even if he is alone in his field, because of the constant threat that another company may introduce a new product or technique that makes his product superfluous. In the field of international trade, free exchange rates and free trade are favored. In this perspective an adequate incentive structure is essential. The entrepreneurs must be sure of reaping the fruit of their labor. This requires a well-developed system of property rights, low taxes, and a frugal system of social assistance. The government should refrain from intervening in the economic process. Active regulation is considered counterproductive, because the government has limited information and no incentive to take advantage of opportunities. Macroeconomic policy, industrial policy, price and wage policy, and competition policy are all rejected. Even in the field of providing public goods and the fight against externalities, government action should be limited, because of the high risk of government failure and the distortions it creates in the market process.

The third perspective, the coordination perspective, is based on the views of John Maynard Keynes (1883–1946), who argued that economic behavior on the micro level can lead to significant and persistent imbalances on the macro level. The future is fundamentally uncertain and this provides room for fluctuations in expectations (animal spirits) that are self-fulfilling and cumulative. If companies face a decline in the demand for their products and dismiss employees, the purchasing power of the employees will fall and this may result in a decline in the demand for products, and eventually recession and a perhaps lengthy period of unemployment. Markets are not self-correcting. Income effects dominate substitution effects (Blaug, 1978). In this perspective there is a potentially large role for the government to correct the short-sightedness of its economic subjects. This provides room for anti-cyclical budgetary and monetary policies, market regulation, subsidies for education, industrial policies, and coordinated decision making in strategic projects with potential long-term gains for national wealth. The most recent example of stabilization policy is the government response to the 2008 credit crisis. All Western governments and many non-Western countries initiated major government programs including tax cuts and reduced interest rates to stop a sudden fall in demand for goods and services, and to restore trust. Externalities and the desire for more equal income distribution also motivate a broad range of policies in health care, social insurance, housing, public transportation, and progressive income tax. In the field of international trade the desire to reduce uncertainty leads to a preference for government-controlled exchange rates and trade policies (quotas, import tariffs, qualitative restrictions, export subsidies, R&D subsidies for emerging industries) to correct any possible short-sightedness of entrepreneurs and protect against a volatile world market or aggressive foreign competition.

The influence of private property rights on economic growth

Particularly in the first and second perspective – perfect market equilibrium and the free market – it is stressed that respect for private property is of fundamental importance to economic development. This thesis is definitely confirmed by empirical research. For example, on a database covering many countries Rodrik *et al.* (2002) estimate a positive and significant relationship between GDP per capita and the so-called Rule of Law index. This index combines several indicators that measure the extent to which agents have confidence in and abide by the rules of society. These include perceptions of the incidence of violent and non-violent crime, the effectiveness and predictability of the judiciary, and the enforceability of contracts. Together, these indicators measure the success of a society in developing an environment in which fair and predictable rules form the basis for economic and social interactions (Van de Klundert, 2005).

Interesting research was recently carried out by Blume and Voigt (2006). They use data from twenty-four different indices (including the so-called Empowerment Rights index, the Physical Integrity index, the Rule of Law index and two indices for economic freedom (see p. 33)). Using factor analysis they cluster these indices into four aggregated indices: civil rights (independent judiciary, freedom of religion, freedom of domestic and foreign travel, political participation), basic human rights (no political killings, no disappearances, protection against torture), emancipatory rights (workers' rights, women's political and economic rights), and property rights. The dependent variable is real GDP growth per capita from 1993 till 2000.[9] Other than the four types of human rights indices, they include twenty-one other explanatory variables that are common in economic growth literature. The regression results confirm that the index of property rights significantly and positively influences economic growth. The other indices – the index of civil rights, the index of basic human rights, and the index of emancipatory rights – do not have a significant positive (or negative) impact on economic growth. This confirms the results of Rodrik *et al.* (2002). When testing for specific components of economic growth, they do find significant positive effects for the civil rights and basic rights index on the ratio of investment in capital (as a percentage of GDP) respectively a positive influence of property, civil and emancipatory rights on productivity. In all regressions no negative influences on economic growth are found for any one of the four clusters of human rights.

The influence of economic freedom on economic growth

Another index that is commonly used in economic research is the Fraser Institute's index of economic freedom. This index includes respect for private property but also captures several other indices of free market operation (see Table 2.3). The index captures what Thomas Friedman has termed the Golden Straitjacket:[10] tight money, small government, low taxes, flexible labor legislation, deregulation, privatization, and openness all around. It thus provides a conceptualization of the economic system that the WARC criticizes.

Table 2.3 Aspects of the index of economic freedom of the Fraser Institute[a]

International trade	Taxes on international trade (−) Size of a country's trade relative to potential (+)	Monetary policy	Volatility of inflation (−) Monetary growth rate (−)
International capital flows	Restrictions on capital flows (−)		
Black market	Differences between an official exchange rate and black market rate (−)	Property rights	Equality of citizens under the law (+) Access to the judiciary (+)
Government intervention	Public consumption as % of GDP (−) Subsidies and transfer payments as % of GDP (−) Role and presence of state-operated enterprises (−)	Banking	Citizens' rights to hold foreign currency accounts domestically (+) Citizens' rights to hold bank account abroad (+)
Taxes	Top marginal tax rates and income threshold at which it applies (−) Conscription (−)	Price controls and regulation and market entry	Price controls (−) Controls on borrowing and lending rates (−) Freedom to compete in markets (+)

Note
a The sign of the influence on the index of economic freedom is presented in parentheses.

Various empirical studies show a significant positive relationship between this index of economic freedom and economic growth (Easton and Walker, 1997; Dawson, 1998; Haan and Sturm, 2000; Sturm and Haan, 2001; Scully, 2002). Nevertheless, there also some differences in results. For example, Dawson (1998) finds that both change and the level of economic freedom impact economic growth. This implies both a direct influence on the productivity of labor and capital and an indirect influence on economic growth through the positive stimulus of investments in physical and human capital.

Haan and Sturm (2000) and Sturm and Haan (2001) find that the index of economic freedom only fosters a higher level of material welfare, not a higher growth in material welfare. An increase in economic freedom thus causes a once-only increase in welfare, not a higher level of economic growth. Hence, steady state growth is not affected by the level of economic freedom. This contradicts Dawson's finding that economic freedom stimulates economic growth by fostering investment and is not in line with the neo-Austrian view. Haan and Sturm (2000) and Sturm and Haan (2001) also test the causality in the relationship between economic freedom and economic growth, because one cannot exclude ex ante an inverse influence of economic growth on economic freedom, as the quality of governance depends significantly on wealth. However, they find no causal influence of economic growth on economic freedom and conclude that the causality runs from more economic freedom to economic growth and not vice versa.

One may wonder whether all aspects of the index of economic freedom are equally important for economic growth. On a sample of developed countries Scully (2002) estimates that economic growth is positively related to the index of free trade and negatively related to the share of government consumption. But he detects no correlation with the other aspects of the index of economic freedom, such as the share of government transfers.

This is also apparent from Table 2.4, which compares various West European countries with the US. Although GDP per capita is substantially higher in the US than in most European countries, this is entirely due to the relatively high average number of working hours per person. If one corrects for this, the income level (productivity per working hour) is lower than in most West European countries, although the share of government outlays is substantially higher in Europe.

Finally, one should be aware that the measurement of institutional characteristics is inherently difficult (Dawson, 1998). The interpretation of the concept of economic freedom depends on the subjective judgment of the researcher or of those who have to fill in the questionnaires on which the indices are based (UN, 2006). This is illustrated by comparing the index of economic freedom of the Fraser Institute with a similar index of the Heritage Foundation and *Wall Street Journal*. Although this alternative index is based on a similar combination of aspects of economic freedom, Haan and Sturm (2000) find a rather low correlation coefficient when comparing both indices on a sample of seventy-nine countries.

Table 2.4 Income and economic freedom in Western countries

	GDP (PPP) per capita[a]	GDP per working hour[a]	% government (social security) in GDP[b]	Index of economic freedom (Fraser Institute)[c]
Denmark	33.2	43.4	56.3 (16.9)	7.7
Sweden	32.5	43.1	57.3 (18.0)	7.3
Finland	31.9	42.2	50.7 (16.8)	7.6
Norway	41.4	60.5	46.4 (15.0)	7.3
Average	*34.8*	*49.3*	*52.7 (16.7)*	*7.5*
Belgium	32.1	49.7	49.3 (16.0)	7.4
Germany	29.9	47.6	46.8 (19.2)	7.5
Netherlands	32.4	48.5	48.6 (12.3)	7.7
France	32.0	54.1	53.4 (17.7)	6.9
Average	*31.6*	*50.0*	*49.5 (16.3)*	*7.4*
Ireland	39.5	50.6	34.2 (9.2)	7.9
UK	32.9	42.9	43.9 (13.4)	8.1
US	41.9	48.9	36.5 (12.0)	8.2

Notes
a 2005. Source: GGDC database, University of Groningen, www.ggdc.net/dseries/totecon.html.
b 2005. Source: OECD: Public management statistics.
c Economic freedom in the world. Source: http://en.wikipedia.org/wiki/Index_of_Economic_ Freedom#Index_of_Economic_Freedom.

International trade and economic growth

One of the factors in the index of economic freedom is free international trade.[11] As discussed above, Scully (2002) finds that trade openness contributes to economic growth. Open economies benefit more from the knowledge that is available in other parts of the world than closed economies (Lucas, 2000; Klundert, 2005).

Still, integration into the world market does not guarantee sustainable growth patterns (Slaughter, 1997). Statistical analysis of the causal influence of the growth of exports on total economic growth is ambiguous and the results vary from country to country (UN, 2006). In contrast to the expectation of economists like Lucas (2000), there is no convergence between countries that have liberalized their economies. The potential of developing countries to participate in fast-growing markets for products with high technological content is limited. Markets for primary commodities and natural resource-based and labor-intensive manufactures with modest growth prospects are more readily available to developing countries. However, specialization in products of this type limits long-term growth if it hampers structural transformation of the economy through diversification towards products and services in fast-growing markets. Moreover, the markets available to developing countries have witnessed deteriorating terms of trade. Non-fuel prices in commodity markets facing low income elasticities of demand fell by 49 percent relative to prices of manufactured goods exported by developed countries during the period 1980–2000 (UN, 2006). The impact of export growth on domestic economic growth is further limited if the link with domestic sectors is relatively weak. This is particularly the case for countries whose exports are part of large international networks, organized by large transnational corporations producing a standardized set of goods in several locations. Export growth then goes together with an increased import content of domestic production and consumption. Thus, large increases in the manufacturing exports of developing countries may take place without commensurate increases in income and value added. For Mexico, for example, it has been estimated that over the past two decades imports for further processing constitute as much as one-half to two-thirds of total sales of affiliates of US transnational corporations in certain industries (UN, 2006: 75). Similar patterns of specialization are discernible in some North African, Central American, and Asian countries. The added value earned by the developing countries mainly consists of the rewards for low-skilled labor, whereas the much higher rewards for capital, management, and knowhow are reaped by the foreign companies. The increased mobility of capital and the rapid entry into the global labor force of unskilled labor are likely to weaken rather than strengthen the bargaining position of poorer countries, reinforcing the highly asymmetric relations between oligopolistic market structures at the top of the value chain and competitive market structures at the bottom of the value chain.

A divergence in production patterns is also visible in the type of foreign direct investment (FDI) that developing countries attract. Whereas the more successful

East Asian and Southeast Asian countries have been able to attract FDI in manufacturing (electronics, textiles), African countries mainly attracted FDI in natural resources (fuel, minerals), and the Latin American and Caribbean countries in labor-intensive manufacturing. Countries that supply unskilled labor have not been able to attract FDI of a high technological level and the spillover effects to domestic sectors are therefore very limited. In order to profit from FDI, countries need to have the necessary absorptive capacity among domestic firms and institutions. Only countries above a certain level of income, human capital, technological knowledge, and entrepreneurial culture have the opportunity to benefit from technological advances in Western countries and link their economies to markets with a high value added. For poor countries, trade liberalization hardly contributes to their economy (Calderón *et al.*, 2005).

Recent econometric studies indicate that the contribution of trade to growth has declined in recent decades (UN, 2006). Dowrick and Colley (2004) show that the increase in trade between 1960 and 1980 paralleled a growth in production in poor countries twice that of rich countries, but from 1980 to 2000 the marginal influence of trade on production growth in poor countries was negative (see Table 2.5). During 1960–1979 trade openness promoted convergence between poor and rich countries. But after 1980, the role of trade openness reversed. Specialization in the export of primary products has been more harmful than beneficial to poor countries. So, although the trade of developing countries is increasing, the revenues they receive from trade seem to decline.

Government regulation

The empirical research reviewed in the preceding sections supports the free market perspective only to a certain degree. There are indications that the free market does not provide sufficient conditions for the sustainable economic development of developing countries. Those that have opened up to the international free market risk severe and persistent market imperfections. Free international trade requires good governance. Only if the government has the competence and power to limit the market imperfections that may arise in competitive markets can they open up their economy to the world market.

Table 2.5 The contribution of trade to economic growth[a]

	1960–1979		1980–1999	
	Poor countries	*Rich countries*	*Poor countries*	*Rich countries*
Share of trade in GDP	41	60	63	71
Estimated contribution of trade to annual growth rate of GDP per capita	1.1	0.6	–0.5	1.0

Note
a Source: Dowrick and Colley (2004: Table 3).

The need to good governance was recently confirmed by the 2008 credit crisis. One of the origins of this crisis lay within the subprime segment of the US mortgage market. Subprime mortgages are loans given to risky, most low-income borrowers. These loans were based on the expectation that house prices would continue to rise. In 2006 the US house market turned down, however, and as a result many of the mortgages went sour. If subprime mortgages had been subjected to risk regulations by the government, the problem would not have become as acute as it did in the second half of 2008. This also holds for government regulation of banks' investment policies (see also section 5.1 below). The banks which made the mortgage loans did not keep them on their balance sheets, but sold them in the form of securities to investors around the world. This was accompanied by the loss of the information on the underlying risk of these loans. In addition, rating agencies made over-optimistic assumptions about the performance of these securities. Following the fall in the US house market, many financial institutions saw their assets melt away. This led to a complete breakdown of trust in the financial market and of interbank lending.

Governments likewise have an important role in regulating markets in trade relations. For example, if a poor country allows transnational companies unlimited access but does not have experience in good governance, the companies have ample opportunity to use their economic power to drive out local competitors by low price strategies (Klein, 2002). When local competitors have been vanquished, the transnationals can raise their prices and increase their profits. The opening of markets thus only creates short-term benefits to the local population in terms of lower prices and greater wealth. Once the foreign companies have built up a monopoly position, it is very difficult to reverse this situation by regulation policies, particularly in poor countries that lack a strong and incorruptible administration and an independent judiciary. If officials are amenable to bribery, powerful companies have ample opportunity to frustrate antitrust policies and can easily maintain their power.

This is particularly true for economic power that is coupled to or derived from political power. An example is the Soviet Union. The shock therapy of direct price liberalization and privatization induced unprecedented poverty and concentration of economic power. Between 1990 and 1998 production in Russia fell by 43 percent. Oligarchs were able to acquire state companies very cheaply, stripped them and invested their profits abroad. Other former Soviet republics fared even worse. Moldavia and Ukraine witnessed a decline of more than 60 percent in GDP between 1989 and 2000 (Stiglitz, 2002: 152).

Countries that have proven successful in realizing export-led economic growth applied various forms of government regulation. In South Korea the government imposed land reforms that increased the proportion of farmers with their own land from 50 percent to 94 percent, and invested in health and education.[12] In Singapore the government provided training facilities and publicly funded R&D institutions in order to attract multinationals. South Korea and Taiwan protected several domestic industries by forbidding foreign investment until the late 1980s. An important reason for an active industry policy is the so-called infant industry argument. As discussed above, in an open world market developing countries run the risk of specializing in traditional products that feature low growth potential (because of low income elasticities) and render low value added. This may seem attractive in the short run, but may hamper dynamic economic development in the longer run because these countries will not be able to absorb technological progress from the rest of the world (Klundert, 2005). This is exactly why most Western countries have protected weak but promising industries in the past by import tariffs, subsidies, cheap loans, etc. This protection gave them the opportunity to develop economies of scale on the local market. Once they grew strong enough to compete on the world market, the protective measures were abolished (Landes, 1998). For developing countries, temporary protective measures of this kind can prove necessary to enable them to diversify their production successfully and to avoid traditional specialization patterns based on competition based on low wages. They can thus reduce the technological gap with the Western countries.

Bilateral and multilateral institutions have also contributed to diversification policies in developing countries. Mauritius, for instance, was able to upgrade and reform its sugar sector while it received preferential treatment under the EU sugar and bananas regimes. It successfully diversified into textiles and garments. Some Caribbean countries with a traditionally strong position in the production of bananas used multilateral institutions to diversify into tourism (UN, 2006). Other countries failed to benefit from temporary preferential tariff structures to modernize their economies.

The influence of income equality on growth

In the neo-Austrian free market perspective it is assumed that there is a trade-off between economic growth on the one hand and income equality on the other hand. According to Hayek, social and economic rights necessitate a violation of property rights (through taxation) and this diminishes the growth potential of an economy. Recent defenders of globalization have put forward a similar argument. Norberg (2002) argues, for example, that developing countries should be able to develop their economies first, before they respect social and economic rights. As long as they are poor, assuring economic rights, such as the right to subsistence or minimal health care or education, will hamper economic development because it will weaken their competitiveness. Beginning trade with suppliers from Third World countries that use child labor, underpay their workers, and damage their health will only worsen the situation of these workers. If working children are dismissed, they will be forced to accept even more miserable jobs (prostitution). So, according to Norberg, we have to choose the least bad alternative.

In the Keynesian perspective, the government should take measures to reduce income inequality and prevent workers from entering a vicious circle of lack of food, bad health, low productivity, low income, no education, etc. The World Bank presents data that show that countries with greater equality tend to be more prosperous than countries with greater inequality in assets and income (World

Bank, 2006: 108).[13] East Asian countries like Japan and South Korea realized high growth rates without allowing substantial inequality. They actively complemented policies to reduce poverty, limit inequality, and provide everybody with some opportunity for education. By distributing the benefits of economic growth to all population groups, they increased political support for growth-stimulating economic policies. Many empirical studies confirm that human development policies contribute to economic growth.[14] If people become healthier and better educated, they contribute more to economic growth through higher productivity, more creativity, and greater ability to adopt new techniques. Empirical research indicates that education is particularly important. Numerous studies show that increases in earnings are associated with additional years of education. In agriculture, evidence suggests the positive effects of education on productivity among farmers using modern technologies. In Thailand, farmers with four or more years of schooling were three times more likely to use fertilizers and other modern inputs than less educated farmers. If schools are widely accessible through government subsidy, people with a low income can afford to educate their children: this is of decisive importance for the growth potential of the economy in the long run. However, the positive influence of income equality on economic growth has also been challenged,[15] whereas other studies argue that the relationship is non-linear. For example, Barro (1999) only finds empirical evidence for this positive influence among poor countries.

The positive relationship between income equality and economic development induces possible virtuous and vicious cycles. Whereas East Asian countries developed an upward spiral of economic growth and human development through the supply of education and health on a large scale, sub-Saharan countries are characterized by a vicious downward spiral of low economic growth and low human development. Ranis and Stewart (2005) also identify two other possibilities, namely countries that combine a high level of human development with low economic growth and countries with the opposite situation. Combinations of this kind occur when the linkages between economic growth and human development are weak. The history of the eighty-four countries in their sample that fit these patterns indicates, however, that countries of the first type succeed in moving toward a situation of more sustainable economic growth, whereas those in the second type do not. On the basis of this analysis, Ranis and Stewart (2005) conclude that human development through broadly available education and health care is a necessary (though not sufficient) condition for economic welfare. This suggests that human development cannot be postponed until a country becomes wealthier. Rather, economic growth and human development should go hand in hand from the start.

Conclusion

We started this section by distinguishing three theoretical perspectives on economic growth: neoclassical, neo-Austrian, and Keynesian. An overview of the empirical literature indicates that elements of all perspectives are relevant. On the one hand, empirical research leaves little doubt that property rights for all have a causative influence on long-run development processes, as stressed by the neoclassical and neo-Austrian school. However, this is not the whole story. A good infrastructure, a well-educated working population and good competition, industry, and macro stabilization government policies are of eminent importance to make markets work well. The right mixture of neoclassical, neo-Austrian, and Keynesian elements depends on the specific situation of a country. CPB (1992) illustrates this argument by several historical examples. Whereas the free market perspective stressing the importance of autonomy, incentive structures, well-developed property rights, and entrepreneurship proved successful during the industrial revolution in England and later in the US, the coordination and equilibrium perspectives have played a more important role in the rise of Germany and later Japan. To a certain degree, each country had its own way of becoming successful, depending on its national culture and specific circumstances. But it is dangerous to start by neglecting any of the three perspectives.

2.3.2 Does economic growth lead to less scarcity?

Since the industrial revolution the Western economies have witnessed an unprecedented rate of economic growth. As a result, poverty has substantially declined and the average life expectancy has considerable improved.

One would expect the rise in economic welfare to reduce the incentive to further economic growth. In his *Principles of political economy* (1848), John Stuart Mill predicted that economic growth would be a temporary phenomenon, necessary to overcome material scarcity. The best situation is, however, a stationary economy, in which no one is poor and no one wants to become richer or is afraid of the threat of income loss caused by competition.[16] Mill hoped that people would be content with a stationary economy long before earthly resources were exhausted.

But even in our times there are no signs of such a transformation from a growing to a stationary economy. Although Western economies invest more in the quality of life and mitigation of the damage to the natural environment, the priority of economic growth remains indisputable. Why is that?

In Graafland (2007a) I discuss several explanations. A first explanation for continuing restless economic growth is the insatiability of demand because people get used to higher levels of consumption. Many empirical studies show that consumption patterns are subject to habit formation (Brekke and Howarth, 2002; Layard, 2003). The satisfaction obtained from an increase in income is largely temporary, because people get used to the higher consumption level (Clark, 1999). A rise in consumption therefore eventually raises the minimum level of consumption that people feel they need as a minimum requirement (the reference level of consumption). Research shows that the long-term impact of actual consumption on reference or habitual consumption is about two-thirds (Layard, 2003). So the happiness derived from more income is overtaken after a time by a rise in the reference level of needs.

A second explanation to persistent scarcity is supply-induced demand. In a capitalist system, companies can only be successful if they continuously realize competitive advantages by innovation in products or production patterns that reduce costs or increase productivity. In order to sell the increased production, it is necessary for new needs to be created among consumers by marketing strategies.

A third explanation for persistent scarcity is the social phenomenon that people relate their satisfaction from consumption to their relative consumption level (i.e. compared to the consumption level of others) rather than to their own level. Many prominent economists in the past, including Adam Smith, John Stuart Mill, Karl Marx, Alfred Marshall, Thorstein Veblen, and John Maynard Keynes, acknowledged that standards of decency are socially determined. Fred Hirsch (1977) also attributed the relevance of the relative value of consumption growth to social interaction. He distinguished between private goods and goods that confer status which he called positional goods. The satisfaction derived from private goods is independent of the consumption level of others. In contrast, the satisfaction from positional goods is purely relative and only present if others cannot enjoy them. A very interesting aspect of Hirsch's theory is the thesis that the demand for private goods diminishes over time, whereas the demand for positional goods increases with wealth. Economic growth therefore goes together with increasing competition for positional goods. Since only few people are able to acquire positional goods, this kind of competition generates frustration among those who do not succeed in obtaining them. The higher the share of positional competition, the lower the satisfaction economic growth will generate. Recent economic research also confirms the role of social interaction in the creation of new needs. For example, Solnick and Hemenway (1998) found that graduate students of public health at Harvard would prefer a world in which they earned $50,000 annually and others earned half that amount to a world where they earned $100,000 a year while others got more than double that amount. In a similar study based on a more representative sample in Sweden, Carlsson *et al.* (2003) found that only 25 percent of the respondents would prefer the second type of society in which they earned more but less than others. In economics this phenomenon has become known as "keeping up with the Joneses" (Alessie and Kapteyn, 1991).

A fourth cause of persistent scarcity is the inherent tendency of the free market to crowd out public goods through negative external effects. Policy makers believe that these negative externalities will only diminish if economic growth continues. Economic growth provides the necessary means for social policies that invest in public goods, save the environment, and preserve cultural treasures and all other kinds of public goods. Therefore, economic growth remains top priority in economic policy.

A somewhat different explanation of permanent or even increasing scarcity is that awareness that everything is scarce has increased, due to the more efficient use of the resources that result from trade. In a monetary economy everything has a price (Achterhuis, 1988). Before money was invented, a farmer produced as much as he needed for his own household or local community. Much land remained uncultivated, because excess produce was worthless and therefore not subject to the economic law of scarcity. When money was invented and trade made the produce exchangeable, farmers could accumulate money and wealth by cultivating land beyond their own needs and selling its produce on the market. The land that was previously useless as its produce was not marketable now received an opportunity cost and therefore became scarce. The more goods become marketable and can be efficiently used in the economic process, the more things get an opportunity price and become subject to the law of scarcity. This reinforces people's awareness that everything is scarce.

A final explanation of persistence in scarcity is related to Hirsch's concept of positional competition. But instead of focusing on status goods, it is exclusively concerned with power as a mean to guarantee safety. According to the philosopher Hobbes, the need for power is based on people's restless fear of loss of control and finally of death. One can only be saved from the violence of others if one has sufficient power over them. Knowledge, wealth, status and military equipment are all means to gain power. But like status goods, power is a relative good. If others get richer, then one needs more economic means in order to maintain the power balance. Economic growth in order to gain or maintain power and secure one's freedom or safety is therefore endless.

2.3.3 Does economic growth make us happier?

Neoclassical economics assumes that people will always prefer more and are insatiable. The preceding analysis seems to confirm this assumption. However, neoclassical economics also takes it for granted that economic growth causes more satisfaction of needs and thus fosters happiness. The analysis in section 2.3.2 above, however, casts doubt on whether economic growth will really contribute to happiness.

By now, much research is available about the factors that influence happiness. A path-breaking work is a paper written by Richard Easterlin in the mid-1970s. Using data from a broad range of Western and developing countries, Easterlin (1974) established three findings. First, in any given country at a given time, wealthy people report higher subjective well-being (SWB) than poor people. Consumption is essential for well-being. This especially holds true for elementary goods, like being well fed, clothed, and housed. A second finding of Easterlin is that the life satisfaction of a typical member of a Western society remained substantially unchanged during a period of rapid economic growth. Third, he examined the relationship between average SWB and average income for different countries and found that there was no correlation between these variables. Apparently, the SWB of a citizen of a nation is not tied to that nation's material prosperity.

Easterlin's first finding is confirmed by recent research. Layard (2003), for example, shows that 41 percent of the 25 percent richest people in the US state that they feel very happy, compared with 26 percent of the 25 percent poorest people. Econometric analysis of panel data also confirms a positive relationship between happiness and income within countries (Stevenson and Wolfers, 2008). Income is also found to be positively related to alternative measures of subjective well-being, such as feeling pleasure or pride, being relaxed or cheerful, and having the respect of others, and negatively related to adverse indicators of well-being, such as physical pain, sadness, boredom, and depression.

Easterlin's second finding is not confirmed by recent research. In a sample of eighty-nine countries, Stevenson and Wolfers (2008) found that happiness and GDP per capita had moved in the same direction in sixty-two cases. In twenty-seven countries GDP per capita and happiness had moved in opposite directions.[17] Focusing on data for European countries, Stevenson and Wolfers show that the rise in income between 1972 and 2008 was accompanied by an increase in happiness. For Japan they found similar results. This is in contrast to earlier research indicating that the Japanese reported happiness remained at almost exactly the same level between 1958 and 1988, a period in which Japanese GDP per capita in constant dollars climbed from $2436 (about the same as Swaziland's present income per head) to $13,153 (Kenny, 1999). Stevenson and Wolfers show, however, that this result is due to changes in the measurement of happiness. Estimates for sub-periods (in which happiness was measured in the same way) show a significant positive relationship between income and happiness. Only in the case of the US has happiness not risen over time. It peaked in the 1950s and has never recovered since (Schor, 1997; Kenny, 1999). This is in contrast with the trend in GDP per capita. People's incomes are apparently insufficient to support the lifestyles to which they aspire. Perhaps the disruptive effects of modernization on family and community, traditional values, and established ways of life account for this finding. Alternatively, the decline in well-being may be caused by longer working hours, more television watching, a faster pace of life and more income inequality.

This is also illustrated by Table 2.6. Notwithstanding that the purchasing power of the US population is higher than in most European countries, happiness does not differ much. Layard (2003) also reports that the rise in average income went together with a rise in the least amount of money that people state they need to get along in their community. Data collected by Gallup Poll in the US show that this required income rose as much as actual income between 1950 and 1990. This indicates the empirical relevance of the various explanations of persistent scarcity offered in section 2.3.2.

Easterlin's third finding also appears to be less robust. Schor (1997) cites cross-sectional research on the relationship between income and various measures of self-reported happiness. Both within countries and across countries, income and subjective well-being are usually positively and significantly correlated. Stevenson and Wolfers (2008) also find a robust positive relationship between income and happiness. But the relationship between income and happiness shows decreasing returns, happiness being a function of the logarithm of income rather than absolute income. For poor countries there seems to be a substantial positive relationship between happiness and GDP per capita. But if coun-

Table 2.6 Income and happiness in Western countries

	GDP per capita[a]	GDP per working hour[a]	Happiness[b]
Denmark	33.2	43.4	8.0
Sweden	32.5	43.1	7.5
Finland	31.9	42.2	7.5
Norway	41.4	60.5	7.4
Average	*34.8*	*49.3*	*7.6*
Belgium	32.1	49.7	7.3
Germany	29.9	47.6	7.1
Netherlands	32.4	48.5	7.6
France	32.0	54.1	6.6
Average	*31.6*	*50.0*	*7.2*
Ireland	39.5	50.6	7.8
UK	32.9	42.9	7.2
US	41.9	48.9	7.4

Notes
a In 2005. Source: GGDC database, Rijksuniversiteit Groningen, www.ggdc.net/dseries/totecon. html.
b Source: World Database of Happiness, R. Veenhoven, 2006, http://worlddatabaseofhappiness.eur. nl/.

tries grow richer, the marginal impact of more income on happiness diminishes. Stevenson and Wolfers (2008) show, however, that there is no point of satiation. If they split the sample into rich and poor countries, they find that the impact of the logarithm of income on happiness does not differ for the two sub-samples. This is confirmed by recent research by Deaton (2008).[18]

Far more important causal factors behind perceived happiness appear to be social in nature (apart from genetic factors like personality). In his Lionel Robbins Memorial Lecture, Richard Layard (2003) presented some outcomes of recent happiness research. Table 2.7 gives an overview.

Each row of the table reports the partial impact of one factor, other factors being held constant. In the left-hand part of Table 2.7 the unit of happiness is set in accordance with the fall in happiness caused by a relative decline in family income by 33 percent. Compared to the impact of income, unemployment has a much higher (non-income) effect on happiness. People value working independently from the income that it generates, because their work provides them with opportunities to avoid boredom, to participate in creative activities, to exercise skills, and to contribute to society. Job insecurity has a substantial depressing effect. Moving from a secure to an insecure job lowers utility more than a 33 percent reduction in income. This may partly explain why happiness in European countries (with relatively high job security) is comparable to happiness in the US, notwithstanding lower income levels in Europe.

Third, marriage and family are of primary importance, while ties to friends, colleagues, and neighbors are of lesser significance. Brekke and Howarth (2002) cite research based on data from the US that marriage provides subjective benefits equivalent to a $100,000 per year increase in personal income in comparison

Table 2.7 Main factors that promote happiness[a]

	Fall in happiness index		Rise in happiness index
Family income down 33% relative to average	1.0	Family income up 50% relative to average	1.0
Unemployed (vs employed)	3.0	Trust in others (vs no trust)	1.0
Job insecure (vs secure)	1.5	High tax morality (vs low tax morality)	1.0
Divorced (vs married)	2.5	Political, personal, and economic freedom	2.5
Subjective health down 1 point (on a 5-point scale)	3.0	Religious (vs not religious)	2.0

Note
a Source: Layard (2003: Tables 3.1, 3.2).

to being widowed or separated. This empirical finding is very much in line with the high value of marriage in the Christian tradition. The break-up of family relationships has a severe impact on happiness. The benefits of marriage relate to the quality of relationships in terms of mutuality, reciprocity, and giving (Atherton, 2008). People in committed intimate relationships are better able to cope with stressful life events than the socially isolated. Individuals who can identify at least one true friend are much less likely to become depressed than those who cannot. This suggests that the most important source of happiness is not money, but time, because time is the crucial factor that determines the quality of social relationships. Without time, social relationships deteriorate into misunderstandings, feelings of abandonment, neglect, betrayal, and the like (Schor, 1997). This indicates that leisure is of great importance. Leisure spent on family or group activities fosters a sense of belonging. In contrast to material consumption, leisure is hardly subject to positional competition. Carlsson *et al.* (2003) estimate that 60 percent of respondents prefer a society where they work forty hours per week (and others work thirty-six hours per week) to a society where they work 42.5 hours (and others work forty-six hours per week). This provides another explanation of why US citizens are not happier than European citizens. As shown in Table 2.6, higher incomes in the US are entirely due to the greater number of hours worked and consequent trade of leisure for income.

Furthermore, happiness is significantly affected by physical health, trust, tax morality, freedom, and religion. Self-reported health is strongly related to happiness. Layard (2003) argues that it is specifically mental health to which happiness is related: objective measures of health appear to be much less closely correlated with happiness, because physical limitations can be adapted to much more easily than mental disorder. Second, trust (measured by the response to the statement "In general, people can be trusted") and tax morality (measured by the response to the statement "Cheating on taxes is never justifiable") are as important as a rise in income of 50 percent. These findings are particularly important for the discussion of the influence of the market on virtue in Chapter 4 below, since people can trust each other only if others prove trustworthy. Freedom involves a standard of governance in six different dimensions, including political influence, personal freedom, and economic freedom. Both political freedom (Henley, 2003) and economic freedom (Ovaska and Takashima, 2006) substantially contribute to happiness. Furthermore, religious beliefs relieve anxiety and provide a source of joy and peace of mind. A positive confirmation of the statement "God is important in my life" increases the index of happiness twice as much as a 50 percent rise in income. As argued by Atherton (2008), religion is a potentially powerful source of commitment and motivation. Religious activities like prayer have beneficial psychological and social effects among young people, including an enhanced sense of purpose in life that contributes to greater happiness. Finally, education also contributes to happiness, because it equips people with valuable skills that improve their self-esteem and effectiveness (Brekke and Howarth, 2002).

This list of factors that significantly influence happiness summarizes the findings of much research and corresponds to other lists relating to well-being from various disciplines (Atherton, 2008). It is also remarkably in line with Christian ethics, not only because Christian ethics (as discussed in section 2.2 above) attaches a modest value to income (once people have attained a reasonable level of material well-being), but also because labor, social relationships, trustfulness, justice, freedom, and belief in God are among the most important values in Christian ethics (as will be discussed in Chapters 3 and 4 below).[19] Happiness research thus indicates that Christian morality is not detrimental but helpful to fostering human happiness.[20]

Another important lesson to be learned from happiness research is that the free market may affect happiness in various and sometimes contradictory ways. On the one hand, it contributes to happiness by raising income, offering opportunities to work, and providing (economic) freedom. A rise in income may also have an indirect positive influence on happiness by raising levels of health and trust. The poor are more likely to suffer from broken or impoverished relationships, unsafe and low-trust neighborhoods, ill health, and earlier death (Atherton, 2008). But outcomes depend very much on how the market is embedded in other institutions. If the institutional framework allows the free market to operate hand in hand with high inequality, low employment protection, low public health care, and more stress, for a majority of the people, the negative effects of job insecurity, tensions in social relationships because of economic pressure, poor health, and low trust in others may overrule the positive impact of (average) income in happiness. We will elaborate on these effects in Chapter 4 below, where we discuss the impact of market operation on virtues.

2.3.4   Does the market provide a solution for the environmental problem?

In most church documents, stewardship of the creation is a main concern. God created the world and pronounced it to be very good. The dominion which God gave to human beings over creation must be exercised in a way that is responsible to future generations as well as to non-human creation. Economic systems must be geared to maintaining a healthy ecological system. Do free markets contribute to sustainability and the protection of non-human life on earth?

According to defenders of the free market like Norberg (2002), the answer is yes, at least in the long run. They argue that the economic growth generated by the market stimulates a market demand for a clean environment and provides the technology for sustainable production and consumption patterns. Environmental damage initially increases with income per capita, but at a certain point of economic welfare damage to the natural environment starts to decline. Another indirect effect of market operation on the environment is that an increase in income may reduce population growth. This will also diminish the environmental burden, because the high and growing world population is one of the main causes of environmental harm other than the high levels of consumption in Western economies (Randers and Meadows, 1971).

However, there are few signs that this expectation is coming true. The rise in income during recent decades was accompanied by increasing pressure on the worldwide ecological system. The American Index of Sustainable Economic Welfare (ISEW), developed by Cobb and Daly, declined by 25 percent between 1975 and 1990 and the British by almost 50 percent (Atherton, 2008). This is due to the fact that the market is subject to negative externalities. The environment is a collective good. Economic agents driven by self-interest will not take account of the harm their decisions cause to the environment if they do not have to pay for this damage. Although a rise in income also raises the demand for a clean environment, the total net effect of the economy on the environment is still negative.

This is illustrated by Table 2.8. During recent decades, only in the US has the use of primary energy per capita stabilized. Total use of primary energy increased because of the rise in population between 1980 and 2004. In other countries, the use of primary energy per capita and the total use of primary energy increased even more, particularly in Asia because of the booming economies of China and India. Equivalent trends are reported for CO_2 emissions. Although CO_2 emissions per capita (column 5) and per dollar of real income (column 6) declined in rich countries, total emissions increased between 1980 and 2004 as a result of economic growth. In other countries, CO_2 emissions per capita also increased during this period.

In order to reverse these trends and accelerate eco-friendly production and consumption patterns, the market should be embedded in an institutional framework that fosters internalization of negative externalities. Both market-conforming and non-market policies are potentially usable. Well-known

Table 2.8 Energy consumption per capita

	Primary energy per capita (million btu) 1980[a]	Primary energy per capita (million btu) 2004	CO_2 emission (million tons) 1980[b]	CO_2 emission (million tons) 2004[b]	% growth 1980–2004 CO_2 emissions per capita[c]	% growth CO_2 emissions per dollar real income
North America	286.0	280.2	5439	6866	−5.7	
US	343.9	342.7	4754	5912	−3.3	−40.2
Central and South America	39.6	50.8	623	1041	9.8	
Europe	135.7	146.5	4657	4653	−9.6	
Middle East	62.3	116.0	495	1319	38.2	
Africa	14.4	15.7	534	986	0	
Asia	19.9	38.5	3556	9604	86.8	−63.2
Total world	63.7	70.1	18,333	27,043	2.9	

Notes

a Source: www.eia.doe.gov/pub/international/iealf/tablee1c.xls; btu = British thermal unit.
b Source: www.eia.doe.gov/pub/international/iealf/tableh1co2.xls.
c Source: www.eia.doe.gov/pub/international/iealf/tableh1cco2.xls.

examples of market-conforming policies are emissions trading (i.e. redefining property rights such that emission of CO_2 becomes a monetary cost), taxes on energy use or subsidies for the development of ecologically friendly products and consumption patterns. Such policies make use of the price mechanism to stimulate more eco-friendly behavior. In addition, the government could use non-price policies, such as legal requirements with respect to the maximum pollution levels allowed (for example as a condition for licenses) once new environmentally friendly techniques have become mature and marketable. Coercive laws may, however, be more effective if they endorse self-regulation in the market, such as legal requirements with respect to ecological reporting. Greater transparency will confront market participants more directly with the social consequences of their choices and this will improve the reputation mechanism (Auger *et al.*, 2003; Graafland and Smid, 2004). According to the so-called governance or system approach, the government must try to employ and exploit the existing antagonistic forces within society in its thrust toward self-regulating sub-systems (Hess, 2007). This approach may thus involve coercive laws, but in a way that minimizes governing costs by the maximum employment of societal (countervailing) forces. The preferred mixture of the various policies described above depends, among other things, on the cost-effectiveness of each of them.

2.4 A Christian view of the market, economic growth, and welfare

Economic growth seems an indisputable norm that dominates not only economic policy but also other domains in society. According to Goudzwaard (1976), politics, science, and technology are all in the service of raising productivity in order to foster the goal of economic growth in Western society.

One may, however, question whether economic growth really deserves this high priority. If happiness in Western countries is only modestly affected by economic growth and if economic growth harms vital human interests by threatening the natural environment and social relations, would it not be more reasonable to defend a stationary economy? In order to answer this question, we put together the lessons of sections 2.1–2.3 above about the relationship between market operation, economic growth, and happiness. How should we value market operation and the economic growth that it generates in the light of the biblical view on welfare?

2.4.1 Defense of economic growth

Proponents of economic growth argue that it has an important instrumental aspect for social and ecological values, even if one disregards its consumption value. First, economic growth is an important condition for creating employment. As we saw in the previous section, unemployment has a considerable negative impact on human happiness and generates all kinds of negative social effects, such as criminality and political and religious extremism.

Second, economic growth is necessary to fight poverty. Increased productivity has an upward influence on wages and therefore improves the income of the working population. Developing countries also benefit from economic growth in Western countries if they participate in the world economy. Trickle-down effects will reduce absolute poverty in the Third World. Economic growth also provides governments with more tax revenues which they can use for programs targeted at education, housing, infrastructure, and income assistance to combat poverty and inactivity. Proponents also argue that economic growth is necessary to reduce environmental degradation. Only if a country is prosperous will it give sufficient priority to a clean environment. Other social goals determining the quality of life, such as the preservation of culture and the quality of labor, can only be realized if countries become affluent. If wages increase, employees will be less prepared to accept unpleasant, badly paid jobs. Wages for such jobs will have to be increased and this provides companies with an incentive to make them redundant by technological innovation.

2.4.2 Economics of sufficiency

Notwithstanding the logic of this defense of the instrumental value of economic growth in the fight against unemployment, poverty, degradation of the environment, and poor quality of labor, post-Keynesian critics argue that economic growth is not the solution to but rather the cause of these social problems. The high priority given to technological progress to raise labor productivity makes workers redundant and exacerbates the social problem of unemployment. It also harms the quality of labor, replacing secure jobs by temporary, low-skilled ones, because automation creates only few good-quality interesting and creative jobs with primary labor conditions relative to a vast number of simple, routine jobs with secondary labor conditions. This induces a process of polarization between high- and low-skilled labor, creating a dual market of primary and secondary labor (Opdebeeck, 1986).

Goudzwaard and de Lange (1995) also doubt that economic growth is necessary to save the environment. Although economic growth and technological progress generate the economic means to invest in environmentally friendly methods of production and consumption, the rise in consumption puts additional pressure on the ecological system. Even if the environmental harm per unit of consumption declines, the rise in consumption prevents a reduction in total environmental harm. Moreover, stimulating economic growth by fierce competition tends to reduce the financial leeway that companies have to invest in environment-saving programs which are only profitable in the long run (Graafland, 2002a, 2002b, 2002c, 2003). Although rich consumers attach more value to a clean environment, the free rider problem prevents these preferences from really influencing their purchasing behavior.

Goudzwaard (1982) and Goudzwaard and de Lange (1995) therefore propose a drastic revision of economic goals. Instead of maximum economic growth, consumption and incomes should be put in the service of caring for creation, guaranteeing subsistence to the poor in the Third World and improving the quality of labor in the rich countries. This is only possible if the rich countries settle for their current level of wealth and accept a maximum level of consumption of, for example, food and energy.[21] The economic order should be reshaped in such a way that economic resources are used to meet the economic needs of the poor, the unemployed, the natural environment and the human community. The economy of sufficiency will also improve the quality of life in Western countries, because moderation will prevent over-consumption. Future generations in particular will benefit from a reduction in economic growth, because of the lower use of scarce sources of energy.

2.4.3 Growth: yes...

In my view, a stationary economy with no economic growth is not preferable for several reasons. First, I partly agree with the proponents of economic growth that it sustains employment. Although economic growth is not really a precondition of full employment (McCloskey, 2006) – productivity growth can be used to increase leisure times, time for children, etc. rather than to increase income – one may doubt whether all innovation can be directed to these alternative uses. Humans are active beings. Working and creating are essential aspects of human nature in the image of God. They have intrinsic value and are not solely a means to more consumption. Inventing new products and solving problems provide a lot of satisfaction. Participation in productive labor can therefore be considered a human right. Through labor, people develop their capabilities and are able to contribute to society.[22] Technological progress and the resulting growth in labor productivity reduce employment if production is fixed at a maximum.

Opponents of economic growth argue that employment can be secured when the reduction in economic growth is accompanied by diminishing technological progress. But is this feasible? Technological progress is largely determined by international economic developments. If a single country isolates itself, its economy will be disproportionately harmed when other countries continue their technological development. After a while this country will no longer be able to compete with other countries and will be forced to specialize in production sectors with low profitability. I agree that lower technological progress does not necessarily increase unemployment. Applied general equilibrium models (Graafland et al., 2001) show that a fall in the growth of labor productivity does not raise the equilibrium unemployment (except for second-order effects). The main effect will be a decline in wealth. But this result only holds for the long term. Because of labor market rigidities and hysteresis effects (Graafland, 1990), it may take a long time before the economy reaches this new equilibrium. In the meantime, lower production will increase unemployment and cause major social problems. Therefore, prudence is required by a country which is reducing technological progress when other countries are not.

But even when other countries would cooperate and reduce technological progress in order to stabilize production and employment levels, I doubt the desirability of an economics of sufficiency. Growth in labor productivity springs from the gift of human creativity and the ability to accumulate knowledge and apply it to improving production techniques and inventing new products that meet human needs. When one rejects technological progress, one forbids people to express the image of God as creator in their daily economic life. We noticed in the previous section that education and development contribute to human happiness. When wealth increases, Western countries are able to use a larger share of their economic means for investment in education and research. There is no reason to reject the economic growth that results from these investments (provided that its benefits are allocated in the right way; see below).

Whereas the creativity argument in favor of economic growth relates to the supply side, one can also defend economic growth from the demand side. Demand for products also has a natural vitality because of the need for variation. God himself created endless variation. In economic life, variation is expressed by product innovation. Insofar as economic growth can be interpreted as a way of creating variation by product innovation, there is no need to reject it. The idea that human needs are limited does not seem justified from this point of view. There are many examples of product innovation contributing to human happiness. The fact that economic growth hardly diminishes scarcity because it creates new needs does not necessarily imply that one should reject economic growth, as the quality (rather than the quantity) of needs can increase. The goal of the economy is not complete fulfillment of all needs, as moderate scarcity is in line with the Christian ideal.

2.4.4 ... but selective

Instead of rejecting economic growth, a Christian economic ethics should be much more concerned with the type of economic growth, whether it really serves the needs that have priority in a Christian view of the economy. Instead of an economics of sufficiency I therefore prefer the concept of selective growth.[23]

From a Christian point of view, reduction of poverty takes priority over increased wealth for Western countries. Economic growth and poverty reduction in developing countries also requires economic growth in Western countries, but this is not a sufficient condition because trickle-down effects are too uncertain. Economic growth in Western countries should therefore be selective and directed towards stimulating developing countries. As Atherton (2008: 153) states, economic growth has to be targeted to addressing the needs of the poorest (so-called pro-poor economic growth). Concrete examples are the reduction of trade barriers that protect the North and block the exports of developing countries, as well as special and differential treatment programs for developing countries as a tool to foster their exports. This does not mean that all economic growth in Western countries should be used to stimulate economic development in developing countries. The citizens of Western countries should also benefit from the fruits of their economic growth. Both prudence and justice demand that part of the revenues of economic growth in Western countries should accrue to those who generate it.

The priority of needs over luxury wants applies not only to international relations, but also to the allocation of resources in Western countries. This allocation should be directed to meeting real needs that contribute to people's capacities and serve their freedom. As argued by Sen (1984), a person's freedom depends on his or her ability to perform functions, and social policy should focus on helping to develop these abilities. A concrete example is cosmetic surgery (Graafland, 2004, 2007a). If plastic surgeons are attracted by the high salaries that private clinics offer for cosmetic surgery, the supply of plastics surgeons for basic plastic surgery for patients who really need it decreases.

Selective economic growth is also needed to sustain the natural environment (i.e. pro-environmentally sustainable economic growth). Although economic growth is necessary to finance investments in decreasing polluting production and consumption patterns, economic policy should provide large incentives to channel economic growth toward more sustainability. Although the exact effects and the speed of progress are highly uncertain, the rich countries cannot risk the collapse of the ecological system by just hoping that greater wealth in the future will provide the necessary techniques and willingness to reduce pollution before it is too late. Since the happiness-generating effects of continued economic growth in Western countries are very modest, redirecting economic growth to more sustainability should take an extremely high priority.

Selective economic growth is also needed because of the bounded rationality of consumers. The production and (excess) consumption of products that create addiction and harm the health and happiness of consumers in the long run, such as alcohol, tobacco, and other drugs, should be minimized, as should gambling. Cosmetic surgery is another example where regulation could reduce the market imperfection resulting from bounded rationality. Clients often have unrealistic expectations, partly because of television programs that show the most favorable results. An optimistic mindset reduces the client's objectivity and ability to take into account the considerable risks of cosmetic surgery. To illustrate, the probability of serious side-effects from breast enlargement varies from 30 to 50 percent (Gimlin, 2000).

Christian ethics will also be critical of economic growth resulting from the satisfaction of perverse preferences. Which preferences are perverse depends on the religious view. Take, for example, prostitution. From an economic utilitarian point of view, voluntary and well-paid sexual services contribute to overall utility.[24] If the negative externalities of prostitution (health risks and criminality) could be contained, economic utilitarianism would legitimize this kind of economic activity because free trade between a prostitute and a client contributes to the utility of both. However, from a Christian point of view on sexuality, fostering economic growth by allowing this kind of activity is immoral, because satisfaction of sexual needs by economic transfers is contrary to the purpose of sexuality. According to the Christian view, legalizing and accommodating prostitution will not foster human happiness in the long run. Of course, any policy to contain prostitution should be informed by prudence, because of the persistent sinful nature of man. Bluntly forbidding prostitution can elicit even more harmful effects. But in a Christian view of economic growth, promoting prostitution just because of the economic benefits should be rejected. Rather, the target of policies should be to minimize this sector without causing greater harm to all those who are involved. More generally, Christians should always be critical of the argument of Mandeville (1714) that vices like greed, voluptuousness, gluttony, and envy are necessary to sustain employment. Preservation of employment cannot be a valid argument for tolerating all kinds of vices.[25]

Furthermore, a Christian ethics will restrict economic growth that harms social and community relations. The happiness research reviewed in the previous section shows that people need enough time for social interaction in a family and social environment and for relaxation. One should therefore be wary of encouraging labor market participation as the main solution to societal problems like the aging of the European population.[26] For there are also many adverse effects that offset the economic benefits in the long run. High pressure of work increases the probability of stress, burn-out, and disability. This has a negative external impact on the welfare of others, and may harm the quality of the upbringing of children and therefore future human capital. But equally important is the loss of leisure to enjoy the company of partner, children, and friends and other forms of social interaction and recreation. As discussed above, economic research shows that leisure is less subject to positional competition than material consumption. The economic models that predict that a rise in labor supply will increase wealth often do not take sufficient account of the loss of well-being caused by the loss of leisure.

Another restriction on economic growth that serves Christian priorities concerns collective rest times. Proponents of the free market argue that restrictions on labor time reduce economic growth and the opportunity for individuals to plan their activities to meet their own preferences. Another advantage is that business capital (buildings and machines) as well as public goods (roads, beaches, etc.) can be used more efficiently if leisure, work, and travel time are spread over seven days. From a Christian point of view, however, the loss of collective rest has also severe drawbacks. It harms the cohesion of social networks because collective moments of leisure facilitate community activities. Collective restrictions on labor time also protect the least advantaged groups in society against employers and (richer) consumer groups that want labor services at inconvenient times (during the weekend, evening or night). The restriction on labor time prevents the poor from being forced by their poverty to take on several jobs and allows them to maintain community relations with their family and others. It forces society to find a more human and fair solution to guaranteeing subsistence welfare and creating full employment for the poor. Finally, respecting collective moments of rest also protects people against bounded rationality. During times of collective rest, it is easier to relax and to distance oneself from daily work routines and associated worries. The economic benefits of additional employment and economic growth caused by liberalization of working time are far too modest to counterbalance the reduction in quality of life caused by the erosion of community.[27]

The example of collective rest days illustrates another priority in Christian economic ethics, namely that economic growth should not harm spiritual life. The command to keep the Sabbath holy is part of the Decalogue and therefore belongs to the core of the Bible. More generally, if tough competition seduces economic actors into focusing on economic success, there will be less time for reflection and spiritual life. Alienation from God will also harm human happiness, as shown by the happiness research discussed in the previous section.

2.4.5 The free market as a risky ideal

The argument for selective economic growth has implications for our view of the market. Although markets contribute to wealth, they do not guarantee that the type of economic growth generated by market operation is in line with Christian priorities and the Christian view of happiness. The persistence of market imperfections makes that highly unlikely. The perfect free market is a beautiful and inspiring ideal, but in economic reality it is particularly useful for identifying the imperfections of market operation and correcting the market accordingly. Liberalization and privatization without institutions that correct market imperfections are highly risky and can be extremely harmful to sustainable economic development.

2.4.6 Limits to the government

Well-functioning markets therefore require good governance. The government has various means that help to reduce market imperfections, as stressed in the neoclassical and Keynesian perspectives, including competition policies, environmental regulations, and taxation and subsidies.

However, although the government can and should play an active role in structuring markets, there are also limitations to what governments must or can do. As stressed by neo-Austrian economics, costs are involved in frequent and varying government interventions in the market. It may foster uncertainty if the government regularly changes property rights. This creates a negative incentive to private investments. The advantages of regulation should therefore be carefully weighed against the disadvantages. This creates the dilemma of the intervention paradox: if the government intervenes in order to improve market operation, the intervention may violate private property rights and diminish the incentive to invest (Bovenberg, 2000).

Lack of information further reduces the effectiveness of government regulation. This is exacerbated by globalization. In a dynamic international economy, the task of regulating markets is extremely complex. Globalization also limits the reach of government regulation, since the power of national governments is usually limited to their own area. Governments should respond to this challenge by international coordination, but the power of international organizations is restricted because of diverging interests among countries. So, whereas on the one hand the need for government regulation only seems to increase, the internationalization of markets actually erodes the position of governments. Because of worldwide population and productivity growth, economies are ever more constrained by social and ecological limits. Take fishing, for example. Because of the enormous capacity of fishing boats, fishing species are threatened with extinction. Coordination is needed to protect the fish stock and hence fishing in the longer run. However, international coordination often proves to be very difficult because of varying interests, cultures, and phases of economic development.

Finally, government regulation can lessen individual responsibility and induce free rider behavior. Although modest external pressure can certainly encourage the internalization of externalities, beyond a certain level a command and control policy may also have a negative effect by feeding an attitude of minimal compliance and distrust. It can be more efficient to delegate responsibility to private agents in order to encourage commitment to common welfare and corporate social responsibility. Only when companies do not live up to their social responsibility should the government intervene in order to prevent too much harm (Bovenberg, 2000; see also Chapter 4 below).

2.5 Summary

2.5.1 Utilitarianism

Utilitarianism combines consequentialism, welfarism, and sum ranking. It has great practical value and is compatible with how people often make decisions, namely by looking at the beneficial and harmful consequences of an institution.

Utilitarianism does not, however, take full account of Christian moral intuitions. It is subject to several serious moral criticisms. We should add other ethical standards that set constraints on utilitarianism in order to secure fairness.

2.5.2 Wealth and welfare in the Bible

In the Bible absolute poverty is rejected. Because poverty is substantially harmful to people's happiness, the fight against it deserves high priority.

The value of wealth is ambiguous. On the one hand, material wealth is perceived as a blessing that one may (even should) enjoy. One should not pass over the gifts of creation on a continuous search for more. Excessive wealth may seduce people into a sense of independence of God and the community of fellow humans.

Nature should not be used merely as a mean of increasing human wealth. It should be intrinsically respected as the creation of God.

The biblical ideal is consistent with a situation of moderate scarcity.

2.5.3 The influence of markets on welfare: outcomes of economic research

The protection of property rights and equality under the law contribute significantly to economic growth.

Economic freedom is positively related to level of income, but not necessarily to economic growth.

The effect of trade liberalization is mixed. Countries can only benefit from trade liberalization if they possess a sufficiently advanced state of technology and infrastructure, are able to diversify their production structures, absorb the technology from foreign investments, and have established a strong link between export-led and domestic sectors.

Liberalization and privatization provide insufficient conditions for economic growth. Market operation should be embedded in institutions that prevent severe market imperfections.

Developing countries have made various types of government intervention in the free market which have contributed to their economic development.

Income inequality is not a necessary condition for economic growth. Rather, it impedes a sustainable economic growth path.

Empirical research confirms that the neoclassical market equilibrium perspective, neo-Austrian free market perspective, and the Keynesian coordination perspective all have some relevance for fostering economic growth. The right mixture of these three perspectives depends on the particular situation of a country.

Economic growth has hardly reduced scarcity in Western countries during recent decades. This can be explained by habit formation, positional competition, supply-induced demand, increasing awareness of scarcity because of the commercialization of society, the crowding out of public goods and fear of losing control.

Rich people are on average happier than poor people. In particular the consumption of elementary goods – food, clothing, shelter, etc. – is significantly related to human happiness.

In cross-country analysis, happiness is found to be a function of the logarithm of income rather than absolute income. This relationship is robust for poor as well as for rich countries. There seems no point of satiation.

During the post-war period of economic growth, happiness has increased in a majority of countries. However, in the US growth in income has not been accompanied by growth in happiness.

On the micro level, a rise in income has a significant but relatively small impact on happiness. Other factors appear of much greater importance, such as stable employment, good family relations, freedom, faith in God, trust, moral attitudes, good health, and education.

Historical trends in the use of primary energy and CO_2 emissions indicate that free markets provide insufficient incentives to sustainability. Although growth in income increases the demand for sustainable products and lowers energy intensity per unit of consumption, the total use of energy and CO_2 emissions still increase as a result of economic growth.

2.5.4 A Christian view of the market, economic growth, and happiness

An economics of sufficiency in Western countries is neither feasible nor desirable. It induces a risk of high unemployment and social problems in the short and medium terms. More importantly, it denies human creativity and the ability to accumulate knowledge and apply this knowledge to improving production techniques and inventing new products that meet human needs. It also disregards a natural and legitimate human inclination to variation. The thesis that human needs are limited seems not justified from this point of view.

In a Christian view economic growth should be selective. It should be directed at serving real human needs, such as alleviating poverty, improving human capacities, reducing environmental harm, minimizing the satisfaction of immoral preferences, and fostering community relations and spiritual life.

It is unlikely that free markets optimally serve Christian priorities, because market imperfections are often highly persistent. Liberalization and privatization without government institutions that correct market imperfections are highly risky and can be extremely harmful to sustainable economic development.

The government can and should play an active role in structuring markets. However, there are also limitations to what governments must or can do. Government intervention creates uncertainty, is costly, often lacks up-to-date information of market dynamics, has insufficient international support, and may erode the responsibility of private agents.

3   The market and justice

In Chapter 2 we evaluated the market from the point of view of aggregate welfare or happiness. The distribution of wealth and standards of justice and rights were not explicitly taken into account, although various notions, such as the priority of the reduction of poverty and of meeting needs rather than providing luxuries, do relate to justice. In this chapter, we evaluate market operation from the perspective of justice. In addition to consequentialist standards, such as utilitarianism, we introduce deontological ethical standards. In deontological standards, consequences are important but not decisive. These standards criticize utilitarianism, because it does not respect people's individuality and legitimizes measures that sacrifice essential human rights if they serve overall utility.

In this chapter we first give a short description of standards of rights and justice and compare the main deontological ethical standards with utilitarianism and other consequentialist standards. In particular, we distinguish between positive and negative rights of freedom as well as between twelve different standards of distributive justice. We also briefly discuss the scope of the principles in terms of cross-national solidarity with people in other countries and intertemporal solidarity with future generations, as well as animal rights.

Next, we investigate which standards of justice are supported by biblical concepts of rights and justice. For that purpose, we distinguish between two main categories of standards of justice, namely egalitarian principles and capitalist principles. Furthermore, we also deal briefly with justice toward strangers as well as with animal rights. This analysis of Bible texts sheds light on the question of whether and in what sense the Accra declaration is right to state that extreme poverty is unjust in the eyes of God.

Section 3.3 researches economic knowledge on the impact of market operation on respect for human rights and distributive justice. Is it true, as claimed in the Accra declaration, that the free market system causes wealth to accumulate to the rich at the expense of the poor? And does the free market system with unrestricted competition, respect for private property, openness to world trade and international capital flows, and privatization of state enterprises, cause extreme poverty? To answer this kind of question, we review some empirical economic literature on the impact of market operation on poverty and on income inequality within and among countries.

Section 4 concludes by formulating a Christian view of the market from the perspective of justice.

3.1 Principles of rights and distributive justice in ethics

Justice is a complex concept with many alternative meanings. Ethics has developed many different standards of human rights and justice. In this section we present a short overview of some of the main standards, without claiming to be comprehensive.

3.1.1 Positive and negative rights

The ethics of justice is closely intertwined with the ethics of rights. One's view on fair distribution is closely connected to one's view on the type of rights that people have. Conversely, what rights citizens should be granted is a matter covered by principles of justice and just social institutions.

In rights ethics, there are different opinions about the type of rights people have. A useful and major distinction is respect of negative rights versus respect of positive rights (see Table 3.1). In the libertarian tradition, people have negative rights. Negative rights are those that impose a duty on others not to interfere in certain activities of the person who holds a given right. They require other people to refrain from acting in certain ways – to do nothing that violates the rights of others.

In the libertarian tradition, which goes back to John Locke, free markets are supposed to preserve two types of negative rights: the right to freedom and the right to property. According to Locke, these are natural rights. Each person has a right to liberty and a right to ownership over his own body, his own labor, and the products of his own labor.

Libertarian philosophers like Robert Nozick (1974) have built on Locke's theory of rights and claim that the only basic right that every individual possesses is the negative right to be free from coercion by other human beings.

Table 3.1 Examples of rights in the Declaration of Human Rights

Negative rights	Positive rights
No slavery or servitude (art. 4)	Right to effective remedy of violation of fundamental rights (art. 8)
Right to freedom of movement (art. 13)	Right to social security (art. 22)
Right to own property, no stealing of private property (art. 17)	Right to work and protection against unemployment (art. 23)
Freedom of thought, conscience, and religion (art. 18)	Right to minimal standard of living (art. 25)
Freedom of association (art. 20)	Right to free primary education (art. 26)

People must be left free to do what they want to do with their own labor and property. They must be free to acquire property, to use it in whatever way they wish, and to exchange it with others on free markets. An important implication is that no one is entitled to force people to contribute to collective funds for the sake of the overall social good. Hence, Nozick defends a minimal state that should only protect its citizens against violence, theft, and the breaking of contracts. A collective tax and social security system to reduce the poverty of the least advantaged is not permissible.

Critics of the libertarian negative rights approach have argued that securing freedom requires more than merely the protection of negative rights to freedom. Real freedom is only realized if people have sufficient means to act. Respect for freedom therefore implies positive rights as well. A positive right imposes a duty on others to provide the holders of positive right with what they need to pursue their interests freely (Velasquez, 1998). Real freedom and the exercise of certain capacities require some minimal resources. This means that economic rights, such as the right to minimal subsistence, belong to the rights that have the highest priority. This is defended by Shue (1996) among others. By minimal subsistence, Shue means a minimal standard of clean air and water, adequate food, adequate clothing, adequate shelter, and minimal preventive public health care: all things that one needs for a decent chance of a reasonably healthy and active life of more or less normal length, barring tragic events. According to Shue, the right to subsistence is a basic right. He defines a basic right as one that is essential to the enjoyment of other rights, such as the right to free association. People who lack subsistence are sick and utterly helpless and cannot enjoy other rights.

3.1.2 Rights of animals

Sometimes it is argued that animals also have moral rights. This means that animals have not only instrumental value to human interests, but also intrinsic value as ends in themselves. Because of their intrinsic value, animals deserve moral consideration entailing a human moral duty to protect their lives and to refrain from harming them (Manenschijn, 1988). Although the moral rights of animals are not the same as the moral rights of human beings, people have a moral duty to care for them.

3.1.3 Principles of distributive justice

As argued above, one's view of human rights is closely connected to one's view of distributive justice. However, rights and justice theories have different focuses. Whereas the ethics of rights is mainly concerned with the protection of individuals' vital interests against possible threats by other people or the state, the ethics of distributive justice is about balancing the interests of different people. In cases where different people make conflicting claims to property rights which cannot all be reconciled, questions of distributive justice arise.

The formal principle of distributive justice requires that equals should be treated equally and unequals should be treated unequally in proportion to the degree to which they are unequal. The question is then: When are people equal and when are they unequal? Which criteria should be applied to compare different persons? There are several answers to this question, ranging from those based on socialist principles that stress equality in income to those based on the libertarian principle that gives priority to individual freedom (see Table 3.2).

The first norm is absolute egalitarianism, which holds that all people are equal in all aspects. There are no relevant differences that justify unequal treatment. This implies an equal share in benefits and burdens. An example of an economic application of this principle would be a strict communist system in which everyone obtains an equal income. Such a system requires that all incomes are taxed at a rate of 100 percent and are then equally redistributed to all citizens.

An absolutely communist system of income distribution could, however, be very harmful to the economy. If everyone received the same income, the lazy person would earn as much as the industrious person. Hence, there would be no economic incentive to work. A less extreme variant of egalitarianism, the difference principle of Rawls (1999a), acknowledges that allowing some inequalities will benefit everyone, including the least advantaged. The difference principle requires that the primary social goods of the least advantaged group be maximized. Primary social goods are those that any rational person wants.

Table 3.2 Twelve alternative standards of distributive justice

Principle	*Description*
Absolute egalitarianism	Everybody an equal share
Difference principle	Inequalities allowed up to the point where the least advantaged get most in comparison to other distributions
Needs and ability principles	People get in accordance to needs, people should contribute in accordance to ability
Capability	People who need more to develop capabilities get more
Weighted priority view	Benefiting people matters more the worse off those people are
Utilitarianism	Equalize marginal utility of all individuals
Respect for positive basic rights	Redistribution is fair if it improves the absolute circumstances of people below an absolute threshold
Equal opportunity	Positions are open to all under conditions of fair equality of opportunity
Reward to effort	Distribution according to the efforts of individuals
Reward to productivity	Distribution according to the productivity of individuals
Reward to market price	Distribution according to the market mechanism
Respect of negative rights	Distribution by free transactions

They include income and wealth (besides rights, liberties, opportunities, and self-respect). The difference principle may still require substantial redistribution, although less than 100 percent, because some inequality will render everyone better off, including the least advantaged.[1] Rawls assumes a strong correlation between the various dimensions of the social primary goods and that it is not problematic to identify the worst-off. The least advantaged are simply those with the fewest social and economic advantages, the class of people with the most modest place in the distribution of income and wealth. The expectation of the lowest representative person is defined as the average taken over this whole class. Or more accurately, it is not the lowest score actually achieved, but the expected score of the incumbent of a social position accessible to the least fortunate. This means that the difference principle is responsibility-friendly (or ambition-sensitive) rather than egalitarian (in outcome terms) in individual cases: it does not require us to equalize the individual outcomes, but only to maximize what the representative incumbent of the worst social position can expect.

The Rawlsian difference principle is, however, insensitive to special needs, such as those of the disabled, the old, or the ill. These groups may be unable to produce anything worthwhile and at the same time they need more income than the healthy to obtain a similar level of well-being. This notion is captured by the third principle which states that benefits should be distributed according to people's needs and the burdens should be distributed according to people's ability (Velasquez, 1998).

A standard that is closely related to the needs principle is the capability approach of Sen (1984). His theory concentrates on the realization of certain powers or capabilities. The cripple's entitlement to more income arises in this view from the lack of ability to move about unless he or she happens to have more income or more specialized goods (for example, a vehicle for the disabled).[2] There are, according to Sen (1984), some specific differences between a needs approach and his own capability approach. First, in the needs approach needs are defined in terms of commodities. Particular goods and services are required to achieve certain results, even though it is acknowledged that different people need different commodities to satisfy their needs. However, the relation between commodities and capabilities may be a many–one correspondence, with the same capabilities being achievable by more than one particular bundle of commodities. A second difference is that the needs approach tends to focus on basic needs, i.e. on a minimum quantity of particular goods. This may lead to a softening of the opposition to inequality when the average level of welfare increases. Equality of capabilities is not prejudiced by the special concern with basic needs and can be used for judging justice at any level of development.

Another serious criticism of the difference principle is that it does not allow a major improvement in the benefits of some groups if it reduces the benefits of some worse-off groups. The maximin principle, like Rawls' difference principle, allows the smallest benefit to the worst-off to trump any benefit, however large, to any but the worst-off. In order to prevent this outcome, Crisp (2003) and

Arneson (2002) press for a number-weighted priority view, which holds that benefiting people matters more the worse off those people are, the more of those people there are, and the greater the benefits in question. This permits us to benefit those who are better off if the benefit to them is significantly greater than to the worse-off, or if they are greater in number.

In utilitarianism, all that matters is the maximization of the total amount of happiness or desire fulfillment. It differs slightly from the weighted priority view because it gives equal priority to the marginal utility of all persons, rich or poor. Still, utilitarianism does not exclude a high degree of equality, because the utilitarian criterion of maximizing total utility prescribes that income should be redistributed until the marginal utility of all persons is equalized. As Singer (1972) argues, this implies a moral duty to give money if it is in one's power to prevent poverty without thereby sacrificing anything of comparable value.

The seventh principle is respect for positive basic rights. Respect for positive basic rights implies that redistribution is fair if it improves the absolute circumstances of people below an absolute threshold (Anderson, 1999). If the basic rights of all are secured, there is no further need for redistribution. In contrast to the difference principle, this principle implies that we should not be concerned about the inequality between the rich and the super-rich.

The principle of equal opportunities is also proposed by John Rawls (1999a). This principle focuses not on outcomes but on opportunities, and although it is more liberal in nature than the preceding principles, it is still closely related to them, because the principle of equal opportunity requires that the influence of social contingencies should be mitigated. Arneson (1999) argues that equality of opportunity can be broken down into two principles: First, openness to talents, which requires that selection to positions of advantage in society should be made impartially according to the criteria of merit that are reasonably predictive of successful performance; second, fair background which requires that measures be taken which entirely eliminate the effect of social background on competition for positions of advantage, so that any two persons with the same native talent and the same aspiration to succeed should have exactly the same prospects of success. This may require, for example, affirmative action to rectify the effects of past discrimination. A possible objection to these principles is that they incorporate a compromise with the norm of meritocracy, i.e. that those who are naturally more talented should enjoy greater prospects of fortune in life. Such reward of natural talents may be morally arbitrary. Effort is a responsibility factor, but talent is not (Cappelen and Tungodden, 2006). A more egalitarian interpretation of the principle of equal opportunities is therefore that the redistributive mechanism should also eliminate income differences due to differences in talent. More generally, one could argue that it is morally reprehensible if some are badly off through no fault or choice of their own (Arneson, 2000). Vallentyne (2002) distinguishes three factors that (together with choices) jointly determine what outcomes are realized: brute luck in initial opportunities, brute outcome luck (if an agent could not have reasonably deliberately influenced the possibility or probability of its occurrence), and option outcome luck (resulting from the uncertainty of choice outcomes). Justice does not demand compensation of the latter kind of luck: a tax on lottery winners (option luck) to help those who lose their money on lotteries is not a matter of justice. Compensation for brute luck is likewise doubtful. According to Anderson (1999), the proper end of justice is not to eliminate the impact of brute luck from human affairs, but to end oppression. Although the capacities for responsible choice – foresight, perseverance, calculative ability, strength of will, self-confidence – are partly a function of genetic endowment and of the good fortune of having decent parents, granting aid to those with bad brute luck is disrespectful, because it passes negative judgments on their worth. This is incompatible with respecting the dignity of others. Furthermore, to implement brute luck egalitarianism, the state must make judgments on moral deserts or responsibility in assigning outcomes. These judgments are grossly intrusive and moralizing. Thus, equality of fortune interferes with citizens' privacy and liberty. Furthermore, it also gives individuals an incentive to deny personal responsibility for their problems and generates a huge deadweight loss to society. For these reasons, we only focus on equality of initial opportunities in our analysis below.

The next three principles reflect capitalist norms of fairness, which distribute benefits according to the value of the contribution that individuals make. This is also called distribution according to moral deserts (or rendering to each his or her due). The principle states that each person should obtain that which he or she deserves. When a person has performed labor on some property, he or she has engaged in an activity that either displays some sort of human excellence (such as working hard), or confers a needed benefit on surrounding others (like making an object they want to buy) (Christman, 1998). Thus, if a worker adds value to the lives of others in some permissible way and without being required to do so, he or she deserves a fitting benefit. There are several ways of measuring this value. A first approach is to relate benefits to the individual effort a person has made. However, this approach encounters several problems such as measurement of effort and lack of compensatory justice if people work hard but not in a productive way. For this reason, it might be better to relate value to a person's productivity. This criterion of justice is consistent with Locke's property concept whereby each person has a right to ownership of his own body, his own labor, and the products of his labor. However, just as with effort, it is often difficult to determine the exact productivity of workers, especially if their work is complementary to that of others. The third approach, the market mechanism, determines a worker's contribution on the basis of market price. In a perfect market each factor of production will be paid its marginal product. The total income reaped by an owner of production factors is the sum of the price of the goods and labor he or she holds and the amount of his or her endowment of that factor.

The final and most liberal principle of justice is Nozick's entitlement theory.[3] Nozick does not accept any end-result principle. Justice only consists of an unhindered operation of the just procedures of justice, so-called procedural justice. The most important of these are justice in transfer and justice in rectification. Justice in transfer requires that parties involved in a transfer voluntarily agree to it. This means that their negative rights to freedom should be respected. Justice in rectification requires that any injustice resulting from a violation of the negative right to freedom should be rectified. Nozick's theory differs slightly from the capitalistic principle of income in accordance with contribution. For example, Nozick also accepts voluntary transactions that do not allocate income according to merit, for example by inheritance or gifts, provided that these transactions are voluntary.

3.1.4 Scope of principles

Differences in concepts of distributive justice pertain not only to the type of standards but also to the scope of the standard: do they hold for all people world-wide or do they only apply to the distribution of goods within a certain type of community (nation)? To illustrate, Rawls considers that the difference principle as defined above only holds for distribution within well-ordered states and within one generation. Rawls has offered various reasons for not using the difference principle across generations and across people and for elaborating instead a distinct principle of just savings and assistance among peoples. These distinct principles are less egalitarian than the difference principle. Rawls' just savings principle allows a situation whereby the first and poorest generation saves in order to benefit later richer ones, evidently making this poorest generation worse off (Parijs, 2003; Wall, 2003). The difference principle would favor a savings schedule that requires no savings from this generation, since to do so would be to benefit later and better-off generations at the expense of the worst-off group in the first generation. Furthermore, in the *Law of peoples* Rawls (1999b) argues that rich countries have a duty to assist poor countries until they have an ordered society and sufficient all-purpose means to make effective use of their freedom and to lead worthwhile lives. When this situation exists, there is no further need to narrow the gap between the rich and the poor nations, no matter how great this gap may be. This conception of fairness between nations evidently implies a duty of assistance of poorer nations by richer ones that falls far short of the difference principle that Rawls formulates for the distribution within ordered nations (Parijs, 2003).

3.1.5 Intergenerational justice and the environment

The rights and justice ethics also imply a moral duty to preserve the natural environment. A sustainable natural environment is essential for the right to freedom. Current and future generations have a right to protection of their lives and this requires care for the environment.

Conflicts between the interests of current and future generations evoke questions of intergenerational justice. The World Commission on Environment and Development (1987: 43) gives a well-known definition of intergenerational distributive justice: "Sustainable development is development that meets the needs of the present without compromising the ability of future generations to meet their own needs." Obviously, intergenerational justice sets limits to the welfare of current generations: the use of non-renewable resources reduces the opportunities of future generations. On the other hand, the growth of knowledge, techniques, and welfare provides future generations with the means to satisfy their own needs.

3.2 Principles of justice in the Bible

Section 3.1 describes many alternative standards of justice. Which of these standards is compatible with biblical notions of justice? Does the Bible only demand respect for negative rights, or does it give more priority to equality in outcomes?

In order to research this question, we cluster the various standards of justice in two main groups: capitalist justice (reward should be in accordance with effort, productivity or market price, and procedural justice) and egalitarian justice (absolute egalitarianism, difference principle, needs principle, capability theory, weighted priority view, utilitarianism, and respect for positive rights).[4] In this section we first show that the concept of freedom is central to biblical ethics. But this leaves open which type of freedom rights should be respected. Next, we discuss biblical support for capitalist and egalitarian principles of justice. Finally, we reflect on the question of whether biblical solidarity is universal and reaches out to all humans or mainly to one's own community.

3.2.1 Freedom

Freedom is a central value in the Bible. It comprises not only spiritual freedom (John 8:36; Rom. 6:18; Gal. 4:26, 5:13) or freedom from sin (Tit. 2:14), but also social freedom (Lev. 25:10), like emancipation from slavery (Exod. 21:2; Job 3:19) and imprisonment (Isa. 61:1; Luke 4:19), or freedom from paying taxes (Matt. 17:26). The liberation of Israel from slavery in Egypt is one of the most important events in the Old Testament and is often cited as a reason to respect the freedom of others (Exod. 22:21, 23:9; Lev. 25:38; Deut. 24:18). Just as God liberated Israel, He wants Israel to be a society of free people (Meeks, 1989). The laws in Exod. 21:16 and Deuteronomy 24:7 required the death penalty for whoever kidnaps someone to sell or to keep as a slave.

Freedom is intrinsic to human dignity. Men and women derive this dignity from being created in the image of God (Gen. 1:26). This central biblical text provides a religious foundation for human dignity and respect for human rights. Human dignity is not a matter of social convention or a self-grounded possession, but is essentially conferred by God. Every person counts and has an intrinsic, inalienable value. Job witnesses that he has not despised the rights of his servants, because: "The same God who created me created my servants also" (Job 31:13–15). A human being may not be used merely as a production factor (Monsma, 1999). Any human has a right to a life that can express the image of God. Freedom is a necessary condition. To be a human person means having freedom of decision without being coerced by others. That is foundational for many other values in human interaction, such as love and responsibility. If people do not have freedom of choice, they cannot be held morally responsible for their deeds. In Christian ethics, individuals are responsible for their own deeds (Gal. 6:4–5). Human freedom does not mean dissoluteness. It is the kind of freedom that is directed at serving God and others: "You were called to be free. But do not let this freedom become an excuse for letting your physical desires control you. Instead, let love make you serve one another" (Gal. 5:13). God respects the individuality of human beings and allows them sufficient room to express their individuality, even if they abuse their choice of freedom. He voluntarily took the risk that humans would choose against Him when He created man. The commandment not to eat from the tree of knowledge of good and evil already provided humans with freedom of choice (Safranski, 1997).

Slavery

Many Old Testament laws refer to the liberation from slavery in Egypt. The people of Israel should remember that they were once foreigners themselves and delivered by God (Exod. 22:21–7, 23:9; Lev. 19:34). Nevertheless, the liberation from Egypt did not effect the complete abolition of slavery. Although slavery was not perceived as a natural fact of creation and did not have religious status, it was still part of the social-economic life of Israel. Still, slavery was regulated by laws that guaranteed basic protection and dignity for slaves. Hebrew slaves had to be released after six years. Mistreatment of slaves was condemned (Lev. 25:46). Slaves should not be sold to foreigners (Lev. 25:42). Leviticus 25:39–40 commands that Hebrew slaves should be treated well. They should not be made to do menial work such as taking off their master's shoes or turning the mill stone. Hebrew slaves belonged to the family household. They could participate in the religious community and feasts (Deut. 12:12; Exod. 12:44) and even share in the inheritance of their owner (Gen. 15:3; Prov. 17:2). The Israelites should never forget that they were slaves themselves in Egypt (Exod. 23:9; Deut. 15:15). And, once a week, slaves should have a day of rest on the Sabbath (Exod. 20:10, 23:12). This law was also motivated by the deliverance of Israel from Egypt (Deut. 5:15). Slavery can therefore be interpreted as a way for impoverished people to stay alive during times of hardship.

Furthermore, some perceptions in the Old Testament change in character. Whereas Exod. 21:20–1 still assumes that the slave is the property of the slaveowner, Deuteronomy 15:18 rather perceives slaves as wage laborers and arranges the reward accordingly. Leviticus 25:53 actually interprets slavery in this sense: "as if he had been hired on an annual basis."

But it remains a matter of fact that slavery is not condemned either in the Old Testament or in the New Testament. This illustrates the cultural context of the Bible.

3.2.2 Capitalist justice

The priority given to freedom in the Bible still provides insufficient insight into the implications for economic order. Both positive and negative rights ethics and the various standards of distributive justice assume the right to freedom. An important question for the evaluation of the free market therefore is: Which of the various standards of justice are supported by the Bible and which are not?

Church declarations often seem to apply egalitarians standards of justice. To illustrate, according to the WARC declaration (see section 1.1 above), the root causes of massive threats to life are predominantly the product of an unjust economic system. The globalized free market system is in opposition to the covenant that God has made with all of creation. In article 20 of the declaration, the WARC states that the covenant is an inclusive one in which the poor and marginalized are preferential partners. It calls on us to put justice for the "least of these" (Matt. 25:40) at the centre of community life. Jesus did not only identify himself with the poor (Sider, 1977), but proclaimed that he would deliver justice to the oppressed, give bread to the hungry, free the prisoner, and restore sight to the blind (Luke 4:18). In article 24 the WARC declares that God is a God of justice. God calls for just relationships with all creation. More specifically, God is in a special way the God of the destitute, the poor, the exploited, the wronged, and the abused (Ps. 146:7–9).

These statements indicate that the concept of justice that the WARC declaration assumes is egalitarian. The poor and marginalized are the focus of justice. They are preferential partners in the covenant of God. In Christian ethics, defining justice in terms of the so-called privilege of the poor is, however, not uncontested. There is discussion as to which standard of justice is endorsed by the Bible. In Christian ethics, two opposing views can be distinguished. On the one hand, libertarian Christians like Beisner and Novak defend capitalist or libertarian views on justice. According to Novak (1982: 345), God is not committed to equality of results. The Bible stresses ultimate competition: there are winners and losers. According to Beisner (1994), the biblical concept of justice can be summarized as rendering impartially to everyone his or her due in proper proportion. This would lend support to the last four standards of distributive justice described in section 3.1 above. Other Christian ethicists defend the priority of the poor. The Bible favors special treatment for the poor in justice and law, and acknowledges their special needs. The poor are given priority, not because God loves them more, but because their wretchedness requires greater attention if the equal regard called forth by the equal merit of all persons is to be achieved (Mott, 1994). In this section we will discuss both views and investigate whether the Bible supports the last view, which is also expressed by the Accra declaration.

Let us start with the libertarian principle of procedural justice. The Bible indeed mentions many texts that command equality under the law (Exod. 23:3, 23:6; Lev. 19:15; Deut. 16:19; Isa. 5:23, 10:1–2; Jer. 5:26–8; Mic. 3:11; Zeph. 3:3; Job 13:10; Prov. 18:5, 24:23, 28:21; 1 Tim. 5:21), the right to private property (Exod. 20:15; Lev. 19:11; Prov. 23:10; Job 24:2; Ps. 35:10; Eph. 4:28), compliance with contracts (Jer. 22:13), and rectification if property rights are violated (Exod. 22:4–7; Lev. 5:14–16, 6:1–5, 22:14; Num. 5:5–8; Prov. 6:30–1).

There are also many texts that support the capitalist principle of moral deserts (or rendering to each his or her due) (see Table 3.3). God rewards a person according to what he or she does (Prov. 24:12). This implies for human economic relations that trade should be honest. One should use true and honest weights and measures and not cheat one's trading partner (Lev. 19:36; Deut. 25:13–16; Ezek. 45:10, Mic. 6:10; Amos 8:5; Prov. 20:10). Hence, one should be rewarded in accordance with what one actually brings to the market. Many texts in the Old Testament and New Testament support the idea that effort or productivity should be rewarded. Jesus applies this principle in the parable of the three servants (Matt. 25:29; Mark 4:25; Luke 8:18; Luke 19:26) and the parable of the gold coins (Luke 19:26). In the Kingdom of God also, everybody shall be rewarded in accordance with his or her deeds (Matt. 6:3, 16:27, 19:29; Luke 6:38, 18:29–30; Rev. 22:12). The apostle Paul defends a similar standard (Rom. 2:5–6; 1 Cor. 3:8, 3:12–15; 2 Cor. 9:6; Gal. 6:5–9; 1 Tim. 5:18; 2 Thess. 3:10).

So, basically, the Bible supports the capitalist principles of justice. But is that all? According to Calvin Beisner (1994) it is. Beisner (1994) argues that if justice defined along libertarian and capitalistic lines had really been taken seriously in biblical times, the poor would not have been abused and in many cases they might not have become poor. In this view, in the Bible unjust oppression of the poor is always linked to violation of their (negative) rights to freedom. The complaints of the Old Testament prophets should be read against the background of a hierarchical structure that developed during the reign of Solomon. During this time, the pressure of the royal court on the population increased (Leeuwen, 1956; Soggin, 1993). For example, 1 Kings 5:13 reports that 30,000 men were forced to labor on Solomon's building. In addition, 80,000 men were forced to work in quarries and another 70,000 were porters. This forced labor and the high taxes for the royal household hit small peasants especially (Davies, 1989). This situation continued under the kings following Solomon. Excavations have shown that during this time the royal court inhabited large palaces, whereas the common people had to live in slums (Vaux, 1989).[5] According to Beisner, the key point of injustice to the poor is violation of procedural justice. He refers to Psalms 72:4, 74:21, 82:3, 109:31; Proverbs 22:22, 28:3, Isaiah 3:14, 10:2, 11:4; Jeremiah 5:28 and Amos 2:6, 5:12. The call to help them by administering justice on their behalf is based on the procedural injustice done to them, and is not because they are merely materially in want. For those who are materially in want, independent of any violation of their property rights, we are only to exercise charity or grace. It is not a matter of justice.

Table 3.3 Examples of capitalist standards in the Bible

Old Testament

Reference	Standard	Text
Lev. 19:15	Equal opportunity	Be honest and just when you make decisions in legal cases; do not show favoritism to the poor or fear the rich (see also Exod. 23:3, 23:6).
Prov. 24:12	Moral deserts	Don't hesitate to rescue someone who is about to be executed unjustly. You may say that it is none of your business, but God knows and judges your motives … and he will reward you according to what you do.
Lev. 19:35	Procedural justice	Do not cheat anyone by using false measures of length, weight, or quantity. Use honest scales, honest weights, and honest measures (see also Deut. 25:13–16; Ezek. 45:10; Mic. 6:10; Amos 8:5; Prov. 20:10).
Lev. 19:11	Private property	Do not steal or cheat or lie (see also Exod. 20:15).
Jer. 22:13	Respect for contracts	Doomed is the man who … makes his countrymen work for nothing and does not pay their wages.
Prov. 23:10	Respect of private property	Never move an old boundary mark or take over land owned by orphans (see also Job 24:2; Ps. 35:10).
Prov. 6:30–1	Rectification	People don't despise a thief if he steals food when he is hungry. Yet if he is caught, he must pay back seven times more – he must give up everything he has.

New Testament

Reference	Standard	Text
Matt. 16:27	Moral deserts	For the Son of Man is about to come in the glory of his Father with his angels, and then he will repay everyone according to his deeds (see also Matt. 6:3, 19:29; Luke 6:38, 18:29–30; Rom. 2:5–6; 1 Cor. 3:12–15; 2 Cor. 9:6; Gal. 6:5–9; Rev. 22:12).
Matt 25:29	Moral deserts	For to every person who has something, even more will be given, and he will have more than enough; but the person who has nothing, even the little that he has will be taken away from him (see also Luke 8:18, 19:26).
1 Cor. 3:8	Moral deserts	God will reward each one according to the work he has done.
1 Tim. 5:18	Moral deserts	A worker should be given his pay (see also Matt. 10:10).
2 Thess. 3:10	Moral deserts	Whoever refuses to work is not allowed to eat.
Eph. 4:28	Private property	The man who used to rob must stop robbing and start working, in order to earn an honest living for himself.

3.2.3 Egalitarian principles in the Old Testament

Violation of negative rights of freedom was, of course, not the only cause of poverty. An example is Naomi. Others did not harm her negative rights to freedom. Nevertheless, she was impoverished as a result of the early death of her husband and sons. Periods of drought could also impoverish small farmers. According to Frick (1989), the general climatic patterns in Palestine have not changed significantly since around 6000 BC. Palestine suffers from occurrences of a series of abnormal years. Three consecutive dry years are often part of the experience of farmers. Coincidentally, this explains the possibility of disastrous drought in the time of Elijah (I Kgs. 18:1). Whereas a farmer could weather a single dry year, a series of such years caused severe want.

God commands the rich to show mercy to the poor who have been impoverished as a result of bad luck (rather than violation of their negative rights). Mercilessness is a sin (Deut. 15:7–11). According to Beisner, relief of this kind of poverty is a matter of caritas, not of justice. In his view, the poor do not have an unqualified positive right to assistance by others just because they are poor. There is no absolute duty for the rich to guarantee a subsistence level of welfare for the poor that can or should, if necessary, be enforced by the state.

In contrast to Beisner, I think assistance to the poor was not only a matter of charity, but also a matter of justice. A first reason for rejecting the distinction between justice and charity in relation to helping the poor is the close connection of both in Bible texts. Mott (1994) refers, for example, to Deuteronomy 10:17–18. This text stresses the impartiality of God, but also describes God as the one who takes care that orphans and widows are treated fairly and foreigners are given food and clothes (see also Ps. 146:7). Orphans, widows, and foreigners all belonged to the group of poor people who could not meet their basic needs. Hence, there is little scope for making a strict distinction between charity on the one hand and justice on the other hand. Tracing the meaning of the word *tsedaqa* shows that the link between justice and charity only became stronger during the times of the prophets. In Ezekiel 18:5–9 the virtue of justice is expressed by one's social attitude: "he doesn't cheat or rob anyone, he returns what a borrower gives him as security, he feeds the hungry and gives clothing to the naked … he is righteous and he will live." Both the duty to respect negative rights (not cheating or robbing anyone) and the duty to respect positive rights (feeding the hungry) are mentioned under the heading of justice.

Another reason, even more decisive, for rejecting the idea that the state has no responsibility for taking care of the poor is that the Bible commands several arrangements to protect the poor, independent of the causes of their poverty (Mott, 1994). For example, the poor were entitled to receive food during sabbatical years (Exod. 23:11) and to take what was passed over in the harvest (Deut. 24:19–22). The hungry were to be allowed immediate consumption of food in the grain fields (Deut. 23:24); farmers should not cut the corn at the edges of fields, but leave them for the poor (Lev. 19:9–10). Other examples are the law of tithing (Lev. 27:30; Num. 18:21; Deut. 12:6, 14:22–9, 26:12; Amos 4:4), the law on sharing food with the poor at the harvest festival (Deut. 16:11), and the prohibition on demanding interest from the poor (Exod. 22:25; Lev. 25:36; Deut. 23:19; Prov. 28:8, Ezek. 18:8).[6] Thus, aid to the suffering is not merely a matter of a personal duty to be merciful. It should be embedded in the institutions of society and everybody had the duty to obey these institutional rules. Justice is not merely a matter of respecting procedures, but also pertains to outcomes that should be corrected at the institutional level if they do not meet essential needs. Political leaders are made responsible for this (Ezek. 34:4). The just king will have his eyes open for the needs of the people (Isa. 32:3). In Ps. 72:12–13 the justice of the king is connected to helping the poor:

> He rescues the poor who call to him, and those who are needy and neglected. He has pity on the weak and poor, he saves the lives of those in need. He rescues them from oppression and violence, their lives are precious to him.

It should be acknowledged, however, that the various institutions providing help to the poor also require them to be active on their own behalf. Collecting the corn that was left in the fields after the harvest or cutting the corn at the edges of the fields involved laborious, time-consuming work with low productivity. Hence, rather than a right to subsistence they were allowed a right to labor to provide themselves with subsistence. These laws remain, therefore, to a large extent closely related to the principle of rendering to each his or her due. Still, there is a difference. The farmer must allow the poor the opportunity to help themselves, even if it would be more profitable to let his own laborers do this work.

The needs principle and other egalitarian principles

These rules are compatible with the needs principle of distributive justice and the positive right to subsistence. There is no qualification in any of these texts stating that the poor people thus provided for are victims of procedural injustice. They merely are needy. The needs principle is also behind prohibitions on delaying the payment of a worker's wage (Deut. 24:14–15; Lev. 19:13) or on hoarding grain during times of hunger (Prov. 11:26). Many other texts confirm the relevance of the needs principle. An example is how God provided Israel with manna in the desert: "Every morning each gathered as much as he needed" (Exod. 16:15–18).[7]

What about the other standards of distributive justice? Does the Old Testament support these as well? First, some texts can be used to defend Sen's capability theory. The poor should not only receive aid to keep them alive, but also be provided with the means to develop their capacities and maintain their freedom. Only then would they be able to live a life of dignity. An example is Deuteronomy 15:13–14, which commands slaveowners to free their slaves in sabbatical years and to provide them with sheep, corn, and wine. This would enable the released slave to build up a new independent life. With deliverance from slavery, the exploitation of the weak by the powerful is rejected. Like many social laws, this is motivated by Israel's own deliverance from slavery in Egypt (Meeks, 1989). Another example is the prohibition on demanding a working tool such as a millstone as security for a loan because this would take away a family's means of preparing food to stay alive (Deut. 24:6). A third example is the law of the jubilee year (Lev. 25:8–22). In this year, all property that had been sold should be restored to the original owner or his descendants. The text justifies this prescription by the principle that God is the owner of the land (Klenicki, 1997). The land was a gift of God imparted to all the people of Israel. No member of the community was to be denied the privilege of enjoying the benefits of the land and its produce (Graafland, 2001). One can interpret this institution as an application of Sen's capability principle, since land was a necessary means for people to develop their capabilities and exercise real freedom. It did not only provide people with the capital needed to earn an income, but also offered the possibility to participate fully in the community. Loss of land meant not only economic hardship but also loss of representation in the local assembly (Davies, 1989).

The law of the jubilee year can also be interpreted as an application of the principle of equal opportunities. Land was the main capital in Israel. The jubilee year implies that once in fifty years the next generation should have the opportunity to start anew. They received the capital that they needed to be economically successful. But, of course, the assigned land was just a start. They had the responsibility to use the capital in the right way to build a prosperous life.

There are no biblical texts that support the weighted priority view, utilitarianism, or the difference principle. The Bible is largely unfamiliar with the modern concepts of (marginal) utility and efficiency. It does not propose some kind of maximization of total happiness or of the social primary goods of the least advantaged group. Nor does the Bible defend absolute egalitarianism, because it does not force everybody to have exactly the same. Nevertheless, it should be acknowledged that the egalitarian ideal is not completely unfamiliar. For example, after the occupation of Canaan, the Israelite tribes were each allotted their territorial areas. It is clear from Joshua 13–19 that the land was allocated on a broadly equitable basis, so that each clan and each individual household had a right to a share in the inheritance of God's people (Wright, 1983). The eschatological ideal, as expressed, for example, in Micah 4:4 ("Everyone will live in peace among his own vineyards and fig trees"), pictures a situation where everybody equally will be happy and will enjoy life. That does not allow very unequal positions.

There are also several similarities between biblical justice and Rawls' difference principle. First, both the difference principle and Old Testament ethics respect the right to private property. Second, in both Rawlsian and Old Testament ethics the right to private property is not absolute. In Rawls' theory of justice, the right to private property constitutes only a very weak constraint on the rules that govern ownership and transfers of material goods, and is perfectly consistent with tax arrangements that spread wealth widely across society.

It would only exclude a radical form of communism in which all consumption goods are held in common (Parijs, 2003). Similarly, biblical ethics seem quite egalitarian in nature. Although the Bible does not demand forced redistribution to realize a situation of absolute egalitarianism, it still points to a considerable degree of economic equality. The Old Testament envisages several institutions that aim at establishing a reasonably egalitarian distribution of livestock and capital. Third, in both concepts of justice, the ideal of economic equality leaves much scope for individuals' personal responsibility in accordance with the principle of moral deserts; that is, it could be achieved independently, by their own labor, and by respecting the right to private property. As noted above, several institutions in the Old Testament that aim at securing basic subsistence for the poor, assume that they also take responsibility for their own situation by actively using the opportunities thus offered them. Economic independence furthers human dignity, as is expressed in the eschatological text in Isaiah 65 that describes people on the new earth fully enjoying the things they have worked for. In Rawlsian justice theory, the personal responsibility of individuals is also very important. This is evident from the priority that Rawls gives to the principle of equal opportunity above the difference principle.[8] But the difference principle allows ample scope for personal responsibility as it seeks to maximize the expectation of the lowest representative individual, defined as the average of this class as a whole.

Notwithstanding these similarities, there are some notable differences between the difference principle and the principles of justice reflected in Old Testament economic ethics. Rawls' difference principle is much more systematically developed and more precise in the determination of the degree of equality. Although it is in practice very difficult to estimate how institutions should be structured in order to meet the difference principle because of the uncertainty involved in the effects of institutions on the social primary goods of the least advantaged, the principle itself is quite accurately defined. In contrast, the egalitarian justice reflected in Old Testament ethics is less systematically developed and leaves open more alternative interpretations. In Old Testament texts the egalitarian principles focus particularly on meeting the needs of the poor and preventing absolute poverty. The institutions in the Old Testament do not necessarily imply maximization of the social primary goods of the least advantaged. They may well be interpreted as reflecting other egalitarian principles of justice described above, such as the needs principle, the basic positive rights view, or the weighted priority view. In contrast to the difference principle, these principles allow improvements in the benefits of richer groups without benefiting the worse-off groups as long as the latter's basic needs or basic positive rights are met. Instead of fostering equality and fighting relative poverty, the focus is on reducing absolute poverty. Biblical ethics therefore offers a broader spectrum of egalitarian principles than the difference principle. However, given this spectrum of distributive principles, the difference principle may be perceived as a legitimate variant of justice, without denying that more or less egalitarian principles can also be defended from a biblical point of view.

3.2.4 Egalitarian principles in the New Testament

Section 3.2.3 shows that the Old Testament acknowledges egalitarian principles of justice besides capitalist principles of justice. The New Testament seems to be even more egalitarian because, going further than the Old Testament, it calls on people to renounce their property and give it to the poor (Santa Ana, 1977). In this section we discuss some texts that point in that direction. But we also find that the principle of moral deserts and the right to private property are supported by the New Testament as well.

As already argued in Chapter 1 above, many texts in the New Testament refer to the Kingdom of God. Earthly life is often put into the perspective of eternal life. This does not necessarily imply that the principles of justice that are implicit in these texts are not relevant to the economic order here and now, but it does mean that one should be careful with direct applications of these principles. The words of Jesus in his defense of Pilate ("My Kingdom does not belong here," John 18:36) also indicate that the Kingdom of God has another origin and character than societal life here and now.

The priority of the poor in the preaching of Jesus

The preaching of Jesus indeed seems to support a radical choice in favor of the poor. Jesus describes his mission in Luke 4:18–19 as: "The Spirit of the Lord is upon me, because he has chosen me to bring good news to the poor ... to set free the oppressed." This is the very first preaching of Jesus. In this text he refers to Isaiah 61:2. He mentions the poor explicitly in relation to the bringing of the good news. A similar message is given in Luke 7:22:

> Go back and tell John what you have seen and heard: the blind can see, the lame can walk, those who suffer from dreaded skin-diseases are made clean, the deaf can hear, the dead are raised to life, and the Good News is preached to the poor.

The connection between the poor and the preaching of the good news can be explained by the correlation between the poor and the pious already developed in the Old Testament. Still, Luke 4 does not refer to poverty only in a spiritual sense. Jesus' deeds show that he interpreted his mission not merely in spiritual terms. He healed the sick, the lame, and the blind and fed the hungry.

The solidarity of Jesus with the poor is most forcefully expressed in Matthew 25:35–40:

> I was hungry and you fed me, thirsty and you gave me a drink; I was a stranger and you received me in your homes, naked and you clothed me; I was sick and you took care of me, in prison and you visited me.... Whenever you did this for one of the least important of these brothers of mine, you did it for me.

Some interpret "the least important" as poor fellow believers, but others argue that it means all needy persons, not only Christians (Gutiérrez, 1972). Jesus identifies himself with the poor and destitute. He wants believers to take care of the hungry and the desperate with whom he identifies.

The priority given to the poor is also shown in the beatitudes in Matthew 5:3:"Happy are those who know they are spiritually poor; the Kingdom of heaven belongs to them!" and Luke 6:20: "Happy are you poor; the Kingdom of God is yours." When Jesus says that the Kingdom of God will be for the poor, he means that it will be their future; their poverty and misery will be over. In the Kingdom of God, there will no longer be any poverty. This kingdom is the future, but it is also already among them (Luke 17:22). Jesus' acts show signs of the coming kingdom: he heals the sick and motivates rich people like Zacchaeus to care for the poor.[9]

The special place of the poor in the preaching of Jesus can also be illustrated by the parable of the great feast (Luke 14:15–24). The message of this parable extends beyond its spiritual meaning (that the self-satisfied will not partake in the Kingdom of God). This is also evident from the preceding text in which Jesus calls on his audience to invite the poor, the crippled, the lame, and the blind, who cannot repay them, when they give a feast.

Another intriguing parable is the workers in the vineyard (Matt. 20:1–16), about a landowner who gives workers who have only worked some hours the same wage as those who have worked all day. Although the latter are paid the wage they had agreed to, they are dissatisfied with this arrangement that seems unfair following the capitalist principle of rendering to each his or her due. The owner, however, argues that he has the right to be generous to the others. One can interpret this parable as a defense of absolute egalitarianism: everybody gets an equal reward, independent of his or her contribution to production. However, one may doubt whether we can disconnect the reward and the effort completely. The laborers who were hired at the end of the day were unemployed and had been available to work all day. A more plausible interpretation therefore is that this parable shows that workers should receive what they need (Gorringe, 1994). The owner wants to give all workers a wage that is sufficient for their subsistence. Alternatively, one could also interpret the parable in a libertarian way: any transfer is fair if it has been voluntarily agreed to. The owner respects the contract with the laborers who have worked all day and he is free to give the others what they need: "Don't I have the right to do as I wish with my own money? Or are you jealous because I am generous…. So those who are last will be first, and those who are first will be last." In the last verse, Jesus puts the capitalist principle of reward in accordance to contribution into perspective. This verse repeats Matthew 19:30 in the text preceding the parable of the workers in the vineyard. Although Jesus does not want to deny the principle of moral deserts, as stated in Matthew 19:29, he does stress that people should not exalt themselves because of their efforts. They remain dependent on an attitude of humility (Loonstra, 2000).[10]

Finally, the parable of the three servants (Matt. 25:14–30) and the related parable of the gold coins (Luke 19:11–27) are both significant. In the parable of the three servants, the third servant who hid the money in the ground is condemned. The master characterizes him as a lazy servant. All the money is taken from him. Jesus adds: "For to every person who has something, even more will be given, and he will have more than enough; but the person who has nothing, even the little that he has will be taken away from him" (Matt. 25:29). So here Jesus seems to confirm the capitalist principle of rendering to each his or her due. Although the context of this parable is service to the Kingdom of God (as appears from the text after this parable), it is difficult to see why the principle should not hold for our current economic order as well. This is also confirmed by the parable in Luke 19, which follows immediately after Jesus' meeting with Zacchaeus. In this parallel parable the principle of rewarding one's contribution is even more pronounced. The most productive servant gets the gold coin of the lazy servant. If bystanders object that the productive servant has already received ten coins, Jesus answers in a similar way to Matthew 25, that to every person who has something, even more will be given. From these parables it is clear that Jesus does not support absolute egalitarianism and that people are responsible for what they do with their talents.[11]

Taking all these texts together, it seems difficult to draw an unambiguous conclusion as to which principle of justice is supported by the preaching of Jesus. On the one hand, Jesus seems to confirm the capitalist principle that each should receive in accordance to his or her effort or productivity. Other texts, however, point at a radical reversal of rich and poor (as in the parable of Lazarus). Still, I believe that the two perspectives are complementary. On the one hand, one can conclude that the needs of the poor take priority over private property rights. Just as in the Old Testament, the hungry should be fed and the naked clothed. This supports the needs principle (or parallel principles such as the capability principle). The rich who have neglected their moral duty to help the poor will be punished, whereas those who have taken care of them will be rewarded. This confirms the principle of moral deserts.

The needs principle in the writings of the apostles

Caring for the needy was a top priority in the first Christian congregation:

> There was no one in the group who was in need. Those who owned fields or houses would sell them, bring the money received from the sale, and hand it over to the apostles; and the money was distributed to each one according to his need.
>
> (Acts 4:34–5, see also 2:44–5)

This text shows the application of both the needs principle and the ability to pay principle. Nevertheless, the right to private property was still respected. Ananias, for example, was not obliged to sell all his property and hand the revenue to the apostles (Acts 5:4).

Paul does not qualify supporting poor fellow believers as an absolute duty. His efforts to collect money for the congregation in Jerusalem show that such support should be voluntary: "I am not laying down any rules" (2 Cor. 8:8). Nevertheless, his arguments for supporting poor fellow believers confirm the needs principle and the ability to pay principle:

> But since you have plenty at this time, it is only fair that you should help those who are in need. Then when you are in need and they have plenty, they will help you. In this way both are treated equally.
>
> (2 Cor. 8:13–14)

Paul refers in this text to the manna in the desert: "As the scripture says: The one who gathered much did not have too much, and the one who gathered little did not have too little" (2 Cor. 8:14). Exodus 16:15–18 states that each gathered just what they needed. According to Carter (2005) this reflects the true God-given, abundance. Just as the Israelites received in accordance to their needs, there should be no needy people in the Christian community. Those who have the ability should provide for this need in accordance with their ability (see also 1 Cor. 16:12).

However, one can also interpret Paul's call to support needy believers in Jerusalem in a capitalist way, because he argues that they have shared their spiritual blessings with the gentiles. Then, the gentiles have a moral obligation to use their material blessings to help the Jews (Rom. 15:27). The principle of moral deserts is also present in the spiritual reward for solidarity: "Remember that the person who sows few seeds will have a small crop; the one who sows many seeds will have a large crop" (2 Cor. 9:6). Doing good to others is like an investment, the return on which depends on one's benevolence.

3.2.5 *The position of the stranger*

Until now we have focused on the controversy between capitalist and egalitarian principles of fair distribution. We have neglected the communitarian principle whereby solidarity with the needy should be shown to members of one's own community in particular and less to those living in other communities. In our society, this communitarian principle is expressed, for example, by the welfare state that provides subsistence levels of income for its own citizens, but not for those of other countries.

Adam Smith (1759) already distinguished several degrees of solidarity. After caring for oneself, one is naturally most concerned with the happiness of one's own family. Next come friends, colleagues, and people living in the same neighborhood and same country. Finally comes universal benevolence to the unfortunate far away. This universal benevolence is the business of God, not of man (Smith, 1759: 348).

Christian writers like John Wesley also defended concentric circles of solidarity with other people:

> First, you should provide things needful for yourself; second, provide these for your wife, your children, your servants or any others who pertain to your

household. If, when this is done, there be an overplus left, then do good to them that are of the household of faith. If there be an overplus still, as you have opportunity, do good unto all man.

(Stackhouse *et al.*, 1995: 197)

Does the Bible support this kind of partiality in solidarity? Or do we discern a development toward universal solidarity? This question is particularly pressing in our time, because caring for the needy only becomes a really formidable duty if the Bible requires universal solidarity rather than solidarity within one's own community.

Solidarity with foreigners in the Old Testament

Many texts in the Old Testament make a sharp distinction between one's own people and foreigners. An example is the release of slaves in sabbatical and jubilee years. This command only holds for Hebrew slaves, not for foreign slaves. Foreign slaves may be held as permanent property and can even be part of an inheritance (Lev. 25:45–6).

Although the Torah distinguishes between the Hebrew people and foreigners, the Old Testament does not leave foreigners unprotected. On the contrary, many texts require the Israelites to care for foreigners, just as they should for widows and other vulnerable groups in society. As already discussed above, these texts often refer to the situation in Egypt where the Israelites were foreigners themselves (Exod. 22:21–7, 23:9; Deut. 10:19, 24:17–22). For this reason, they should love foreigners as they love themselves (Lev. 19:34).

One should, however, distinguish between two groups of foreigners, the *gerim* and the *nokhri*. The *gerim* were originally connected to the Israelites' family or clan. This institution originated when the Hebrew people were still semi-nomads living in the desert. The *gerim* could ask protection from other clans (Vaux, 1989). For example, Abraham was a *ger* in Hebron (Gen. 23:4) and Moses was in Midian (Exod. 2:22). As a class of landless resident aliens in Israel the *gerim* were mostly poor. As the land was owned by the Israelites, they had to work as laborers (Deut. 24:14–15). Like widows and orphans, they should not be oppressed (Exod. 22:21; Lev. 19:33; Jer. 7:6, 22:3; Ezek. 22:7), robbed (Ezek. 22:29), or cheated (Deut. 24:14). In legal disputes, foreigners should be treated impartially (Deut. 1:16, 24:17, 24:19–21, 27:19). The cities of refuge were also available to them (Num. 35:15). The penalty for killing a foreigner was the same as for killing an Israelite (Lev. 24:22). Apart from these negative rights, foreigners also had the positive right to support when they were impoverished and could not support themselves any more. For example, like widows and orphans, foreigners shared in the harvest during sabbatical years (Lev. 25:6), in the benefits of the tithe (Deut. 14:29, 26:12, 26:13), and rest on the Sabbath (Exod. 20:10, 23:12; Deut. 5:14). They were allowed to gather the crops that were left over after the harvest (Lev. 19:10, 23:22; Deut. 24:19) and glean from olive trees and vines (Deut. 24:20–1). So foreigners had some of the same rights as poor

Hebrews. Their status was comparable to that of the Israelites who had been *gerim* in the land of Egypt and they therefore deserved Jewish solidarity.

The *nokhri* were foreigners who were temporarily in Israel for business and did not belong to the Jewish community (Jospe, 1997). Unlike the Hebrews, they could be charged interest and their debts were not discharged in sabbatical years (Deut. 15:3, 23:20). So there is a certain hierarchy in rights and responsibilities, Hebrew people coming first, next resident foreigners, and finally visiting foreigners. The closer the kinship, the greater the rights. Resident aliens had some but not all the same social rights as Israelites. In all cases, solidarity is only specified for relations with foreigners staying in Israel. There are no regulations that imply some kind of solidarity with foreigners living outside Israel.

Solidarity with foreigners in the New Testament

In the New Testament the community of Israel is replaced by the community of Christians in and outside the land of Israel. Whereas the land of Israel was fundamental for the identity of the people of Israel, the land loses its constitutive value in Christianity (Wright, 1983). The land of Israel no longer held special theological meaning. Not only has spiritual solidarity extended beyond the people of Israel (Matt. 28:19; Luke 24:47; Col. 3:11), but material solidarity has also extended internationally. Still, in the New Testament too, solidarity is communitarian in nature. The holiness of the land of Israel is replaced by the holiness of Christ, and solidarity with fellow Hebrews is replaced by solidarity with fellow Christians. The priority of fellow believers is expressed, for example, by Paul's efforts to provide help for the believers in Jerusalem. His call in Galatians 6:10 also reflects the concentric circles of solidarity: "So then, as often as we have the chance, we should do good to everyone, and especially to those who belong to our family in faith."

3.2.6 Rights of animals in the Bible

In Chapter 2 above we noticed that the creation story has certain general implications for care of the environment. As well as these general notions of stewardship, the Bible also contains several texts that deal more specifically with the relationship between humans and the environment. An example is Deuteronomy 20:19 on the protection of trees. If an army besieges a city, it may not destroy the surrounding fruit trees: "the trees are not your enemies." Only the fruit of these trees may be consumed. Other trees, however, may be cut down and used in siege mounds.

Sabbatical years have an ecological dimension as well as a humanitarian dimension. Letting the land rest one year in seven prevents its exhaustion. Moreover, wild animals could also benefit from its yield in the seventh year (Exod. 23:11) because the produce of the land could not be harvested. People could anticipate sabbatical years, animals could not.

Most specific texts about human responsibility for the non-human world concern the protection of animals. God's care for animals is illustrated in the Bible's very first chapter: "but for all the wild animals and for all the birds I have provided grass and leafy plants for food" (Gen. 1:30). Humans were put in charge of all the animals (Gen. 1:28), but that did not mean that animals were only created to serve human interests. Humans should leave enough for animals to live their own lives.

Animals therefore have some rights that should protect them against abuse. A well-known example is the law that forbids muzzling an ox when it is used to thresh corn (Deut. 25:4). This law requires the farmer to allow the ox to eat some of the corn that it is threshing (Leeuwen, 1975). The ox has a right to a share of the harvest, even to as much as it wants. Paul refers to this text (1 Cor. 9:9) in his defense of the principle of rendering to each his or her due (for his labor as an apostle), although he does not seem to properly value the literal meaning of the text (given his rhetorical question). The text thus complies with the capitalist principle of justice.

In addition, the Old Testament mentions several other rights of animals. One example is their right to rest on the Sabbath (Deut. 5:13–14); another is the duty to get an animal to its feet after it has fallen down (Deut. 22:4). The reason to care for animals is that they are God's creatures. Their lives should therefore be respected. This is also the background of all commands aiming to guarantee the survival of species. For example, if one happened to find a bird's nest in a tree or on the ground with the mother bird sitting either on the eggs or with her young, one should not take the mother bird (Deut. 22:6–7). Similarly, it was forbidden to sacrifice a cow or a sheep together with its calf or lamb (Lev. 22:28). Furthermore, Jewish law also contains commands that protect animals against cruel deaths. It was forbidden to eat the meat of animals that were killed by strangulation or suffocation (Lev. 17:10–16). Torturing animals by using slipknots or hanging was not allowed.

One may question whether respect for the life of animals is not violated by the practice of religious slaughter. The Old Testament prescribes various types of animal offerings that meant killing many animals every year. However, one should consider that most of the animals offered for sacrifice were used for consumption by priests and guests on religious festivals. In everyday life, the Israelites hardly consumed meat. The average consumption of meat was therefore much lower than we are currently used to. Only a small part of the meat of the sacrificial animals was burned on the altar. But this burning testifies to a high respect for animal life rather than the opposite. Nevertheless, it remains a fact that many animals were killed in religious offerings during Old Testament times. In the New Testament, the need for animal sacrifices vanished because of the complete and final sacrifice by Jesus. Jesus thus liberated animals from their sufferings for the sins of humans.

3.3 Markets, rights, and justice: outcomes of economic research

In this section we review some empirical research on the relationship between markets and justice. Is it true, as the Accra declaration claims, that the current economic system allows accumulation of wealth by the rich at the expense of the poor? More specifically, is there empirical information that provides insight into whether the internationalization of the market system helps or harms distributive justice?

3.3.1 Capitalist justice

The free market seems logically coherent with capitalist justice and the protection of negative rights to freedom. If an economic order changes from a collective planned economy to a free capitalist economy, property rights and the principle of moral deserts will be more respected.

However, complete liberalization or privatization may also threaten respect for negative rights, even if the government guarantees private property rights. If the government abstains from active competition policy, market imperfections may emerge that violate the negative right to freedom in transactions. If companies have the freedom to reduce transparency in order to shield their products from competition, the freedom of choice of the consumer is reduced. Market imperfections also limit the principle of moral deserts. If companies acquire economic power by successfully limiting market entrance, prices will go up, enabling companies to get more than their effort or productivity justifies. In Catholic social thought, monopoly profits are therefore rejected as usurious. Only temporary pioneer profits that arise from the creative initiatives of entrepreneurs that ultimately benefit the consumer are allowed, provided that the profit is invested in an economically meaningful way (Höffner, 1983).

A highly debated market segment is the labor market of CEOs of large international companies. This market is highly imperfect because of the low number of members, both on the demand and the supply side. In the Netherlands, only seventeen top CEO positions became vacant during 2002–2005 (Duffhues and Jobson, 2006). The market is best characterized as a bilateral monopoly. The market for CEOs is not homogeneous, because leadership demands very specific qualities that fit the needs and context of the company and these qualities may be highly diverse as well as scarce among CEOs. Hence, CEOs cannot easily be replaced by others. This market structure has caused a substantial rise in the remuneration of top CEOs. In the US, top CEOs earn more than 400 times the salary of the average worker. The effort of CEOs will never amount to 400 times the effort that an average production worker expends on his or her work. Whether this reward is linked to productivity is difficult to ascertain, because the productivity of a top CEO is complementary to that of the other workers in the organization. Furthermore, empirical research yields ambiguous results about the relationship between the performance of companies and the incomes of CEOs (Hall and Liebman, 1998; Bebchuk and Fried, 2005).

Fierce competition in free international markets can also obstruct respect for negative rights, because it may induce companies to do business with undemocratic governments. Trade enables these undemocratic and oppressive regimes to continue ruling their country by selling its resources. According to Pogge (2001), any group controlling a preponderance of the means of coercion within a country is internationally recognized as its legitimate government. The international order confers upon it the privilege of freely carrying out economic transactions (borrowing, selling resources). The economic freedom helps such governments stay in power. This international economic order thus indirectly contributes to the violation of negative rights in these countries. An example is the Dutch off-shore company IHC Caland in Burma in the 1990s. Burma is well known for its violations of political rights. Notwithstanding severe societal protests, IHC Caland continued to operate in Burma. According to its CEO at that time, Mr. Bax, fierce competition had forced the company to accept this kind of business (Graafland, 2006). A similar argument has recently been made by the oil company Total. Total refuses to withdraw from Burma as long as there is no law that forbids it to do business there. Total's argument is that if it puts political pressure on Burma, it will soon be replaced by others who have no concern for human rights. Indeed, that is one of the problems of competition. The possibility of being replaced by others puts limits on what is ethically feasible.

3.3.2 Positive rights

Free market policies are, however, more often criticized because they lack egalitarian justice. In this section, we focus on a subset of egalitarian principles of distributive justice. The number of people living below certain poverty lines and the Human Development Index are used as approximations of the fulfillment of basic human needs. The degree of egalitarianism is approximated by indices of income (in)equality within countries, such as the Gini index, and between countries. For the other egalitarian standards of distributive justice, empirical indicators are much harder to obtain. For the measurement of the degree of market operation, we again use the index of economic freedom (see Chapter 2 above). There is no literature that relates indicators of the degree of competitiveness (such as the relative profit measure, the price-cost margin, the labor income ratio, and the Herfindahl index[12]) to poverty, human development, or income inequality. Since a number of studies find a positive causal influence of economic freedom on GDP per capita (see Chapter 2 above), we also investigate the relationship between GDP per capita and the fulfillment of needs or income equality.

A first indication of the impact of international markets on the fulfillment of needs is absolute poverty. The globalization of the world economy during the last decade has been accompanied by a decline in poverty (see Table 3.4). From 1990 to 2004 the absolute number of people living below the poverty line of $1.08 per day declined from 1.25 billion to 980 million (UN, 2007). Poverty declined particularly markedly in East Asia. An example is China. After the

Table 3.4 Recent trends in poverty[a]

Region	1990	1999	2004
East Asia	33.0	17.8	9.9
Southeast Asia	20.8	8.9	6.8
Latin America and Caribbean	10.3	9.6	8.7
Western Asia	1.6	2.5	3.8
Southern Asia	41.1	33.4	29.5
Sub-Saharan Africa	46.8	45.9	41.1

Note
a Those living on less than $1.08 per day, as a % of population. Source: UN (2007).

change to a market system in 1978, the number of people living in poverty (below $1 per day) declined from 634 million in 1981 to 212 million in 2001 (World Bank, 2006). In Africa the absolute number of poor people remained high, but as a percentage of the population the statistics also show a modest decline, particularly since 1999.

Analysis of the impact of the market on poverty is hindered by the fact that pure market liberalization seldom takes place. China grew because it allowed more private initiative, but flouted many other rules of the free market (Rodrik, 2002). In order to calculate the effects of trade liberalization on poverty, computable general equilibrium (CGE) models are often used (Ackerman, 2005). CGE models, such as the Global Trade Analysis Project (GTAP) model and the World Bank's LINKAGE model, project that full trade liberalization should generate a one-off, not continuing, rise of 0.44 percent (0.8 percent) of GDP in developing countries. Using poverty elasticities calculated by the World Bank,[13] full trade liberalization would lift an estimated 66 million people out of poverty (using the $2 per day poverty line). For the world as a whole, this would represent a 3.4 percent reduction in poverty. Under the lower $1 per day poverty line, full liberalization would reduce poverty by 32 million people. This outcome indicates that trade liberalization may contribute to a reduction in poverty, but only to a very limited degree. It should be noted, however, that these estimates are surrounded by a high degree of uncertainty.

Empirical studies broadly support the view that trade liberalization will be poverty-alleviating in the long run and on average (Winters *et al.*, 2004). Winters *et al.* distinguish several channels. First, trade liberalization will stimulate economic growth, and economic growth tends to reduce absolute poverty. Trade liberalization also fosters productivity growth. Although the effect on poverty reduction is uncertain, productivity growth is seen as a necessary part of any viable poverty reduction strategy for the long term. The empirical evidence for other channels through which trade liberalization may reduce poverty – through more economic stability, through price reduction of consumer goods, through the creation and destruction of markets, through the creation of employment or an increase in wages, through more government revenue – is, however, not unambiguous and highly dependent on local institutions and complementary government policies.

There is quite a lot of evidence that poorer households may be less able than richer ones to protect themselves against adverse effects from more trade liberalization or to take advantage of new opportunities created by openness. Therefore, there is an important role for additional policies to provide social protection and to enhance the ability of poorer households to benefit from new opportunities.

Another indicator of the fulfillment of basic needs is the Human Development Index (HDI).[14] This index combines three dimensions of human welfare: life expectancy (as an indicator of longevity and health); the adult literacy rate combined with primary, secondary, and tertiary gross enrollment ratios (as an indicator of knowledge); and real GDP per capita (as an indicator of the standard of living). Biermans (2005) shows that the first two aspects (health and knowledge) are positively related to the third aspect of the HDI (standard of living). This is particularly true for poor countries. Diener and Diener (1995) provide similar findings for the so-called basic needs fulfillment index (including the percentage of the population having access to safe drinking water, the rate of infant mortality, mean life expectancy, the percentage of the population with sanitary facilities, and mean daily calorie supply per person). They showed that this index is significantly positively related to GDP per capita at low levels of income, but then levels off at higher levels of income.

This positive relationship does not prove, however, a causal influence of economic welfare on human development, because this influence can run in both directions. Ranis and Stewart (2005) present empirical support for both directions of causality by using lag structures that reduce the simultaneity bias. They also argue that the influence of economic welfare on human development crucially depends on the degree of income equality. The propensity of households to spend their income on products that contribute most to the fulfillment of basic needs – food, potable water, education, and health – increases if the incomes of the poor rise. One estimate suggests, for example, that if the distribution of income in Brazil was equal to that in Malaysia, school enrollments among poor children would be 40 percent higher.

3.3.3 Income equality within countries

Income equality is not only important for the fulfillment of basic needs through economic growth, but is also an important condition for economic growth as such. There is now a growing consensus that countries with an initial egalitarian distribution of assets and income tend to grow faster than countries with initial high inequality (Hoeven, 2009). This means that reducing inequality strikes a double blow against poverty. On the one hand, a growth path characterized by greater equality at the margins directly benefits the poor in the short run. On the other hand, an initial high level of equality contributes to economic growth as well. The question that we discuss in this section and the next is how a free market system affects equality.

Equality can be based on income, wealth, consumption, or any other reasonable proxy for well-being (such as job opportunities and social security). Most of the empirical research focuses on equality of annual income, because data for other types of equality are less available. In this section we first consider income equality within countries.

According to the so-called Kuznets curve, income inequality will initially rise with GDP per capita but then fall as countries get richer. The history of the poor and rich countries seems to confirm this relationship (Glaeser, 2005). Cornia (2004) argues that the last two decades have witnessed a rise in within-country inequality in developing countries. The World Bank (2006) also refers to various research that shows that trade liberalization has a positive influence on wage inequality. This is confirmed by a recent overview article by Goldberg and Pavcnik (2007). They show that the exposure of developing countries to international markets as measured by degree of trade protection, share of imports and/or exports in GDP, scale of foreign direct investment, and exchange rate fluctuations has increased inequality in the short and medium run, although the precise effect varies by country and time-specific factors. They research seven representative developing countries that have substantially reduced import tariff levels and non-tariff barriers to trade during the 1980s and 1990s. All these countries have experienced an increase in wage dispersion between high- and low-skilled labor, coinciding with the trade reforms.[15] Goldberg and Pavcnik offer several explanations. First, the recent rise of China and other low-income developing countries (India, Indonesia, Pakistan, etc.) may have shifted the comparative advantage in middle-income countries from low-skill to intermediate- or high-skill intensity and therefore increased the demand and wage for skilled labor at the expense of unskilled labor. Some of the middle-income countries started to outsource their production to the upcoming low-income developing countries and this also raised the skill premium in the developing countries. Second, globalization has fostered international capital inflows into the developing countries. Since the utilization of capital normally requires the employment of a higher proportion of skilled labor, the demand for skilled workers increased as well. A similar mechanism is skill-biased technological change. This technological change may have taken the form of increased imports of machines, office equipment, and other capital goods that are complementary to skilled labor. Liberalization may also have raised the demand for skilled labor, because it advantages companies that are operating more efficiently or closer to the technological frontier. Trade shifts resources from non-exporters to exporters and there is ample empirical evidence that exporters tend to be more productive than non-exporters. Trade openness may also have induced an additional upgrading of these firms, which was partly passed on to skilled workers in the form of higher wages. Finally, some research indicates that trade liberalization has increased the prices of consumption goods (such as food and beverages) that form a relatively large proportion of the consumption bundle of the poor, and decreased the prices of goods that are consumed in greater proportion by the rich. The latter effect seems, however, to be relatively small compared to the effects on wage dispersion between unskilled and skilled labor.

In the longer term, the effects are uncertain. Some studies indicate that market operation decreases income inequality in the longer run. Scully (2002) estimates that the index of economic freedom has a small but significant negative impact on the Gini index. Berggren (1999) also finds that sustained and gradual increases in economic freedom influence equality measures positively. According to Berggren (1999), trade liberalization and financial mobility are driving these results, perhaps because poor people are employed in industries that expand and flourish with freer trade.[16]

Market operation does not guarantee, however, that income distribution will become more equal (once a certain level of welfare has been reached). This is illustrated by the US. Initially, the economic process in the US was very much in line with the Kuznets curve. The share of national wealth earned by the top 1 percent rose from 15 percent in 1775 to 30 percent in 1855 and 45 percent in 1935. After 1935 inequality declined, but this process stopped at the end of the 1960s. A similar pattern has been observed for the Gini index. After a substantial decline between the 1930s and the second half of the 1960s, inequality has increased significantly since 1975, partly as a result of economic factors (skill-based technological change, increased trade and globalization,[17] the decline of unions) and partly as a result of political factors (less progressive taxation and lower minimum wages and unemployment benefits). Table 3.5 confirms that European countries with large government expenditure show more income equality than the US. Obviously, institutions in the US are less egalitarian and probably do not meet Rawls' difference principle.

The negative relationship between market operation and the Gini index for rich countries is also confirmed if we compare the index of economic freedom of

Table 3.5 Income distribution, government expenditure, and economic freedom

	% government expenditure in GDP[a]	Gini index[b]	Index of economic freedom[c]
Denmark	56.3	24.7	7.7
Sweden	57.3	24.9	7.3
Finland	50.7	26.9	7.6
Norway	46.4	25.8	7.3
Average	*52.7*	*25.6*	*7.5*
Belgium	49.3	25.0	7.4
Germany	46.8	28.3	7.5
Netherlands	48.6	32.6	7.7
France	53.4	32.7	6.9
Average	*49.5*	*29.7*	*7.4*
Ireland	34.2	35.9	7.9
UK	43.9	36.0	8.1
US	36.5	40.8	8.2

Notes

a 2005. Source: GGDC database, www.ggdc.net/dseries/totecon.html.

b Source: United Nations Development Program (2004), http://hdr.undp.org./en/reports/global/hdr 2004.

c Economic freedom in the world. Source: http://en.wikipedia.org/wiki/Index_of_Economic_ Freedom# Index of economic freedom.

the Fraser Institute with the Gini coefficient for the countries reported in Table 3.5. As described in Chapter 2, government intervention (measured by public consumption spending as a share of GDP, subsidies and transfer payments as a share of GDP, and the existence of state-operated enterprises) and top marginal tax rates are elements of the index of economic freedom that lower this index (see Table 2.3). This explains why, among others, this index is higher for the US than for European countries. Estimated results in Scully (2002) for a larger sample of eighty advanced countries confirm that income inequality depends negatively on the proportion of government spending in GDP (both government consumption and transfers and subsidies).

Whether market operation contributes to income equality also strongly depends on the type of institutions governing capital, output, and labor markets (World Bank, 2006). In many developing countries, access to the financial market is highly unequal. A small number of wealthy families exert extensive control over the financial sector. Rapid liberalization and privatization allow powerful insiders to gain control over state banks (Stiglitz, 2002). The poor often have to pay much higher interest rates. Prahalad (2006) mentions the example of Dhavarie (near Bombay) in India, where the interest rate for the poor is 600–1000 percent, compared to 12–18 percent for the rich in Bombay. Labor market institutions can also lead to significant equity gains. Examples are the right to be represented by unions, minimum wage legislation, and labor security regulations. Important product market institutions are antitrust legislation, good infrastructure and low transportation costs, and supply of information (for example by Internet connection in rural areas).

3.3.4 Income equality between countries

According to Milanovic (2005), 70 percent of worldwide income inequality arises from income variation between countries and 30 percent from income inequality within countries. In order to determine the impact of international markets on equality, one should therefore not only look at income inequality measures for individual countries, but also consider the convergence between countries.

Table 3.6 indicates that the expansion of international markets has not contributed to greater income equality between rich and poor countries. From 1820 to 2001 the ratio of per capita income between the richest and the poorest country rose from 3:1 to 15:1. Income inequality has grown in recent decades. This contradicts the expectations of economists such as Lucas (2000) who argue that the spread of technology will diminish income inequality between countries in the long run. The major exceptions are Japan (during 1953–1973) and more recently India and China.

According to the UN (2006), the hypothesis that international markets will bring convergence of income levels across countries is only confirmed on a regional level. For example, in Europe relatively poor countries like Greece, Spain, Portugal, and Ireland were able to adapt to the economic prosperity of

Table 3.6 Trends in worldwide income ratios[a]

	Growth rate real income per capita[b]			Ratio of real income per capita compared to Western countries				
	Total 1820–2001	Annual 1973–1980	Annual 1980–2001	1820	1950	1973	1980	2001
Western countries	19.0	1.9	1.9					
East Europe	8.8	2.1	0.2	0.57	0.34	0.37	0.38	0.26
USSR	6.7	0.8	−1.6	0.57	0.45	0.45	0.42	0.20
Latin America	8.4	2.7	0.3	0.58	0.40	0.34	0.35	0.25
Asia	6.9	2.8	2.3	0.48	0.15	0.15	0.16	0.18
China	6.0	3.5	5.9	0.50	0.07	0.06	0.07	0.16
India	3.7	1.4	3.6	0.44	0.10	0.06	0.06	0.09
Japan	30.9	2.3	2.1	0.56	0.30	0.85	0.88	0.91
Africa	3.5	1.2	−0.1	0.35	0.14	0.11	0.10	0.07

Notes
a Source: UN (2006: World Economic and Social Survey, Table I.1).
b Gross National Product per capita in 1990 international Geary Khamis dollars.

other European countries, due to their geographical location and stronger trade relations with richer European countries, the transfer of technology, and financial support by the EU. Regional convergence also occurred in East and South Asian countries, whereas African and Latin American countries showed convergence in economic stagnation. In fact, 84 percent of worldwide income inequality is accounted for by income differences between regions and only 16 percent by income differences within regions (UN, 2006).

This indicates that market forces alone will not be sufficient to bring about worldwide income equality. Calderón *et al.* (2005) show that financial and trade liberalization generally leads to higher economic growth, but this positive impact appears to be small for poor countries. Only as a country develops, does the impact become substantial (see also Chapter 2 above). According to the UN (2005), a country should have a certain amount of physical and human capital in order to compete on the worldwide market. Without basic infrastructure (roads, railways, harbors, energy facilities, telecommunications, safe drinking water, etc.), good public governance and administration, education, and a minimum of health services, local companies will not be able to compete on the world market.

3.3.5 Worldwide individual income distribution

In the previous section we took countries as units of analysis, measuring inequality between them. However, if one is concerned about income equality between individuals, it seems more useful to consider indices that take the population sizes of various countries into account. A few countries in Asia, like China and India, that have seen a substantial rise in income levels are large and populous, while many of the countries that have stagnated are small.

In order to construct a world distribution of income index, Sala-i-Martin (2006) integrates the annual income distributions of 138 countries (see Figure 3.1). He shows that globally the Gini coefficient of individual citizens remained more or less flat during the 1970s and followed a downward trend over the following two decades. In 2000, the world Gini coefficient was 0.637. Overall, the Gini has declined by almost 4 percent since 1979 (when it peaked at 0.662). Other income inequality indices (Atkinson indices, the variance of the logarithm of income, the ratio of the average income of the top 20 percent of the distribution to the bottom 20 percent, the ratio of the top 10 percent to the bottom 10 percent of the distribution, the Mean Logarithmic Deviation, and the Theil Index) show a remarkably similar pattern of worldwide inequality over time. They remained more or less constant (or possibly increased) during the 1970s but declined substantially during the 1980s and 1990s. Furthermore, when China is excluded from the analysis, the picture reveals that worldwide individual income inequalities increased from 0.620 to 0.648 between 1970 and 2000. Sala-i-Martin also breaks down the decrease in worldwide inequality between individuals into a within-country and between-country component. These components show that within-country inequality increased over the sample

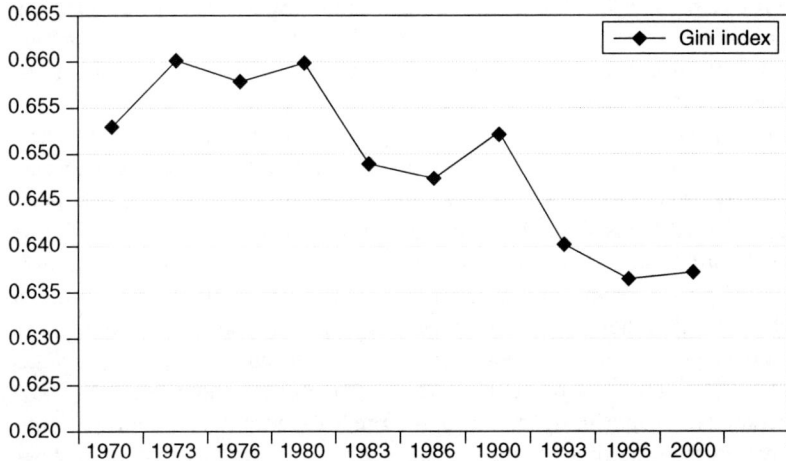

Figure 3.1 World individual income inequality (source: Sala-i-Martin (2006: Figure VIII)).

period, whereas the between-country index declined. Since the latter effect was larger, overall global income inequality declined.

3.4 A Christian view on the market and justice

In this section we bring together the normative standards set out in sections 3.1 and 3.2 and the descriptive analysis in section 3.3 to derive a Christian view on the market from the perspective of justice. First, we discuss the priority position of the poor and how positive and negative rights relate to each other. Next, we discuss redistribution by the government.

3.4.1 The priority of the poor

Section 3.2 shows that many texts in the Bible endorse respect for negative rights and the capitalist principles of distributive justice. During the times of the kings, the violation of negative rights was an important cause of oppression of the poor which evoked protests by the prophets. However, there are also many texts that underline the moral duty to help the poor. Not only in the sense of charity. The Old Testament describes several institutions that seek to secure the positive right to subsistence. In many texts, assistance to the poor is motivated by their needs and not by violation of their negative rights. Likewise in the New Testament, fulfillment of the essential needs of the poor has a high priority. This is particularly reflected in the preaching of Jesus where he identifies himself with the sick, the lame, and other unfortunate groups in society. The Gospels attach extremely low value to accumulation of wealth and condemn the rich if they do not care about the poor, or even worse, violate their negative rights to freedom.

On the basis of this analysis, I conclude that the economic order should guarantee positive basic rights, while, at the same time, respecting negative rights as much as possible. This requirement holds for all Western countries, because they can easily afford to meet the basic needs of all their citizens by provision of minimum subsistence, health care, education, etc. Empirical research shows that Western countries with a high collective supply of these goods do not perform worse economically than countries that do not guarantee these social-economic rights. For poor countries, provision of goods that meet basic social-economic rights is not always possible. However, respect for positive rights should not be postponed until these countries have reached a high welfare level on the grounds that meeting positive rights slows down their economic development. Empirical research shows that these countries cannot develop in a sustainable way without human development. So in developing countries too absolute side-constraints should be set on economic practices. It is unacceptable if women are fired when they become pregnant (Südwind, 2000), if large Western multinationals pay substantially less than the living wage (Klein, 2002), or if employees have to work twelve hours a day and seven days a week (Musiolek, 1999). The argument that developing countries should have the opportunity to develop just as Western countries have in the past is also disputable because the current world economy is very different from that of 200 years ago. At that time, there were no rich countries that could assist the Western countries in their economic development (or hamper their economic development because of their economic power). Now developing countries have to develop in the presence of other countries that are rich and powerful. This creates a responsibility to help the poor countries to a level where human rights can be guaranteed. Stimulating free trade is insufficient for that purpose, because for poor countries it remains difficult to benefit from international trade if they lack the minimal level of health, education and infrastructure that they need to upgrade their economies by product differentiation and absorption of technological developments from abroad. The rich countries should therefore play an active role in the development process of the poor countries.

3.4.2 Redistribution in rich countries: can we define an acceptable range?

As already stated, Western countries should give priority to meeting the basic needs of their own citizens. Economic growth should be instrumental to this goal. In the Christian view, the government should, if necessary, guarantee that basic positive rights to minimal subsistence, basic health care and primary education are met.

But what if this situation is realized on a larger scale, as in the Scandinavian or other European countries? Is further redistribution then necessary from a Christian point of view? If yes, how far should the government go?

In section 3.2 we noted that the Bible does not demand compulsory redistribution to realize a situation of absolute egalitarianism. Nevertheless, eschatological texts like Zechariah 3: 10 and Micah 4: 4 still imply a considerable degree of economic equality. "All will enjoy peace and security and be surrounded by their vineyards and fig trees." That does not indicate that all should own the same amount of property, but still requires that all should be equally happy and receive the opportunities to reach this state of happiness. That puts limits to the economic inequality between rich and poor.

Ideally, economic equality is realized by respecting negative rights to freedom and in accordance with the principle of moral deserts. That means people should achieve it independently, by their own labor, and respecting private property. Economic independence furthers human dignity. This is expressed in the eschatological text in Isaiah 65 that describes people on the new earth fully enjoying the things they have worked for. In such a free capitalist society people would also have the opportunity to conclude insurance contracts that protect them against unexpected setbacks. The ideal society would also feature voluntary solidarity with those who, against their own will and notwithstanding their efforts, lag behind others in society (see the standard of virtue ethics in Chapter 4 below).

However, it is illusory to expect the free market, in which the government only guarantees a minimum subsistence level of welfare, to realize this ideal. In a free market economy, only people with a similar risk profile can be insured against comparable conditions. Nor will the egalitarian ideal of reasonable income equality materialize by voluntary solidarity. Although rich people can be very generous, income inequality in countries with low government expenditure remains much higher than in countries with high collective solidarity.

Therefore, the ideal of reasonable income equality requires an additional violation of the negative rights to private property. But how far can one go? Obviously, two basic rights conflict. It is dangerous to try to compose an ideal society by force. Collectively forced solidarity can erode voluntary solidarity (see also Chapter 4 below). I therefore see two important side conditions. First, the violation of negative rights (by taxing private income) should really improve the situation of the least advantaged (by providing collective resources for their economic development). This is also expressed by Rawls' difference principle that accepts a certain degree of inequality, but not beyond the point where greater inequality would make the position of the least advantaged deteriorate further. If collective means are effective in improving the primary social goods of the least advantaged, redistribution beyond a minimum level of state welfare provision is justified. The economies of Scandinavian countries show that such redistribution is also economically feasible. However, the effectiveness of redistribution policies and their impact on overall economic growth will differ by country.

Another important side-constraint is citizens' preferences. Cultures differ greatly in their valuation of freedom versus equality. To illustrate, the divergence in democratic support for redistribution policies shows that US citizens place relatively higher priority on individual freedom than on equal income in comparison to European citizens. If a majority of the population does not want substantial government redistribution, then this kind of policy is much more harmful to the respect of the negative right to freedom. Because of these cultural differences, the range of income inequality that is still legitimate from a Christian point of view is quite large.

3.5 Summary

3.5.1 Principles of rights and distributive justice in ethics

Ethics has developed many different standards of human rights and justice. I distinguish between twelve standards of distributive justice: (1) absolute egalitarianism (everybody has an equal share); (2) the difference principle (inequalities are allowed up to the point where the least advantaged get most in comparison to other distributions); (3) the needs and ability to pay principle (people receive according to their needs, and contribute according to their ability); (4) the capability principle (people who need more to develop capabilities receive more); (5) the weighted priority view (benefiting people matters more the worse off they are, the more numerous such people are, and the greater the benefits in question); (6) utilitarianism (equalize the marginal utility of all individuals); (7) respect for positive basic rights (redistribution is fair if it improves the absolute circumstances of people below an absolute threshold of income); (8) the principle of equal opportunity (positions are open to all under conditions of equality of opportunity); (9) reward of effort (distribution is according to the efforts of individuals); (10) reward of productivity (distribution is according to the productivity of individuals); (11) reward to market price (distribution is according to the market mechanism); (12) respect for negative rights (distribution is by free transactions).

Differences in concepts of distributive justice pertain not only to the type of standards, but also to whether they hold worldwide (universal) or only apply to the distribution of goods within a certain type of community.

3.5.2 Principles of justice in the Bible

The Exodus story shows that freedom and liberation are central themes in the Old Testament. God released Israel from slavery in Egypt. He wants Israel to be a society in which people are not oppressed.

The Bible supports several standards of distributive justice. On the one hand, capitalist standards of justice are amply supported by biblical texts. Many texts in the Old and New Testaments reflect respect for negative rights, respect for private property, equality under the law, the principle of moral deserts, respect for contracts, respect for freedom in transactions (no deception in trade), and justice in rectification (in case of violation of justice in transactions).

In the libertarian view, biblical justice pertains to respect for negative rights and procedural justice. In this view, helping poor people who have been impoverished for reasons other than violation of their negative rights should be perceived as a matter of charity, not as a matter of justice. However, unlike this Christian libertarian view, biblical justice is not limited to these capitalist standards. There are several texts that also prescribe a positive duty to fulfill the basic needs of the poor, independent of the cause of their poverty. This confirms the view of the Accra declaration that extreme poverty is unjust according to Christian faith.

God is so much attached to preserving the lives of the poor that whether they are helped through charity or through justice following violation of their negative rights does not make any difference with respect to the morally obligatory character of this kind of help.

The positive right to subsistence was embedded in Old Testament society by various institutions, such as the right of the poor to harvest the land during sabbatical years, to glean olive trees and vines, to gather corn left after the harvest and at the edges of the fields, the tithing law, the law on sharing food with the poor at the harvest festival, and the prohibition on demanding interest from the poor. These laws support the needs principle of justice. However, in most cases the poor could only receive this subsistence welfare by their labor. Thus, these laws remain closely related to the principle of rendering to each his or her due.

The capability principle was also supported by various institutions in the Old Testament, such as sabbatical years and jubilee years. Jubilee years could also be interpreted as an application of the principle of equal opportunities, because it provided people with access to the most crucial capital factor in an agricultural economy, land.

Although there was no compulsory absolute egalitarianism, one can still maintain that the ideal of the Old Testament was an economy with small differences in income and wealth.

There are no biblical texts that support the weighted priority view, utilitarianism, or the difference principle. The Bible is largely unfamiliar with the modern concepts of (marginal) utility and efficiency. It does not propose any kind of maximization of total happiness or of the social primary goods of the least advantaged group. Still, the difference principle does not conflict with the biblical view on distributive justice. It may be perceived as a legitimate variant of justice, without denying that more or less egalitarian principles can also be defended from a biblical point of view.

The radical preaching of Jesus supports both the needs principle and the principle of moral deserts. Both principles are also found in the writings of the apostle Paul.

Although solidarity is universal, both the Old and New Testaments confirm communitarian principles of distribution that give higher priority to those who are part of one's own community. In the Old Testament the Hebrew people have more rights than foreigners, in the New Testament fellow believers take precedence over non-believers.

Animals should not merely be treated as means to human interests. They have certain rights – food, rest – and should be respected as creatures of God.

3.5.3 Markets, rights, and justice: outcomes of economic research

If markets function well, negative rights and capitalist principles of justice will be respected. Market imperfections distort respect for negative rights and capitalist justice.

If competition is fierce, negative rights to freedom can be wiped out by trade with undemocratic regimes.

Empirical research generally supports the hypothesis that trade liberalization reduces absolute poverty in the long run. Thus, we find no evidence that free international markets have been a major cause of poverty in the developing countries, as suggested by the Accra declaration.

Human development (measured by life expectancy and education) is strongly positively related to economic welfare in developing countries. Whether economic growth contributes to respect for positive human rights depends on the allocation of the revenues of growth and income distribution.

Since empirical research has shown that free markets (approximated by the index of economic freedom) contribute to economic growth, we may conclude that markets are a necessary condition for human development and the fulfillment of basic needs.

The econometric evidence that economic freedom reduces income inequality is mixed. Econometric evidence shows unambiguously, however, that income inequality decreases with government redistribution policies.

Western economies with a larger proportion of government spending meet the needs principle, capability principle, and difference principle better than economies with a small proportion of government spending.

Trade liberalization tends to increase income inequality within poor countries in the short and medium terms. In the longer term the effects are uncertain. The effect of market operation on income equality depends on the various types of institutions governing the capital, labor, and product markets.

There is no indication that the globalization of the economy has reduced income inequality between countries. Insofar as convergence takes place, it is mainly on a regional scale, wealth being spread among all countries in rich regions and lack of wealth being spread in poor regions.

Global income inequality between individual citizens remained more or less flat during the 1970s and followed a downward trend over the following two decades. Although within-country inequality increased in the period from 1970 to 2000, overall inequality declined because of the rise in average income in populous poor Asian countries like China and India.

4 The market and virtues

The moral standards in Chapters 2 and 3 judge the moral value of the market by applying certain principles. Ethics is, however, concerned with more than a system of principles. It is also about the development of certain characteristics that people need if they are to put values and norms into practice. This aspect is stressed in virtue ethics. Principles are distinct from the people who are to apply them. Virtue ethics focuses on what people should be like (Desjardins, 1984). Only if people internalize ethical principles by developing a moral character can these principles function in daily reality.

In recent years economists have become more interested in how virtues influence the interaction of economic agents in imperfect markets. Sen (1977) argues that societies are only viable if they uphold social norms and rules of conduct. To run a society entirely on incentives to personal gain would be pretty much a hopeless task. A great many virtues are relevant to the economy (Solomon, 1992). Virtues like honesty, loyalty, trustfulness, and justice facilitate efficient coordination if individual and common goals are not perfectly aligned and if information is imperfect. According to Arrow (1972), virtually every commercial transaction has within itself an element of trust, certainly any transaction conducted over a period of time. Frank (2004) gives several examples of how integrity contributes to profitable business opportunities and wealth.

In economic theory social norms and trust that sustain implicit contracts are labeled social capital. Social capital refers to the networks, norms, and trust that enable participants to act together more effectively to pursue shared objectives. The World Values Survey shows that higher social trust is associated with low corruption, higher tax compliance and the efficiency and integrity of the legal system (Atherton, 2008). The economic importance of social capital has by now been firmly established by empirical research. Knack and Keefer (1997) and Zak and Knack (2001) posit a strong and significant relationship between social capital and economic growth. Beugelsdijk *et al.*'s (2004) "robustness analysis" reveals that the results of Zak and Knack (2001) are highly robust in terms of statistical significance, although the effect of trust on growth may vary in extent, dependent on the set of variables and the sample used in the analysis. In this kind of research, trust is measured by the answer to the question: "Generally speaking, would you say that most people can be trusted, or that you can't be too careful in dealing with people?"[1]

The recognition that trust contributes importantly to efficient market operation has generated interest in the determinants of trustfulness, civic cooperation, and other virtues. It is this question that concerns us in this chapter. More specifically, we are interested in the inverse impact of market operation on virtues. For, as Knight (1923) argues, while men are "playing the game" of competition, they are also molding their own and other personalities. From an economic point of view, insight into the determinants of virtues is important for securing economic welfare. But from an ethical point of view, the research interest in the determinants of virtues is not primarily driven by the potential economic benefits that virtues may bring about, but rather by the more general goal, a good individual and community life. Even if virtues reduced economic growth, they should be fostered because they contribute to the overall quality of human life. In virtue ethics, the main criterion to judge capitalism is therefore not whether it serves economic growth, but whether it serves the good life by fostering virtues and restraining vices.

In order to analyze the impact of markets on virtues, I first present an elaborate scheme of virtues derived from Aristotelian virtue ethics. In section 2 I compare Greek virtue ethics with biblical notions about virtue. In section 3 I present an overview of the literature that sheds light on the empirical effects of market operation on various virtues. Section 4 puts the pieces together and derives a Christian view of the market from the perspective of virtues. Section 5 summarizes the main conclusions.

4.1 The classical virtue ethics of Aristotle

4.1.1 The concept of virtue

Virtues are character traits that are socially valued. Examples are patience, attentiveness, concern, humility, honesty, integrity, self-control, and the like. They are habits of the heart, stable dispositions, durable characteristics acquired by a person who has exercised her will to be good (McCloskey, 2006: 64). This does not exclude that a virtuous person may do wrong in extreme circumstances: none of us are unfailingly good. The reason why a person acted is crucial: those who act in a virtuous way, but intensely dislike considering the interests of others, should be judged as deficient in virtue. Like Kantian ethics, virtue ethics is a *Gesinnungsethik*, but in contrast to Kant's philosophy, virtue ethics implies that acting out of duty is not sufficient. Virtue ethics focuses on the conformity between right thinking and desire (Koehn, 1995). The virtuous agent is the person habituated to desire to do what is good and noble. Virtue ethics thus has the merit of not demanding a divided attitude. It does not compel people to do what duty dictates, irrespective of whether they want to or not.

A virtue is praiseworthy in part because it is an achievement. We are not born virtuous, but must be trained so that virtuous activity becomes habitual, just as we must be trained in other skills (Velasquez, 1998). Its development requires effort. For example, the virtue of courage or temperance is only acquired after training oneself or being trained by others, especially during one's youth, by a good upbringing by parents and education at school. Everybody should try to develop virtues so that they become second nature.

The acquisition of virtues is necessary because every person has a natural tendency to do wrong (vices). If one is optimistic about the natural capacity of human beings to do good, there is no need for a struggle to become virtuous. Virtue ethics assumes that human beings do not have a spontaneous will to be good, either to themselves or to others. Any person is open to temptation to do evil and succumbing to such temptation makes that person or other people unhappy (Graafland, 2007a).

4.1.2 *The virtue ethics of Aristotle*

The source of virtue ethics is to be found in the classical Hellenistic tradition represented by Plato and Aristotle. The standard work of Aristotle on virtue ethics is *Ethica Nicomachea* (EN). In contrast to Plato, who argued that the standards for goodness are transcendental, Aristotle followed an inductive approach. His studies in biology made him believe that every being aims at a goal that is specific to the nature of that being.

Aristotle uses the word *telos* to refer to the end or good toward which a thing is moving. For human beings the *telos* is well-being or happiness (eudaimonia). "Now happiness more than anything else seems unconditionally complete, since we always choose it because of itself, never because of something else" (EN: 1097b20). In Aristotle's view, a human being is happy if he performs activities in an excellent or virtuous way. Excellences relate to one particular type of function or work in which persons engage. An example is the excellence of a good doctor who gives a good diagnosis. Moral virtues, by contrast, are universally praiseworthy features of human character that have been fixed by habituation (Beauchamp, 1982).[2]

Aristotle distinguishes between two sorts of virtues: the virtues of thought and the virtues of character. The virtues of thought are the practical and theoretical intellect that arises from teaching and experience. The virtues of character are the ethical virtues. They arise as a result of habit: we become just by performing just actions, temperate by performing temperate actions, brave by performing brave actions.[3] Hence, we must display the right activities, because differences in these imply corresponding differences in the qualities of character. For Aristotle, character is thus an inevitable outcome of action. No true description of what an action is can be given without considering what further consequences that action has for the agent's ability to perform future actions appropriately (Koehn, 1995). This generates an interesting spiral: good actions generate a good character, and a good character makes it easier to perform good actions. This also implies that a human being is responsible for his or her character. Hence, if after a long series of bad actions one develops a bad character and

therefore becomes insensitive to or ignorant of what is good, one is still responsible for one's bad actions (EN: 1114a14, 1115a4). The importance of habit formation further implies that one cannot change overnight from a bad person into
a good person. As one's character changes only slowly, it is not possible to stop
being bad. Although one initially has a choice between performing good or bad
actions, once one is used to bad actions, it is not possible not to be a bad person
any more, according to Aristotle.

Aristotle enumerates several virtues of character (see Table 4.1 below). The
common characteristic of the virtues of character is that they keep a middle
ground between the vice of going too far and the vice of not going far enough in
one's actions. In each situation one must take stock of what is required. The
mean is what an intelligent person would find reasonable (EN: 1107a2). This
requires the virtue of prudence. McCloskey (2006: 253) defines prudence as
good judgment or practical wisdom.[4] The quality of a character tends to be
ruined by excess or deficiency. To illustrate, temperance is the middle ground
with respect to pleasure derived from the sense of taste that human beings share
with animals. Temperance holds the middle ground between the vice of indul-
gence and the vice of austerity. Temperate people enjoy the right things and take
the right quantity. When they lack food or drink, they do not become dissatisfied, or at least not more than is appropriate. Only temperate people have the
ability to be happy, because the longing for pleasure is insatiable. Therefore, our
desires must be tempered and be low in number and consistent with reason.
Another example is generosity. Generosity is the mean between avarice and
extravagance. Avaricious persons devote too much attention to their property.
On the other hand, extravagant people squander their property. Property is a tool.
A person who has a virtuous attitude with respect to material property uses it in
the best way, and such people are generous . Their gifts are in proportion to their
property. Generous people do not give against their will. They give with pleasure the right amount to the right people. They will also not be inclined to acquire
property in an unjust way, because they are not greatly concerned with getting
rich. On the other hand, they will not waste their property either, because they
want to use it to serve others. Because of their generous attitude, generous
people will not easily become rich. Avaricious persons take what they can get,
more than is appropriate. In order to earn money, they are even prepared to lose
their good reputation. Although extravagant people are less depraved than the
avaricious, they too run a risk of becoming corrupt. As they like to spend too
much, they often need more money than they can earn in an honest way.

In the literature, the four cardinal virtues – courage, temperance, justice, and
prudence – often get the most attention. Economists even tend to reduce all
virtues to the virtue of prudence or rationality. Justice, honesty, and all other
virtues are perceived as prudent ways of acting for the sake of long-term self-
interest. McCloskey (2006: 282) argues, however, that the virtues cannot be
reduced to prudence or aggregated to some overall concept of one highest good.
The various virtues are complementary and incommensurable. Virtues are also
context-dependent: which virtues deserve priority depends on the situation. One

should stay calm when a friend becomes angry, brave if others become fearful. Because virtues cannot be reduced to one dimension, dilemmas can arise between different virtues. In this respect, virtue ethics differs from utilitarianism, which assumes that all utilities can be aggregated and that the solution of the choice problem is unambiguously determined by maximizing total utility. Virtue ethics accepts fundamentally conflicting impulses that do not allow rational solutions without dilemmas (McCloskey, 2006: 359). It acknowledges that ethics is more about building bridges than about mathematics.

4.2 Christian virtues

Like Greek ethics, Christian ethics stress the importance of virtues. "A healthy tree bears good fruit, but a poor tree bears bad fruit" (Matt. 7:17). Christians derives their identity from the life story of Jesus. The imitation of Christ means exercising the virtues that characterized Jesus' character (Loonstra, 2000). Christian ethics acknowledges the power of evil and the human tendency to do wrong (vices). The Bible sketches the high origin of the human being as an image of God, but also his fallen character that is more evil than the *homo economicus*, who is neither altruistic nor envious. The apostle Paul gives the following concise description in Romans 3:10–16: "There is no one who is righteous ... no one does what is right, not even one ... they leave ruin and destruction wherever they go." Disregarding the reality of evil is harmful to society. A society that does not want to know about the evil character of humans, easily falls prey to evil powers (Verbrugge, 2004). There is need of a struggle to become virtuous.

4.2.1 Comparing Aristotelian and Christian virtues

Christian virtues are derived from the Bible. There is much overlap between Greek and Christian virtues. To illustrate, an envious and insatiable attitude is rejected in the Decalogue. This is apparent from the tenth commandment: "Do not desire another man's house ... or anything else that he owns" (Exod. 20:17). This commandment states that we should not place ourselves in a competitive relationship to our neighbors by wanting what they have. Such competition can never be won and is a source of dissatisfaction, because there are always people who have more than we have. Table 4.1 presents an overview of the Greek and biblical virtues. Aristotle often used similar wording to the bible. The meaning of Christian virtues is, however, colored by Christian theology. The linguistic field of meanings does not therefore fully overlap with that of the meanings of corresponding virtues in Greek virtue ethics. Take, for example, the virtue of long-suffering. In the Bible this means that a person will not easily become angry (Noordegraaf *et al.*, 2005). Thus it is similar to the virtue of self-possession in Greek virtue ethics. But it can also indicate an attitude of waiting for God. Thus it refers to patience and spiritual perseverance. Furthermore, the virtue of long-suffering can be connected to love. Love is patient (1 Cor. 13:4). This means that one endures others, notwithstanding the harm that others do to one.

Table 4.1 Aristotelian and biblical virtues and vices[a]

		Deficit	Middle ground	Excess
Daring	Greek	Cowardice	Courage	Recklessness
	Bible	Cowardice, fearfulness	Courage, bravery	Overconfidence, frivolity
Pleasure/pain	Greek	Insensitivity	Temperance	Excess
	Bible		Temperance, moderation, sobriety, contentment	Desire, licentiousness, lust, gluttony, insatiableness
Anger	Greek	Inertia	Self-possession	Short-temper
	Bible	Resignation	Calmness, quietness, self-control, long-sufferingness	Irritability, impatience, vengefulness
Particular emotions	Greek	Malicious pleasure at the misfortunes of others	Righteous indignation	Envy
	Bible	Shamelessness	Righteous indignation	Jealousy
Giving	Greek	Avarice, niggardliness	Generosity, handsomeness	Extravagance, vulgarity
	Bible	Avarice, niggardliness, greed, selfishness	Generosity, benevolence, unselfishness, willingness to make sacrifices	Extravagance, wastefulness, ostentation
Status	Greek	Humility	Pride	Arrogance
	Bible	Humility, meekness, simplicity, modesty, shyness	Frankness, candidness	Arrogance, patronizingness, conceit, complacency
Social interaction	Greek	Grumpiness, false modesty, rudeness	Friendliness, honesty, wit	Unctuousness, boastfulness, foolery
	Bible	Dissatisfaction, meanness, quarrelsomeness, insincerity, slanderousness, unfaithful, faithlessness, rudeness, incivilitude	Faithfulness, peace-lovingness, tolerance, inoffensiveness, sincerity, genuineness, hospitability, civilitude, cheerfulness	Derision
Trade relationship	Greek	Injustice, deceit	Justice, trustworthiness	Injustice, submissiveness
	Bible	Predatoriness, partiality, misleading, fraudulence, falsity	Fairness, reasonableness, faithfulness, impartiality, clarity	Enduring

Note

a The vices that are underlined are virtues in the Bible.

Some Christian virtues are not mentioned in EN, but still fit quite well into Aristotle's framework. Examples are hospitality and tolerance, which relate to Aristotle's category of friendship, because he placed friendship in the context of the continuation of community relations (chapter VIII in EN). Another Christian virtue not mentioned in EN is diligence. According to the wisdom writers laziness causes poverty: "But while he sleeps, poverty will attack him like an armed robber" (Prov. 6:11).[5] In *Politics* (Book I), one can observe that Aristotle also supported the virtue of diligence, because in this book he used it as an argument in defense of private property. Communal ownership of goods would generate laziness and disinclination to work, since each would seek to shift his or her work onto others. Similarly, some Aristotelian virtues are not explicitly mentioned in the Bible, but are not in conflict with biblical virtues. An example is insensitivity that is somewhat related to the biblical concept of indifference, although the biblical concept of indifference often concerns spiritual attitude whereas Aristotelian insensitivity is concerned with pleasure.[6]

Notwithstanding a substantial overlap between Greek and Christian virtues, there are also some evident divergences. For example, whereas humility is a vice in Aristotle's account, it is considered a virtue in Christian ethics. The great example is Jesus, who, according to the Bible, took the nature of a servant, was humble, and walked the path of obedience all the way to his death on the cross. He knelt before his disciples and washed their feet, as a slave would. In this, he left an example of the command he gave his disciples: "The greatest one among you must be your servant. Whoever makes himself great will be humbled, and whoever humbles himself, will be made great" (Matt. 23:11–12; see also Phil. 2:6). Humility amounts to a slave mentality and stands in contrast to the Greek virtue of pride. In Christian ethics, humility does not only relate to the proper attitude of man toward God, but also implies an attitude of meekness toward one's fellow humans and of modesty. The Christian virtue of humility also explains why endurance or submission is not a vice. Because of the value of love, one must be prepared to endure injustice.

The virtue of humility is closely connected to the most central Christian virtue, namely the virtue of love, and related virtues such as helpfulness, mercifulness, self-sacrifice, compassion, and mildness. The Christian virtue of love differs from Aristotelian friendship. In Aristotle's account of the virtues, friendship is based on reciprocity. According to Aristotle, friends receive more or less in equal degree from each other. If there is a substantial imbalance in excellence, welfare, or goodness, or something else, it will not be possible to maintain the friendship (EN: 1158b35). Aristotle therefore considers friendship between God and man impossible. How different is Christian virtue ethics on this point. In the Bible God's love for the sinner is the most central message (MacIntyre, 1985). Instead of reciprocity, God loves humans and responds to their sins by gracefully providing reconciliation by the sacrifice of Christ.

The virtue of love has some similarity with the virtue of generosity in Aristotle's account in the sense that both require a willingness to make sacrifices. But Aristotle's account of generosity concerns one's attitude to wealth and money, whereas the scope of the virtue of love in Christianity is broader and also concerns other aspects of human relationships. Another difference is that the virtue of generosity in Aristotle's account is related to nobility and one's place in society (EN: 1122). One's sacrifices must be proportionate to one's wealth and based more on reciprocity than on mere giving. Generous people receive gratitude and honor from the community in return.

The virtue of love is closely connected to other specific Christian virtues such as mercifulness, helpfulness, self-sacrifice, forgivingness, kind-heartedness, and compassion (Table 4.2). The Hebrew root of "merciful" is *rechem*, which originally means "womb." It expresses the compassion of the mother for her child. It is a movement from the higher to the lower, just as God cares for the weak, the poor, the oppressed, and those who have no helper. In the New Testament mercifulness is particularly connected to the grace of God, as for example in the parable of the prodigal son (Luke 15:20), but it also has a social meaning. Jesus is often described as having pity for the poor, the sick, the hungry, the possessed, and the sinners. The virtue of forgivingness is clearly expressed by the parable of the unforgiving servant which ends with: "You should have had mercy on your fellow-servant, just as I had mercy on you" (Matt. 18:33). This resembles the fifth term in the prayer in Matthew 6:12: "Forgive us the wrongs we have done, as we forgive the wrongs that others have done to us." Kind-heartedness is one of the fruits of the Holy Spirit. In the Old Testament kind-heartedness (*anava*) is related to humility (*ani*). *Anan* and *ani* are used in close connection. Both words have a social as well as a spiritual meaning. Jesus himself is described as kind-hearted, humbly riding on a donkey to Jerusalem.

Another difference between Christian ethics and classical ethics is the focus on God. Table 4.3 gives several examples of virtues and vices connected to the relationship between man and God. The believer should remember the great deeds of God. Faithful acceptance of the grace of God further requires an atti-

Table 4.2 Specific biblical virtues and vices

Virtues	Vices
Loving, merciful, serving, helping, self-sacrificing, gracious, forgiving, kind-hearted, compassionate	Loveless, selfish, merciless, heartless

Table 4.3 Spiritual virtues and vices

Virtues			Vices		
Mindful	Regretful	Grateful	Forgetful	Unremorseful, impenitent	Ungrateful
Holy, pious, obedient, pure	Faithful, god-fearing, respectful	Hopeful, without worry	Unholy, impure, disobedient	Faithless, godless, idolatrous, blasphemous	Without hope, overanxious

tude of penitence. Regret is crucial to the process of reconciliation. In turn, the grace of God elicits an attitude of gratitude. The essence of the Christian virtues is the attitude of total surrender of one's will to that of God. The model of the Christian life is the life of Jesus, his radical obedience to God and his love for his fellow humans (Phil. 2:5; Col. 3:13). Greek ethics was not primarily God-oriented, nor did virtue connote surrender to God's will. In Greek ethics, virtues consist of regulating the passions and leading a rational life. A properly acquired knowledge of the workings of reason will bring with it a virtuous and happy life (Kellenberger, 1980). Christianity does not share the Greek belief in the self-sufficiency of human beings, but rather puts its hope in the redeeming love of God. It regards the achievement of a virtuous life primarily as a gift of God, beyond the powers of man without the grace of the Almighty.

This is also evident in the two other cardinal Christian virtues, faith and hope. Faith is trust in God and respect for God. It is closely connected to the virtue of hope: "To have faith is to be sure of the things we hope for, to be certain of the things we cannot see" (Hebr. 11:1). Whoever trusts in God has hope in His care, also as regards material needs (Matt. 6:30). There is therefore an inherent tension between the classical virtues and the more specific Christian virtues. This is especially true for the theology of Augustine and Luther. Other Christian theologians have tried to reconcile the Greek concept of self-fulfillment with the concept of grace. For example, Thomas Aquinas accepted the four cardinal virtues of Aristotle. He then added the three cardinal Christian virtues (faith, hope, and love) and proposed a division whereby the intellectual and moral virtues perfect the human intellect and appetite in proportion to human nature and the theological virtues the supernatural.

McCloskey (2006) also tries to reconcile the typical Christian virtues with an economy driven by reciprocity rather than by love. To illustrate, McCloskey (2006: 189) interprets humility as selfless respect for reality and an attitude of willingness to listen to others. This interpretation makes it easier to fit humility into the context of the market, as any businessman can only succeed by listening carefully to his clients. She mentions McDonalds and Wal-Mart as examples of companies that have become successful due to offering humble products and listening carefully to what customers want. However, categorizing Wal-Mart as an example of humility takes us quite a long way from the Christian meaning of humility, that one considers others to be better than oneself, that one is modest, meek, simple-hearted, humble, or ready to submit oneself to another. Likewise, McCloskey extends the meaning of faith and hope, and adds a more secular interpretation by arguing that every person has a conviction about reality beyond what can be known. This conviction is faith. It integrates the unknown and the known into a living whole. Hope is interpreted as the virtue of the energetic person who seeks a future difficult but attainable good, whether as a saint or an entrepreneur (2006: 159). Again, this interpretation is attractive because it brings Christian virtues nearer to daily life, but it also takes us farther away from the theological meaning of the Christian concept of hope.

4.2.2 How legitimate is self-interest?

In the virtue ethics of Adam Smith, prudence has a meaning that differs slightly from in Aristotelian ethics. Adam Smith defines prudence as "the careful and laborious and circumspect state of mind, ever watchful and ever attentive to the most distant consequence of every action ... to procure the greatest goods and to keep off the greatest evils" (1759: 434). It is superior reasoning and understanding which make one capable of discerning the remote consequences of all one's actions for one's own happiness (Smith, 1759: 271). Prudence is the central virtue of *homo economicus*. The virtue of prudence aims at self-interest. The prudent man thus combines rationality and self-interest, which are two conditions for a perfect market (see Chapter 2 above). Self-interest is not only a descriptive assumption that economists often use when describing economic behavior, it is also a normative assumption that underlies the market morality.

How does the assumption of self-interest relate to Christian ethics? As we have seen above, selfishness is a vice in Christian ethics that stands in contrast to the Christian virtue of self-sacrificing love (*agape*) and the related virtues reported in Table 4.2. Indeed, it is obvious that a focus on self-interest is condemned by the Bible. This also holds for rational self-interest (prudence) that takes account of the long-term consequences of choices informed by one's own interests. The virtue of love is not directed to one's own long-term interest, but is focused on the interest of others, without wanting any kind of compensation (Matt. 5:43–7).

However, this does not imply that self-interest is immoral. Rather, the Bible requires that self-interest should be in balance with the interest of others: "And look out for one another's interests, not just for your own" (Phil. 2:4). The great command to love your neighbor as you love yourself (Matt. 22:39) also strikes a balance between self-interest and the interest of others. Since people tend to love themselves more than others, both texts stress love for others, but this does not imply that one should not love oneself. This is also implicitly assumed in texts that promise a reward for active faith, such as Galatians 6:5, 6:8

> "For anyone has to carry his own load ... If he sows in the field of his natural desires, from it he will gather the harvest of death; if he sows in the field of the Spirit, he will gather the harvest of eternal life.

Although this text refers to spiritual recompensate, it nevertheless illustrates the legitimacy of minding one's own future. 1 Corinthians 3:12–15 also speaks of rewards for spiritual efforts to build on the foundation laid by Christ. Jesus himself more than once calls on believers to consider their own interest. An example is Matthew 19:29: "And everyone who has left houses or brothers or sisters or father or mother or children or fields for my sake, will receive a hundred times more and will be given eternal life."[7]

Agape *as a catalyst*

Can we also justify placing limits on self-sacrificing love? How realistic is this type of love in economic life? Isn't it too utopian for trade relations that are often based on reciprocity (Fehr and Gächter, 1999; Gächter and Fehr, 1999)? In Christian ethics the requirement of love has often been played down. An example is the two kingdoms doctrine in neo-Lutheran theology that makes a clear-cut distinction between secular life and spiritual life. This theology was inspired by the discovery of Weiss that the eschatology of Jesus was apocalyptic. In this view, it cannot be applied to current economic and political reality (Duchrow, 1987). The economic domain is ruled by its own laws that oppose the requirement of love.

Calvinist theology has likewise developed its own way of placing the radical command to love others as oneself outside harsh economic reality by arguing that the sinful nature of earthly reality renders perfect obedience to the law of God impossible. The true virtuous life will only materialize on the new earth.

A third way of making the radical requirement of self-sacrificing love less demanding is by interpreting it as a voluntary commitment to develop excellence in spiritual life. It is not an absolute moral duty. This is, for example, implied by the Catholic distinction between commands and so-called evangelical counsels (the advice given by Jesus in the Gospels, in particular the three counsels of obedience, voluntary poverty, and celibacy). An example is the command of Jesus to the rich young man: "If you want to be perfect, go and sell all you have and give the money to the poor, and you will have riches in heaven, then come and follow me" (Matt. 19:21). However, it is difficult to reconcile this interpretation with Jesus' statement in verse 23 that in general it will be very hard for rich people to enter the Kingdom of Heaven.

Rather than weakening the radical command of self-sacrificing love in economic life, I think it is more in line with biblical teaching to maintain the moral stringency of this command, but to apply it in balance with other moral values such as justice. Indeed, there is a serious dilemma between love and justice. If other people do not live up to their moral duties, we are faced with legitimate limits on our own duty to love others. For example, if you invest in cooperation with others who use your effort for their own purposes without reciprocation, it will be difficult to continue the cooperation, because their response has violated justice. Justice thus sets limits on self-sacrifice.

Another restriction on self-sacrificing love is that it can diminish the dignity of the beloved (Brümmer, 1993). If my wife loves me because it is her duty to love me, and not because I am a source of happiness to her, then her love will eventually not satisfy me because I cannot derive self-esteem from it. This kind of self-sacrificing love also discourages the personal responsibility of the beloved. I therefore suppose that Christian self-sacrificing love is rather meant as a catalyst to change people and stimulate them to a mature human relationship of reciprocity, as, for example, expressed in Romans 12:20–1: "If your enemy is hungry, feed him; if he is thirsty, give him a drink; for by doing this you will make him burn with shame. Do not let evil defeat you; instead, conquer evil with good." This parallels the ability of the love of Jesus to change the believer. God loves man, but He also wants him to enter a relationship of reciprocity and respond to God's love by loving others. As John remarks: "We love because God first loved us" (1 John 4:19). One needs patience to love others until they start to respond in the same way. But there is also a limit to God's patience, as is very well expressed by the parable of the unforgiving servant:

> The king was very angry, and he sent the servant to jail to be punished until he should pay back the whole amount.... That is how my Father in heaven will treat every one of you unless you forgive your brother from your heart.
>
> (Matt. 18:34–5)

This also holds for economic relationships. If entrepreneurs are prepared to go one step further and dare to trust others, deadlocks can be broken. If others do not respond to the opportunities provided, it is legitimate to step back in order to protect one's own interest.

4.3 Markets and virtues: outcomes of economic research[8]

4.3.1 Background

The Dutch national newspaper *NRC* of September 29, 2006 presented a remarkable article about the experience of US morticians, who are increasingly troubled by the lack of care for the deceased by their relatives. In Pittsburgh, the number of deceased persons nobody wanted to take care of doubled in five years. This phenomenon does not only occur in poor areas, but extends to other population groups as well. Children of deceased persons sometimes plainly say: "I'd like to have my father's money, but a funeral is not necessary."

One of the questions that may be triggered by such social manners is whether they have anything to do with the free operation of markets. In a seminal paper, Hirschman (1982) distinguishes various theses concerning the influence of the market on social preferences. The best known are two opposite theses, the so-called doux commerce thesis and the self-destruction thesis. Whereas the *doux commerce thesis* states that commerce has a favorable impact on human manners, the *self-destruction thesis* posits that the market undermines the social preferences that are essential for it to function well.

Scientists often take sides, backing one of these opposing hypotheses. Among the authors defending the doux commerce hypothesis are Florida (2002) and McCloskey (2006). In their view, virtuous people may be more successful in the marketplace and the normal operation of market rewards will therefore reinforce their virtue. Moreover, the wealth generated by the market will make people less greedy in the long run.[9] This resembles the view expressed by Keynes in his essay "Economic possibilities for our grandchildren" whereby after 100 years of economic growth, scarcity would be definitely eradicated, allowing us to become "free, therefore, to return to some of the most sure and certain principles of religion and traditional virtue – that avarice is a vice ... and the love of money is detestable" (Keynes 1930: 372).

Authors supporting the self-destruction thesis include MacIntyre (1985), Hirsch (1977), Putman (2000), Sennet (1998), and Layard (2003). According to MacIntyre (1985: 196), "We should expect that, if in a particular society the pursuit of external goods were to become dominant, the concept of virtues might suffer first attrition and then perhaps something near total effacement."[10]

External goods such as fame, power, or profit are characterized in MacIntyre's work as objects of competition, in contrast to internal goods, which are derived from practices. MacIntyre argues that much modern industrial productive and service work is organized so as to exclude the features distinctive to practices and the virtues that sustain them. MacIntyre(1985: xiv) also believes that capitalism institutionalizes injustice and therefore "provides systematically incentive to develop a type of character that has a propensity to injustice." Elsewhere MacIntyre (1995: xiii) writes that "what constitutes success in life becomes a matter of the successful acquisition of consumer goods, and thereby that acquisitiveness ... is further sanctioned. Unsurprisingly pleonexia, the drive to have more and more, becomes treated as a central virtue."

Hirsch (1977) argues that the social morality that underpins the operation of markets has been a legacy of the pre-capitalist and pre-industrial past. This legacy has diminished with time due to the emphasis on self-interest as well as to the greater mobility and anonymity of industrial society. As a result, habits based on communal attitudes and objectives have lost out. In this view, the market is living on borrowed virtues and on borrowed time: in due course, the string will run out, the ethical capital will be depleted, and the moral foundation of the market hollowed out. Putman (2000) shows in his book *Bowling Alone* that many forms of community life declined enormously over the second half of the twentieth century and that people have become increasingly disconnected from one another. People are less inclined to be part of civic groups like churches, unions, neighborhood organizations, political parties, and recreational leagues. As a result, virtues like trustfulness, mutual respect, and civic-mindedness are disappearing. He mentions four factors that have contributed to this development: longer working hours, suburban sprawl, television, and the increasing predominance of orientation on the self. Sennet also bemoans the impact of capitalism on individual character. He gives various examples of how the flexibility demanded by markets induces a short-term focus and corrodes trust, loyalty, and people's long-term commitments. Because of regular job changes, people lack a narrative identity. The flexible labor market enforces shallowness that erodes family and community relations. According to Layard (2003), flexibility and geographical mobility – often defended by economists because they facilitate economic efficiency – increase family break-up and criminality and decrease mutual trust and therefore trustfulness.

The dividing line between these two camps has its historical roots in classical political economy. The first group builds on the writings of classical authors like

David Hume (who considered wealth to be a friend of virtue), Adam Smith (who argued that people who seldom deal with others are more disposed to cheat), and Montesquieu, famously quoted by Hirschman (1982: 1464) as saying that "wherever there is commerce, manners are gentle." The second group can be traced back to Aristotle, who viewed commerce as hostile to the virtues, and Karl Marx, who predicted that capitalism would cause alienation and immiseration, and that this loss of identity would be a source of greed, egoism, avarice, and lack of respect for other people.

The persistence of the debate shows that it is highly ideologically loaded. Present empirical research is not able to settle this ongoing debate, though new insights continue to emerge. In this section I want to contribute to this debate in two ways. First, I will develop a more balanced view of the influence of market operation on virtues by distinguishing various types of virtues which may be affected in different ways. For this purpose, I use the detailed schema presented in Table 4.1 on p. 102. Second, I develop the thesis that the impact of market operation on virtues is curvilinear and depends on the degree of market operation. If competition is limited, market operation will replenish the moral basis of society by stimulating the classical virtues of courage, temperance, justice, and prudence. In this situation, the doux commerce thesis is likely to hold, implying that more competition will contribute to the social manners of economic agents. But if competition is very fierce, more competition will deplete the moral basis of the society by eroding virtue. Then self-destructive forces become more likely.

4.3.2 Methodology

As already noted in the Introduction, empirical research into the effects of market operation on the various virtues is relatively scarce. This has to do with the fact that the link between virtue and the market is, for several reasons, hardly measurable.

Measuring virtue

First, analyzing the impact of the market on virtue is hindered by the fact that inner attitudes or character traits that are not directly observable are at stake. Empirical observations only relate to behavioral patterns. Behavioral changes do not necessarily indicate changes in character traits, since other, external, forces may be at work. For instance, an increase in consumption as a result of the market does not necessarily imply that people have become more intemperate. A market simply provides more opportunities for expressing consumer needs. Similarly, if the market provides more incentives to work (as it will, see p. 125), one cannot derive the conclusion that it stimulates diligence. The rise in working hours may be caused by economic incentives without any change in the character of individuals.

Another problematic issue that hampers empirical analysis of the relationship between virtue and the market concerns the development of virtues over time.

Since virtue is a result of habit formation, change takes a long time. In order to identify the impact of the market, one therefore needs long time series of changes in market operation and changes in virtue, which are often lacking. Experimental research is generally ill-suited to such analysis. Since experiments focus on how a particular feature of the market affects human choice during the short time period of the experiment, the link with character formation remains uncertain.

One possible way of escaping these two problems is to assume that external factors will impact characters in the long run through changing behavioral patterns.[11] As argued above, virtue is a result of habit formation. It is learned by the regular repetition of correct actions. Extrinsic motives will therefore slowly become intrinsic and internalized in the attitudes of individuals. For instance, Macneil (1986) argues that relations with others that were entered into as means to economic ends become transformed into ends in themselves. Sharing in so-called relational contracts thus results, in time, in full-blown social solidarity. As argued by Frey (1998), these effects will not only pertain to behavior on the market, but also spread beyond to non-market areas over time. Where we interpret the outcomes of experimental research in terms of changes in virtue, we thus implicitly make this assumption that behavioral patterns influence virtue, but one should be aware that this need not be true in all cases.

Measuring market operation

Measuring the extent of market operation is also problematic. In theoretical arguments about the impact of the market on virtue, indicators often relate to general instances, such as the number of market transactions, the existence of price incentives, competitiveness, the reputation mechanism, or work on piece rate schemes (rather than fixed wages). In empirical analyses indicators are sometimes used that are also used in the Fraser Institute's index of economic freedom (see Chapter 2 above). Furthermore, the literature also uses variables other than indicators of market operation that are closely related to or influenced by the market and that may affect virtue. Examples are the number of advertisements, the number of choices, watching television, mobility, mandatory overtime, wealth, and income equality. In most cases, there exists a direct relationship with market operation. To illustrate, as described in Chapter 2 above, a number of studies find a positive causal influence of economic freedom on GDP per capita. It is therefore reasonable to assume that the market may affect virtue through the increase in wealth that it creates.

In our analysis of the literature, we do not exclude research on the basis of specific measures of the market. Since empirical research is already scarce, we prefer to consider a broad range of studies. But, obviously, the variety in measures makes it more difficult to derive unambiguous conclusions from the literature reviewed. Rather, they provide us with a basis for formulating hypotheses that should be tested by more narrowly defined conceptual, theoretical, and empirical analysis.

Other problems

There are several other problems I would like to mention. First, because of the limitations of empirical research, the debate about the impact of the market on virtue is partly based on theoretical arguments. Although these are of great value in the formulation of hypotheses, they are, of course, provisional as long as empirical testing is lacking.

Another problem that stands in the way of developing economic knowledge of the influence of the market on virtue is the problem of causality. As stressed by social capital theory, virtue may have an important impact on the workings of the market. Empirical research should therefore take into account the possibility of simultaneity bias, not only for intermediate variables like wealth, but also for the institutions of the economy.[12]

A final complication of analyzing the causal influence of the market on virtue is the possible interaction between different virtues. They can reinforce each other but can also oppose each other; they may combine into new virtues,[13] provide dilemmas because of their incommensurability and context-dependency, and they are also context-dependent in their effect on happiness. It is the details that count in virtue ethics and there are many context-specific details which are more or less significant in particular situations (Solomon, 1992).[14]

These complications should make one way of deriving too definite conclusions from the literature researched in the next section.

4.3.3 Impact of markets on virtue: indications from the literature

In this subsection I present an overview of literature on the market and virtue. Using the structure of Table 4.1, I discuss the influence of the market on the virtues of character (courage, temperance, self-possession, righteous indignation, generosity, pride, honesty, and justice) as well as the virtues of prudence, diligence, love, faith, and hope.

Daring: fear – courage – recklessness

One of the elements of a free, competitive market is a small collective system of social security. In a generous welfare state, unemployed or disabled people who become dependent on a social benefit may lose the motivation to look for jobs and may develop behavioral patterns of learned helplessness, according to which the individual becomes unable to control his or her own situation (Lindbeck, 1995). Learned helplessness has a negative effect on future motivation to try. In a free market people attribute their situation to their own choices, because market transactions require mutual consent. The numerous transactions on the free market therefore teach them self-confidence (Kreps, 1997) and make them more inclined to take risks, which encourages the virtue of courage.

From these arguments, I infer that it is likely that free markets will stimulate courage. However, under certain conditions the free market may elicit fear. If competition is very fierce and the stakes are very high, people will be in constant danger of losing a lot. The globalization of free markets has made jobs more insecure. Most American are well aware that the industrial-era model of secure jobs with good wages is giving way to a more cost-conscious and global competitive workplace marked by stagnant wages and growing threats to outsource jobs abroad. In a survey by the Pew Research Center (2006), 62 percent of the workers said that they have less job security than twenty or thirty years ago. Nearly a third of all workers said they believed it would be possible for their employer to hire someone outside the country to do the job they were currently doing. According to 56 percent of the respondents, employers are less loyal to workers now than they were a generation ago (another third say employers show the same loyalty now as they did then).[15]

Very strong competition and economic incentives may also induce recklessness. According to Rezaee (2005), economic pressure and incentives to meet Wall Street forecasts are the fundamental motives for publicly traded companies to engage in financial statement fraud. Since the costs of corporate fraud can be very significant, these activities are very risky. The economic incentives for corporations to engage in financial statement fraud must be very strong. Grant and Visconti (2006) show that a striking feature of the recent major companies involved in accounting scandals, like Enron, WorldCom, Ahold, and Parmalat, was their reckless and flawed strategy, including over-reliance on acquisition-led growth, misguided vertical integration, penetration into sectors with limited globalization potential, and diversification in the absence of synergies. Acquisitiveness meant for all these companies that cash flow into investment activities exceeded cash flow from operations, causing rapid growth in their indebtedness. Mergers and acquisitions were the other indicator of the companies' appetite for risk. Furthermore, the fact that so many of their acquisitions involved entry into new sectors and geographical markets emphasizes the extent to which these companies were willing to take on additional risk. Once both profits and share prices were in decline, then the incentives to manipulate accounting data increased in the desire to buy time in the hope of some magical turnaround (Grant and Visconti, 2006: 381). This indicates recklessness.

The current credit crisis also indicates that financial markets free of government regulation (of the banking and housing markets) may result in too risky investment patterns. In the packaging and selling of mortgage loans for the subprime segment to investors around the world, information about the risks of the underlying loans was lost. In addition, rating agencies made over-optimistic assumptions about the performance of these securities. Because of the competition between these agencies, they gave double-A ratings to what were almost junk bonds. Furthermore, the market incentives of high bonuses pushed portfolio managers to invest too many funds in risky assets. Once again, this indicates a clear link between fierce competition and the elimination of the virtue of courage.

Pleasure/pain: insensitivity – temperance – excess

An important condition for market operation is that all sellers should have free access to the market (see Chapter 2 above). Competition stimulates productivity growth and innovation, because this allows companies to gain a (temporary) advantage over their competitors. In order to sell the increased output, firms have a high stake in stimulating demand for their goods. Continuous product development, spurious model changes and planned obsolescence all serve the output of the company. The current Anglo-American version of capitalism therefore fosters a tendency to excessive consumption as an inherent part of the system (Moore, 2005). Business management can never rest content in the secure knowledge that enough is enough. In order to secure the demand for their products, firms seek to influence market demand through sales strategies such as advertising. According to J.K. Galbraith's well-known criticism, advertising is the creation of desires in consumers for the sole purpose of absorbing industrial output. Because of its manipulative power, it seduces consumers to more consumption. According to Waide (1987), the most important theme of the cumulative effects of thousands and thousands of advertisements is that you are what you own.[16] The not very surprising result is that people neglect non-market methods of satisfying their desires and this discourages non-market cultivation of virtue. Group pressure makes other people into enforcers so that there are penalties for not going along with the popular currents induced by advertising. Novak (1982) admits that virtue is harder to find once wealth has been attained. In particular, hedonism and decadence should be resisted, because lack of discipline in personal life is potentially damaging to the market economy. Commercial values are not capable of providing their own defense and require correction by a moral-cultural system independent of commerce. In this respect, Novak sees an important role for communal institutions, including churches and families.

Value studies indicate, however, that the current trend is no longer toward more materialism, but toward lifestyle values (Inglehart, 2000). The shift in values is driven by the affluence of modern society, which makes it possible to give higher priority to quality of life than to economic growth. However, if we look at actual consumption patterns, it is difficult to discern any substantial change toward greater temperance. Frey *et al.* (2005) estimate that too much television watching leads to lack of self-control and balance, presumably because those watching television see many more advertisements than others. One very visible form of overconsumption is obesity, which has severe negative consequences on national health, including diabetes, heart problems, and some forms of cancer.[17]

Another way of overstretching consumer's capacity is the choice overload that the market provides. The supermarket economy provides consumers with abundant choice. Psychological research shows, however, that a large array of options reduces rather than increases satisfaction from consumption (Iyengar and Lepper, 2000; Carmon *et al.*, 2003; Schwartz, 2004). Iyengar and Lepper find that an extensive array of options (of exotic jams) can at first seem highly appealing to consumers, yet can reduce their subsequent motivation to purchase this product.

In another experiment, they also found that people perform better in a limited-choice context than in an abundant-choice context. One possible explanation is that the experience of opportunity costs of the option that consumers finally select increases the more choices there are. The existence of multiple alternatives makes it easy to imagine other alternatives that do not exist by combining the attractive features those that do exist. The more options are available, the less satisfying each of them is. The availability of choice also increases personal responsibility for missing a good opportunity, which exacerbates feelings of post-decision regret. Unattainable expectations plus a tendency to take intense personal responsibility make a dangerous combination, raising the probability of dissatisfaction. A final explanation was offered by Carmon *et al.* (2003). In five experiments, they found that consumers become attached to the options during the deliberation process before choosing among them; i.e., they develop a sense of pre-factual possession of the options they deliberate. Once they make a selection, they can no longer think of themselves as potentially owning the non-chosen options. This induces a feeling of loss and post-choice discomfort. As they stated (2003: 28), choosing feels like losing. This also contributes to dissatisfaction and continuous striving at more consumption in order to diminish the discomfort.

It is not clear whether the market feeds the vice of insensitivity. On the one hand, it can be argued that over-consumption damages people's taste. Moreover, since markets stimulate rivalry between consumers (see below), the satisfaction derived from the intrinsic qualities of a product is eroded. On the other hand, wealth created by the market allows more luxuries and cultural goods and enables people to develop a more sensitive taste for quality.

Anger: inertia – self-possession – short-temper

Since markets teach self-reliance and perceived self-confidence (see p. 112), it is likely that they reduce the vice of inertia. Because of competition, the market disciplines economic actors. They have to convince others of the quality of their products and this demands the ability to place oneself in the situation of the transaction partner. The market demands empathy, because it is in a firm's interest to avoid putting features into a product which are not regarded as useful by consumers, and this requires self-control. Furthermore, because of the commercial interest of a good reputation, traders should have a long-term horizon and develop the virtue of trustworthiness (see p. 121). Trustworthiness, in its turn, also presupposes self-restraint, because keeping promises requires the ability or disposition to forgo an immediate advantage (Maitland, 1997). Hence, the market provides ample opportunities for training oneself in self-control.

Particular emotions: malice – righteous indignation – envy

Justified indignation is the middle ground between envy and malicious pleasure. These feelings concern the pleasure and pain that we experience from the fortunes of others. We feel indignant about the undeserved success of some people. Envious people go too far by being annoyed by any success achieved by others, whereas malicious people enjoy others' lack of success (EN: 1108b1–5).

Much has been written about the impact of the free market on envy. Some argue that the causal impact runs in the opposite direction, in the sense that envy distorts the workings of the free market because of government redistribution. Crisp (2003) believes that the preference for redistribution has its ultimate source in envy, generalized through sympathy. This means that envy, through a process of cultural evolution, may be at the root of the principle that it is bad if, through no fault of his or her own, one individual does worse than another. This may have motivated compulsory government redistribution which distorts the free market. Nozick (1974) considers that egalitarianism is motivated by envy. According to Nozick, people are very ingenious in rationalizing their emotions by arguments drawing on justice. However, according to Nozick, self-esteem is based on differentiation. If wealth or income were equalized, society might agree that some other dimension, like attractiveness or intelligence is more important so as to differentiate oneself from others. Then the phenomenon might repeat itself. Therefore, envy might not decrease if incomes were equalized. On the contrary, as the number of differentiating dimensions of life diminishes when some of them are equalized, people have to compete on a smaller number of dimensions. Assuming that people especially value those dimensions on which they perform very well, reducing the number of differentiating dimensions will make fewer people able to gain self-esteem. The most promising way for a society to avoid differences in self-esteem is therefore a high diversity of differentiating dimensions. This would imply that the free market reduces envy, because free markets imply no forced government redistribution.

In contrast, Rawls (1999a) argues that large disparities in wealth and income can give rise to "excusable envy": excusable, since it is a reasonable response to the loss of self-respect occasioned by having less when others have so much more. Often we evaluate how well off we are by comparing ourselves with others. Inequalities in income or position rankle so much because of the feeling that they are undeserved and therefore make the least well-off feel less worthy. If people feel inferior because they do poorly, redistribution may reduce their feelings of inferiority.

Envy is also related to Hirsch's (1977) theory of positional goods (see Chapter 2 above). Hirsch develops the thesis that as the economy grows, demand shifts from private goods to positional goods. According to Hirsch, economic growth will therefore intensify what he terms positional competition, i.e. competition for a higher place within some hierarchy that yields gains for some only by dint of losses for others. This will increase envy, and result in mounting consumer frustration as people compete for this fixed supply of positional goods. While capitalism has raised expectations – partly by its record in raising performance – the opportunities to fulfill these expectations diminish, because the things aspired to are restricted by their very nature. Economic growth in advanced societies thus carries elements of built-in frustration: the growth process fails to deliver its full promise because it runs into social scarcity.

Although the relationship between market operation and envy is a highly debated topic, little empirical research has been done to test it. There is a lot of research on positional competition (Solnick and Hemenway, 1998; Brekke and Howarth, 2002; Carlsson *et al.*, 2003; Alpizar *et al.*, 2005), but there are hardly any results for the link with competitiveness or free market operation. According to Schwartz (2004), although concern for status is nothing new, the problem is more acute now than in the past because of the plethora of choices that the market offers. With the explosion of telecommunications – TV, movies, the Internet – almost everyone has access to information about almost everyone else. Research that throws some light on this relationship was carried out by Bruni and Stanca (2006). Using data from the World Values Survey, they find that the effect of income on both life and financial satisfaction is significantly smaller for heavy television viewers. One possible reason is that when watching television, people are overwhelmed by images of those wealthier than they are. This contributes to raising the benchmark for people's positional concerns. Likewise, Layard (2005) reports that television viewing is negatively related to perceived relative income and happiness, whereas Frey *et al.* (2005) estimate that television consumption lead to higher material aspirations.

Giving: avarice – generosity – extravagance

One would expect the rise in welfare caused by market operation to enable people to be more generous. If people are richer, they have more opportunities to express their altruistic feelings. Another motivation for charity is the so-called warm glow. In that case, contributions to a public good are not only made for the benefit of others, but also serve the giver's interest. Again, rich people can better afford this kind of luxury than poor people. Furthermore, high economic freedom is often the counterpart of small government. In countries with a high proportion of government transfers, there is less need for voluntary generosity to meet the social needs of the poor.

On the other hand, the literature on intrinsic motivation provides considerable empirical evidence that the market also erodes generosity (Frey and Jegen, 2001). For example, there are a number of studies that show that price incentives harm the intrinsic motivation to contribute to a social good. In particular, paying someone to perform a task that he or she might willingly have done without pay may undermine motivation. For example, individuals who give blood for altruistic reasons may suffer a utility loss when blood is priced. Well-known research by Titmuss (1970) found that the market allocation system for blood in the US proved less efficient than the gift allocation system in England. In terms of price per unit of blood to the patient, the market system was five to fifteen times more costly than the voluntary system in Britain, whereas the risks to patients of disease and death because of contaminated blood were substantially greater. The monetary incentive provided by the market may thus eliminate the intrinsic motivation to help other people. In an extreme case, the use of the price mechanism could completely destroy intrinsic motivation, and when price incentives fail to generate any blood donations at all, the net impact may be negative. This effect remains, even after the monetary incentive has been stopped (Gneezy and Rustichini, 2000). Furthermore, Frey and Oberholzer (1997) tested the erosion hypothesis on fulfilling one's civic duty by analyzing citizens' willingness to accept a nuclear waste repository in their hometown. They found that if citizens were offered financial compensation, the acceptance rate declined from 51 percent to 25 percent.[18] A further statistical analysis of the factors explaining the acceptance rates in case of no compensation showed that civic mindedness and care for the wider social costs of the repository had a significant positive impact on willingness to accept the waste repository. If compensation was offered, the impact of these social factors on willingness to accept the repository disappeared. Frey and Oberholzer conclude that where public spirit prevails, using price incentives tends to eliminate civic duty. They therefore need to be reconsidered as an instrument to muster support for a social good. Only in policy areas where intrinsic motivations do not exist or have already been eliminated, could offering financial compensation be a promising strategy to win local support. This is confirmed by an experiment by Gneezy and Rustichini (2000) with high school students who were rewarded for collecting money for a good cause. The students were divided into three groups. The first group was not financially rewarded, but was told that society would be thankful to them and that an article about them would be published in the local newspaper. The second group received, on top of that, remuneration of 1 percent of the money that had been collected, and the third group received 10 percent. The results of the experiments showed that the performance of the first group exceeded that of the other two groups, and the third group ended in second place. One interpretation is that small incentives are detrimental to sacrifices to the community, because they can be perceived as insulting. Ven (2003) stresses the element of reciprocity as a motive for this kind of giving. A monetary reward takes away the possibility of social approval for giving, because then the gift is no longer a sacrifice. This would explain the disincentive that monetary rewards can generate. These pieces of evidence, showing that intrinsic motivation is eliminated by price incentives, seem to be replicated in a wide variety of other areas of the economy and society: children's learning behavior; patients' readiness to take prescribed medication; monetary and symbolic rewards for undertaking various laboratory tasks; the reciprocity and level of trust exhibited in a situation of incomplete contracts; the reaction of managers to various forms of supervision by their superiors; the observation of time schedules in daycare centers; on-time flight performance in the airline industry; and tax morality. Moreover, this empirical evidence has been collected in many different countries, over many different time periods, and in different research environments (Frey and Jegen, 2001).

Little empirical research has been done into whether the market influences the vice of extravagance. But if markets encouraged materialism and envy, one would also expect extravagance to increase. In a social environment of positional competition social status is related to relative consumption. It is therefore important to show financial success in order to gain social approval.

Status: humility – pride – arrogance

As discussed in section 4.2, humility is considered a virtue in Christian ethics, but a vice in Greek virtue ethics.[19] We therefore treat both humility and pride as virtues. In both Greek and Christian virtue ethics, arrogance is considered a vice.

One would expect free markets to belittle the virtue of humility. People who are able to present themselves favorably tend to be more successful. Therefore, the market provides a strong incentive for assertiveness. People's capacities will only be recognized if they are clearly communicated to others. Little research is available to assess the impact of markets on the virtues of humility and pride and the vice of arrogance. Nevertheless, there are some indications that the meritocracy that rules market behavior induces arrogance. Florida (2002: 78), for example, argues that those who have qualities that confer merit, such as technical knowledge and mental discipline, may easily start to think that these qualities were inborn, or that they acquired them on their own. Statistics published by the Yankelovitch Report (Klein, 2002: 305) show an extremely high degree of self-reliance. More than two out of three persons born after 1965 subscribe to the statement: "In this world I must take what I can, because nobody else will give me anything." Only 50 percent of older people born between 1909 and 1945 agree with this statement, and only one-third of those born between 1945 and 1965. Furthermore, nine out of ten teenagers agree with the statement "It depends on me whether I get what I want in this life." It thus seems that long experience of free markets in the US has created a more Darwinist attitude of the survival of the fittest. Those who succeed in competition with others are more inclined to take the credit themselves for their success and to blame the unsuccessful for their failure.

If one interprets humility as selfless respect for reality and an attitude of willingness to listen to others, as McCloskey (2006) does, one could argue, however, that the market does teach humility. The famous example of the butcher, the baker, and the brewer in Adam Smith's *Wealth of Nations* (1776: 20) illustrates the importance of placing oneself in the situation of others. Only by listening carefully to the wishes of one's clients can one know which arguments one should use to be successful in business. Bovenberg (2007) also argues that competition provides people with useful and realistic feedback and thus helps them to be humble. Moreover, as the market allows a high division of labor, it increases mutual dependence which also encourages humility.

Social interaction: false modesty – honesty – unctuousness

Aristotle distinguished three types of virtue and their related vices in social relations: friendliness (with the counterparts of grumpiness or quarrelsomeness when it is in short supply, and unctuousness when in excess);[20] politeness (with the counterparts of rudeness when lacking and derision when in excess); honesty (with false modesty when lacking and boastfulness when in excess). Honesty as a virtue in social relationships should be distinguished from faithfulness in economic dealings, which belongs to the virtue of justice (EN: 1127 a 36) and will be discussed below.

Economists often argue that a society in which the market holds a central position for the satisfaction of human wants generates a more polished human type – i.e. more honest, reliable, orderly, and disciplined, as well as friendlier and more helpful, always ready to find solutions to conflicts (Hirschman, 1982). Through commerce, one learns to be honest and to acquire manners and to be reserved in both words and actions. Repeated commercial contacts are likely to generate some minimal level of courtesy, because commercial success depends on the courteous treatment of people who have the option of taking their business elsewhere (Maitland, 1997). Commerce is also a pacific system, rendering nations as well as individuals useful to each other. It attaches one person to another through mutual utility. Moral and physical passions are superseded by interest.

On the other hand, the market economy reduces dependency on traditional relations. Money creates new types of social relations that allow people to have contractual relations with others. They have to relate to them only as long as and insofar they want to (Gay, 2003). A good deal of interest in others becomes functional. Aristotle does not condemn friendship motivated by personal utility per se. It is ethically neutral, unless functional and opportunistic relations harm the structure of the community and depersonalize social relations. Gay cites Peter Berger, who argued in *The Capitalist Revolution* that

> The world created by capitalism is indeed a cold one. Liberating though it may be, it also involves the individual in countless relations with other people that are based on calculating rationality "What is this person worth to me" ... Human relations too become subject to creative destruction of capitalism.

> (Gay, 2003: 65)

Where the interest in others becomes functional rather than intrinsic, the virtues connected to social interaction may also diminish. People will be unctuous towards those they need and prove unfaithful when they do not need them any more. A relationship is liable to be discarded as soon as one of the parties calculates that it has outlived its usefulness. Virtues like truthfulness and loyalty will come under pressure in an opportunistic environment.[21] If people are highly mobile, they invest less in local amenities and social capital (Glaeser and DiPasquale, 1999). Putman (2000) also considers mobility a cause of erosion of social bonds. Illustrative recent research that confirms isolation was carried out by McPherson *et al.* (2006). They found that in the US, the number of people saying there is no one with whom they discuss important matters nearly tripled between 1985 and 2004. The modal respondent now reports having no confidant; the modal respondent in 1985 had three confidants. The number of both kin and non-kin confidants decreased, but the greater decrease of non-kin ties means more confidant networks centered on spouses and parents, and fewer contacts through voluntary associations and neighborhoods.[22]

The market may reduce social interaction not only as a result of flexibility but also as a result of the strong incentives it provides to work (see below). Golden and Wiens-Tuers (2005) estimate that pressure to work overtime is common in the labor market, especially when demand for labor is high. Their econometric analysis shows that working mandatory overtime increases stress and causes greater work–family imbalances. Major *et al.* (2002) also found that working overtime and making arrangements for time spent at work contribute to work–family conflict and are thus indirectly related to depression and stress-related health problems.

Exchange: injustice – justice – injustice

The virtue of honesty is closely related to the virtue of justice. But, as already noted above, Aristotle classified trustworthiness in economic relations as the virtue of justice. Since trustworthiness is related to trust, we also discuss some literature on trust and social capital under this heading.

There are several indications that a free market system may foster trust and social capital. Most important is the rule of law. Knack and Keefer (1997) estimate that the formal institutional structure of a country and checks on executive power are associated with higher levels of trust and stronger norms of civic cooperation. This result is confirmed by Berggren and Jordahl (2006). In their view, economic freedom has a positive effect on trust. This is especially the case for the subindex that measures legal structure and security of property rights. This indicates that a well-ordered legal system (which is one of the elements of the index of economic freedom) fosters justice. Market participation will reinforce this effect: if one repeatedly makes deals with other people that turn out to meet expectations, one may develop a trusting attitude to other people which becomes a matter of habit and is internalized. On the basis of experiments in fifteen small-scale societies, Henrich *et al.* (2001) find that in countries where payoffs to cooperation and market integration are large, the level of cooperation in experimental games is greater. They explained this finding by the fact that the more frequently people experience market transactions, the more frequently they also experience abstract sharing principles of fairness.

Another factor through which market operation may stimulate trust is simply by increasing wealth. Empirical research by Knack and Keefer (1997) and Alesina and La Ferrare (2002) indicates that income raises trust, although other studies have failed to confirm this finding (Zak and Knack, 2001; Uslaner, 2002; Bjørnskov, 2005; Berggren and Jordahl, 2006). As Zak and Knack (2001) argue, for rich people it is more attractive to work and trust than to take time to verify their trading partners. More wealth, in turn, may enable more education and this also contributes to trust according to Knack and Keefer (1997).[23]

As well as the rule of law, likewise market competition disciplines people to adopt trustworthy behavior because of the reputation factor. In order to succeed in competition with others, a firm must maintain a reputation for reliability, integrity, and fairness. As Adam Smith argues, trustworthiness is a distinctively bourgeois virtue: "Wherever commerce is introduced in any country, probity and punctuality always accompany it ... where the greater part of people are merchants they always bring probity and punctuality into fashion and these are the principal virtues of commercial nations."[24] Where people seldom have dealings with one another, we find they are somewhat disposed to cheat, because they may gain more by a smart trick than they lose by the injury to their reputation. When dealings are frequent, less is expected from any one contract than from a general reputation for probity and punctuality. As commercial beings, people shun vice so as not to arouse any adverse judgment on the part of present and future acquaintances. Other traders will punish the dishonest by not doing business with them. If the reputation mechanism works effectively, neither the government nor the courts have to intervene to punish opportunistic behavior (Bovenberg, 2000).

However, the reputation mechanism only works well if three conditions are met (Bovenberg, 2002). First, information about any agent's past behavior must be available to all potential trading partners. Here the media play a positive role. Through ICT, the world has become a global village where NGOs and the media are increasingly able to inform people on what firms are doing anywhere on the globe. An important internal factor is the degree of transparency offered by a company. If companies do not provide information about their performance, it is much more difficult for others to find information about them. Second, as a good reputation only pays off in the future, it is only important to companies with a long time horizon. A company which is mainly interested in short-term profits has less incentive to build up a good reputation and therefore to be virtuous, for it would have to make costs in the short term to acquire the good reputation that would lead to long-term profits. Third, the reputation mechanism is more effective if a good reputation is collectively rewarded and a bad reputation collectively punished. This depends on the reactions of various types of stakeholders on the labor, goods, and capital markets. If there is a high degree of actual or potential competition, this condition is more likely to be fulfilled, as actors are then subject to a disciplinary mechanism of reward or punishment.

Graafland and Smid (2004) carried out a study of the strength of the reputation mechanism. Their research indicates that the media and market actors respond relatively well to infringements of trust. Their role has increased as a result of ICT. However, the possibilities of these countervailing powers are still hampered if companies lack transparency. If companies' transparency tends to be weak, an important condition for a well-functioning reputation mechanism is not fully met. Furthermore, in some countries time horizons seem relatively short (see below). Overall, Graafland and Smid (2004) concluded that the reputation mechanism certainly helps to stimulate virtuous behavior. But too much faith in the self-enforcing effect of the reputation mechanism is unwarranted.

Indeed, according to several theoretical and empirical indications, free markets can reduce the virtue of justice and encourage fraudulent behavior. First, Shleifer (2004) argued that fierce competition may promote corruption. If a government official takes bribes in exchange for reducing the taxes or tariffs that are owed to the government, a corrupt company can reduce its production costs and gain a competitive advantage. Other things being equal, a firm that is burdened by ethical scruples is presumably at a competitive disadvantage in the marketplace compared with a rival with no such burden (Maitland, 1997).

Another example already discussed under the heading of the virtue of courage is accounting scandals. Rezaee (2005) and Choo and Tan (2007) found that the basic incentive for this kind of fraud is economic. Companies bypass accounting rules to show good figures for earnings immediately before making acquisitions or before their executives exercise stock options. Severe competition on the capital market may provide an incentive for this kind of vice. Earnings manipulation reduces the cost of capital, enabling companies to make acquisitions for stock, attract better executives and workers by offering stock options, and even issue new shares. Without creative accounting, the capital costs might have been too high for such companies to survive. Choo and Tan (2007: 209) quote Messner and Rosenfeld who observe that "Given the strong, relentless pressure for everyone to succeed, understood in terms of an inherently elusive monetary goal, people formulate wants and desires that are difficult, if not impossible, to satisfy within the confines of legally permissible behavior."[20] The strong emphasis on monetary success encourages a pronounced tendency for corporate executives to disregard regulatory controls. The root cause of corporate scandals is not that many executives suddenly decide to become crooks; it rather lies within the system in which they are working (Grant and Visconti, 2006).

An additional mechanism through which free markets may influence trust in economic relations negatively is by fostering income inequality. As discussed in Chapter 2 above, economic research shows a negative correlation between income inequality and government redistribution (as indicated by the share of transfers as a percentage of GDP and by top marginal tax rates). Government redistribution is one of the elements hampering free market operation, according to the index of economic freedom. Knack and Keefer (1997) and Berggren and Jordahl (2006) estimate that social polarization caused by income inequality weakens trust. Inequality and social solidarity are deeply incompatible. Hence, freeing the market from government redistribution policies will decrease trust. This also holds for inequalities at the micro level. Micro-econometric research by Bloom (1999) shows that wage dispersion in baseball teams has a negative impact on the performance of both players and teams, because it instills feelings of inequity, promotes dissatisfaction, and therefore undermines cooperation. Similar results have been found by Bloom and Michel (2002) and Wade *et al.* (2006). Bloom and Michel (2002) found evidence that more wage dispersion causes more managerial turnover and lower average tenure. Wade *et al.* (2006) performed a study on how CEOs' remuneration affects commitment at the lower levels of an organization. They observed that excessive CEO remuneration increases turnover at the lower levels. Their impression was that protests over high CEO pay have increased since the ratio of the CEO's pay to that of the average worker rose from 35:1 in 1974 to 400:1 in 2001. A public policy that is committed to promoting social capital should therefore address the presence of grave inequalities (Atherton, 2008).

The flexibility demanded by markets may also corrupt trust. People trust each other more when few people move house and the community is more homogenous (Knack and Keefer, 1997; Zak and Knack, 2001; Berggren and Jordahl, 2006). The Yankelovitch Report discussed on p. 119 illustrates the trend toward lack of trust in help from others.[27] This suggests that the net effects of fierce market competition on trust and the related virtues of justice and honesty have been negative.

Prudence

As already discussed above, it is often argued that the discipline imposed on the market by competition instills a sense of realism. Commerce teaches people to deliberate and be prudent. It requires interpersonal communication which assists individuals to develop a realistic perspective by continually testing their views.

Markets may also increase economic rationality by making products more comparable. Bowles (1998) remarked that markets increase commensurability because they favor thinking of goods both abstractly and more comparatively as representing more or less market value. Markets are thus powerful simplifiers, radically reducing the complexity with which one typically views an assortment of disparate goods. However, in the context of virtue, such simplification may also reduce a broader sense of wisdom. Aristotle drew a sharp distinction between the higher and lower types of pleasure. The use of money tends to reduce all objective qualities to mere quantities. All qualitative differences are expressed in terms of how much (Gay, 2003). This has the effect of stripping the world of color, taste, and texture. In a money economy, everything looks like a commodity.

There are also indications that the market reduces the rationality of economic actors by encouraging a short-term focus. There is empirical evidence that a long time horizon contributes to long-term profitability (Richardson and Waegelein, 2002; Keil *et al.*, 2001). Executive remuneration not based on the long-term performance of the company will ultimately lead to decisions that are detrimental to shareholder wealth (Vogel and Lobo, 2002). This does not guarantee, however, that managers will have a long-term focus. Indeed, many empirical studies show that competition on the financial market induces short-termism. According to Laverty (1996), there are five (partly overlapping) reasons for short-termism in a company: managerial opportunism, stock market myopia, flawed management practice, fluid and impatient capital, and information asymmetry. Some empirical evidence corroborates the first reason, managerial opportunism (Harrison and Fiet, 1999), but other studies failed to confirm this finding (Bizjak *et al.*, 1993). Empirical literature on the influence of managerial opportunism on short-termism is therefore ambiguous. The second cause of short-termism is stock market myopia. Recently, there have been claims that US companies are either unwilling or unable to make investments that are necessary for the future but require short-term profits to be sacrificed. The reason for this that is very often cited is pressure from the stock market (Segelod, 2000). As Rappaport (2005:

65) states, "Financial analysts fixate on quarterly earnings at the expense of fundamental research." For the other explanations of short-termism – i.e. flawed management practice, fluid and impatient capital, and information asymmetry – Brown and Higgins (2001) found that in the US especially, managers manipulate sudden wage changes to raise their stock price. Large information asymmetries in the US may be creating incentives for a short-run management style detrimental to long-term competitiveness. Most investment professionals recognize that discounted cash flow is the appropriate model for valuing equities, but they believe that estimating cash flows in the distant future is too time-consuming, costly, and speculative to be useful. Because they have much less information about a company's operations and prospects than insiders, they tend to attach substantial weight to reported short-term performance (Rappaport, 2005). Fluid capital can also foster short-termism. The average holding period for stocks until the mid-1960s was about seven years. Today it is less than a year in professionally managed funds (Rappaport, 2005).

A final reason why the market may reduce rationality is through the abundance of choices that it creates (already discussed on p. 115 under the heading of the virtue of temperance). If more alternatives are available, it is more difficult to choose because of conflicts between various aspects of the products. Such conflicts create difficult trade-offs and higher psychological costs in the form of mental stress. The emotional cost of making trade-offs does more than just diminish our sense of satisfaction with a decision (Schwartz, 2004: 131). It also reduces the quality of decisions by narrowing people's focus and creating confusion due to the heavier psychological pressure and the resultant weakening in self-regulation and willpower (Mick *et al.*, 2004). Baumeister and Vohs (2003) performed experiments that showed that going through a decision-making process reduces persistence in finishing a task. This also suggests a reduction in prudence as understood by Aristotle, who considered that a rational person not only knows what should be done in a given situation, but also actually does what should be done (EN: 1152a8).

Effort: laziness – diligence – overzealousness

There is general agreement that markets foster industry and inventiveness (Maitland, 1997). Markets stimulate virtues like diligence, punctuality, entrepreneurship, and the intrinsic motivation to work (Kreps, 1997). Being one's own boss makes one work harder than salaried employment (McCloskey, 2006). Goette and Lienhard (2006) found in experiments that piece rate work, as opposed to fixed wages, increases performance. Those doing piece rate felt greater tension than those with fixed wages, but also showed more concern for the quality of work and learned to be more productive. So meritocracy induces diligence. Frey (1998) argued that the market may generate positive effects on intrinsic motivations to work. An example of such a "crowding-in" effect is the motivating power of a good salary. The efficient wage theory predicts and empirical cases show that higher pay tends to result in higher productivity, partly because of the higher motivation of workers. The experience of work can also improve personal efficiency outside the work situation (spillover effect). Longitudinal empirical studies show that job position has causal effects on individual psychological functioning and affects personal values and leisure time preferences. Workers whose jobs are passive become passive themselves in their leisure and political participation.

The downside of the incentive effects of competition is, however, that markets make people work too hard and they become overzealous. To illustrate, Table 4.4 shows that in the US (where the index of economic freedom is 8.2) the number of working hours per person is about 15 percent higher than in the Scandinavian countries (where the average index of economic freedom is 7.5). Competition means that firms have a strong interest in having their employees work long hours, resulting in a heavy workload. Another factor is the lack of social security and minimum wage in a free market. Many low-skilled workers are forced to take on more than one job in order to earn a subsistence wage.

Love

Maybe the most serious criticism of the market from a Christian point of view is that commerce may erode the virtue of love. The market allows self-interested behavior as long as the negative rights to freedom of others are respected. One should therefore not be surprised that humans start behaving as if the world were theirs. Verbrugge (2004) maintains: "The world is there to be consumed by you, to give you a good time." When this kind of individualism becomes generalized, the self-sacrificing love will disappear.

Competition also puts pressure on the virtue of love. Competition leads to a struggle for survival. It teaches people to think of each other as competitors and not as co-workers (Knight, 1925). One is constantly threatened by competitors who intend to gain market share by beating one. However, competitors sometimes cooperate or show reciprocity. McCloskey (2006) refers to a study by

Table 4.4 Labor time in Western countries

	Working hours[a]	Participation rate[b]		Working hours	Participation rate
Denmark	87.6	103.8	Germany	80.3	91.1
Sweden	88.6	99.2	Netherlands	78.7	102.3
Finland	95.8	93.8	France	80.1	82.3
Norway	76.0	103.1	*Average*	*82.2*	*89.0*
Average	*86.8*	*100.0*	Ireland	91.4	91.0
Belgium	90.0	80.5	UK	90.7	96.2
			US	100.0	100.0

Notes
a 2005, US = 100. Source: GGDC database, Rijksuniversiteit Groningen, www.ggdc.net/dseries/totecon.html.
b 2001, US = 100. Source: Klundert (2005: Table 4.1).

Ingram and Roberts in the *American Journal of Sociology* (September 2000) that shows that a fully booked hotel will send customers on to competitors. However, when competition becomes fierce and aggressive market actors predominate, they force less ambitious actors to be more assertive as well. This raises the feeling of insecurity and encourages a need for control and power so as to protect oneself against cut-throat competition from others. The result may be, in the words of Hobbes, a war of all against all. Others can only be overcome if their market position is destroyed. This is what Schumpeter calls the process of creative destruction: the more competitive product replaces the less productive product; there is no mercy.

If competitive attitudes start dominating the economic domain, they will also spill over into the non-economic domains. If the principle of competition becomes dominant in labor relationships and private relations – even within the community of family, friends, or churches – we lose sight of the most important values of love and grace that are central to the Kingdom of God.

Faith and hope

I do not know any empirical research that investigates the influence of the market on the Christian virtues of faith and hope. When comparing the US with Europe, it seems that Americans are much more inclined to put their trust in God. Whereas faith has declined in Europe, the US continues to be a Christian nation where the majority believes in God. Faith in God and awareness of dependency on Him may be the reverse side of lack of faith in help from others (see p. 119). Where people face fierce competition from others and perceive that their success depends on their own efforts alone, they have greater need of the help of an almighty being. In a generous welfare state where life is more secure, awareness of dependence is less developed.

More faith and dependence on God will also reinforce the virtues of hope and gratitude. The effect on the spiritual virtue of penitence is, however, less clear. In a meritocracy where people relate their success to their own effort and ability, the experience of dependence on God will be part of an optimistic attitude rather than one of humility: God as the source of blessing and prosperity rather than the holy being that reminds one of one's own sinful nature.

Christian virtues and happiness

In Chapter 2 above we presented some research on happiness. According to virtue ethics, virtues contribute to the good life. One would therefore expect Christian virtues to foster happiness. According to the well-known psychologist Seligman (2002), engagement (the depth of a person's involvement with family, work, romance, and hobbies) and meaning (using personal strengths to serve some larger end) are much more important for happiness than pleasure. Psychological research shows, indeed, that human happiness is related to the type of virtues described above. The psychologist Sonja Lyubomirsky derives from research findings some practical suggestions that show remarkable similarity with Christian virtues (Wallis, 2005):

1   Count your blessings: take time to conscientiously count the blessings you receive. This raises overall satisfaction with life and raises energy (compare the virtue of gratitude).
2   Practice acts of kindness. Helping and paying attention to others makes you feel generous and capable, and gives you a greater sense of connection with others. You also win their approval and reciprocated kindness (the virtues of serving, loving or benevolence).
3   Express gratitude to anyone to whom you owe a debt of gratitude (the virtue of gratitude and the virtue of justice).
4   Attend to the small wonders of life. Pay close attention to momentary pleasures and wonders, the warmth of the sun, the beautiful flower besides the road (the virtue of respect for the creation of God).
5   Learn to forgive. Let go of anger and resentment against those who have hurt or wronged you, so that you can move on in your own life (the virtue of forgiving).
6   Invest time and energy in friends and family. As already shown in Chapter 2 above, strong personal relationships appear to have significant effects on satisfaction with life (the virtue of truthfulness).
7   Take care of your body. Getting plenty of sleep and exercise enhances your mood.
8   Develop strategies for coping with stress and hardship (the virtues of endurance, faith and hope in God).

Conclusion

In order to put the pieces of the literature research together, Table 4.5 presents an overview of the main results. The first column presents the literature study. The second and third columns specify respectively the type of behavioral pattern that is taken as an indication of the virtue or vice concerned and the type of variable that represents the market. The fourth column describes the basis of the estimated effect (theoretical or empirical) and the fifth column shows whether the market has a positive or negative effect on virtues.

From this overview we can derive four conclusions. First, Table 4.5 shows how fragmentary our empirical knowledge is when assessing the qualitative (let alone quantitative) scale of the influence of the market on virtues. More than half of the studies reviewed above derive positive or negative effects from theoretical arguments without providing empirical estimates confirming them.

A second finding is that the literature summarized in Table 4.5 shows a discrepancy between theoretical and empirical findings. In theoretical literature, the positive and negative effects of market operation on virtues are very much in balance: half of the cases present arguments for a positive impact of market operation on virtues and the other half arguments for a negative impact.

Table 4.5 Impact of the free market on virtues: overview of studies

Study	Type of virtue/vice or behavioral pattern	Type of market indicator or intermediate variable	Method[b]	Effect
Daring: fearful – brave – reckless				
Kreps (1997)	Self-reliance	Number of market transactions	T	+
Lindbeck (1995)	Helplessness	Transfer payments as percentage of GDP	T	+
Rezaee (2005), Grant and Visconti (2004)	Over-ambitious growth rates/ excessive debt financing	Competitive pressure on capital market	T	–
Pleasure/pain: insensitive – temperate – excessive				
Graafland (2007a), Galbraith (1958), Waide (1987)	Excessive consumption	Number of advertisements	T	–
Inglehart (2000)	Quality of life	Affluence	E	+
Frey et al. (2005)	Self-control	Watching television	E	–
Iyengar and Lepper (2000), Carmon et al. (2003), Schwartz (2004)	Satisfaction from consumption	Number of options	E	–
	Insensitivity	Rivalry	T	–
	Insensitivity	Welfare	T	+/–
Anger: inert – self-possessed – short-tempered				
Kreps (1997)	Self-attribution	Number of market transactions	T	+
Lindbeck (1995)	Helplessness	Transfer payments as percentage of GDP	T	+
Maitland (1997)	Self-control	Reputation mechanism	T	+
Special emotions: malicious pleasure – indignant – envious				
Nozick (1974)	Envy	Income equality	T	+
Rawls (1999a)	Envy	Income equality	T	–
Hirsch (1977)	Positional competition	Welfare	T	–
Schwartz (2004)	Concern for status	Number of options	T	–
Bruni and Stanca (2006)	Jealousy	Watching television	E	–

continued

Table 4.5 continued

	Virtue/concept	Effect/context	Type	Sign
Giving: avaricious – generous – extravagant				
Graafland (2003)	Generosity	Welfare	T	+
Ven and Jeurissen (2005)	CSR	Competitiveness	C	–
Titmuss (1970), Frey and Oberholzer-Gee (1997),	CSR	Competitiveness	T	–
Gneezy and Rustichini (2000), Frey and Jegen (2001),	Intrinsic motivation	Price incentives	E	–
Ven (2003)	Generosity	Price incentives	T	–
Status: humble – proud – arrogant				
Florida (2002)	Self-dependency	Meritocracy	T	–
Klein (2002)	Self-dependency		E	–
McCloskey (2006), Bovenberg (2007)	Respect of reality	Competition	T	+
Social interaction: grumpy/falsely-modest – friendly/honest – unctuous				
Maitland (1997)	Courtesy	Repeated commercial contacts	T	+
Gay (2003)	Relations become more functional	Competition	T	–
Glaeser and DiPasquale (1999)	Social capital	Homeownership, mobility	E	–
McPherson et al. (2006)	Confidential relations		E	–
Major et al. (2002), Golden and Wiens-Tuers (2005)	Stress, work–family imbalances	Working mandatory overtime	E	–
Exchange: unjust – just – unjust				
Knack and Keefer (1997), Berggren and Jordahl (2006)	Trust	Respect of property rights	E	+
Henrich et al. (2001)	Fairness	Number of market transactions	E	+
Knack and Keefer (1997), Alesina and La Ferrare (2002)	Trust	Income	E	+
Zak and Knack (2001), Uslaner (2002), Bjørnskov (2005), Berggren and Jordahl (2006)	Trust	Income	E	?
Maitland (1997), Bovenberg (2000)	Honesty	Reputation mechanism	T	+
Graafland and Smid (2004)	Corporate social responsibility	Reputation mechanism	E	?
Shleifer (2004)	Fraud	Competitiveness	T	–

Reference			T/C[a]	
Razaee (2005), Choo and Tan (2007), Grant and Visconti (2006)	Competitiveness	Accounting fraud	T/C	−
Knack and Keefer (1997), Bloom (1999), Bloom and Michel (2002), Wade et al. (2006), Berggren and Jordahl (2006)	Income inequality	Trust	E	−
Knack and Keefer (1997), Zak and Knack (2001), Berggren and Jordahl (2006)	Mobility	Trust	E	−
Prudence				
McCloskey (2006)	Competitiveness	Realism	T	+
Harrison and Fiet (1999), Bizjak et al. (1993)	Competitiveness	Managerial opportunism	E	?
Laverty (1996)	Competitiveness	Stock market myopia	E	?
Brown and Higgins (2001), Segelod (2000), Rappaport (2005)	Competitiveness, fluid capital	Short-termism	E	−
Bowles (1998)	Market operation	Commensurability	TC	+
Effort: lazy – diligent – overzealous				
Kreps (1997), McCloskey (2006)	Market operation	Diligence	T	+
Goette and Lienhard (2006)	Working for piece rates	Performance	E	+
Frey (1998)	High wage	Performance	T	+
	Competitiveness	Overzealousness	T	−

Note
a Theoretical (T), empirical (E), case study (C).

The empirical studies yield a more pessimistic picture. Only in one-third of the cases do we find support for a positive impact of the market on virtues; in the other two-thirds the impact is negative. This suggests a positive ideological bias of the effects of the market on virtues in the literature researched in this chapter.

A third conclusion that we derive from Table 4.5 is that the indicators relating to market operation are highly diverse. In only a few cases indicators are used that also appear in the index of economic freedom (transfer payments as a percentage of GDP; respect for property rights; fluid capital). In theoretical literature, indicators mostly relate to a general concept of the market, such as the number of market transactions, the existence of price incentives, competitiveness, or the reputation mechanism. In empirical studies, intermediate variables are often used (number of advertisements, wealth, number of choice options, income equality, watching television, mobility, working mandatory overtime) that are more or less closely related to the market.

The fourth conclusion pertains to the impact of the market on virtues. As we can derive from the first three conclusions, the overall picture is highly uncertain. I therefore prefer to formulate hypotheses that summarize the tendencies in the theoretical and empirical literature reflected in the right-hand column of Table 4.5 rather than to formulate clear conclusions. The tendencies in Table 4.5 indicate that the impact of the market on virtues is diverse (see also Table 4.6). Three hypotheses point to a positive influence of the free market on virtues – i.e. self-reliance, diligence, and faith – and four hypotheses indicate a negative influence – i.e. encouraging, envy, and discouraging temperance, generosity, and love – whereas the impact on the other five virtues distinguished in our framework is ambiguous. This indicates that the impact of the market on virtues is too diverse for sides to be taken in the debate on the doux commerce or self-destruction thesis.

Table 4.6 Impact of the free market on virtues: hypotheses

H 1	?	The market stimulates **courage**. Fierce competition may encourage **recklessness**.
H2	–	The market crowds out **temperance**.
H3	+	The market discourages **inertia**.
H4	–	The market encourages **envy**.
H5	–	The market discourages **generosity** through price incentives.
H6	?	The market discourages **humility** and stimulates **pride** or **arrogance**.
H7	?	Market competition fosters **social manners**, but makes social relations **functional** instead of intrinsically valuable.
H8	?	A good legal system and security of property rights stimulate **trustfulnessness** but fierce competition encourages **fraud**.
H9	?	The net effect of market operation on **prudence** is ambiguous.
H10	+	The market fosters **diligence**.
H11	–	Fierce competition erodes self-sacrificing **love**.
H12	+	Competition encourages the virtues of **faith and hope** in God.

4.3.4 Curvilinear relation between competition and virtues

Hirschman's definition of the doux commerce thesis and the self-destruction thesis seems to imply that the two are logically incompatible. Nevertheless, Hirschman expresses the belief that both theses could hold at the same time. He even argues that this is overwhelmingly likely. He illustrates his argument with the example where the practice of commercial transactions generates feelings of trust and similar doux commerce feelings, but at the same time permeates all spheres of life with an element of calculation and instrumentality. In this way, the moral basis of capitalist society is constantly depleted and replenished at the same time.

Nevertheless, Hirschman does acknowledge that under special circumstances an excess of depletion over replenishment is possible, resulting in a crisis of the system. He stops short, however, of specifying the type of conditions under which the market economy will erode virtues rather than reinforce them. This is where my contribution of hypothesizing a curvilinear relationship between competition and virtues comes in. The case for curvilinearity is a variation on Etzioni's (1988) hypothesis of curvilinear relationship between social bonds and competition. Competition is nothing but contained conflict, which can be sustained only within a moral, societal, and governmental context that ensures that conflicts remain within prescribed limits. If competition is left to itself and social bonds are absent or very weak, it will escalate into a destructive, all-out conflict. At the opposite extreme, where social bonds are very powerful, economic competition is likely to be restrained, if not suppressed. Consequently, competition does not thrive in impersonal, calculating systems of independent actors unbound by social relations, or in the close-knit social world of communal societies. According to Etzioni, it thrives best in the middle range, where social bonds are strong enough to sustain mutual trust.

In this section, I want to argue a similar but slightly different thesis, namely that up to a certain point (point A in Figure 4.1) more market competition

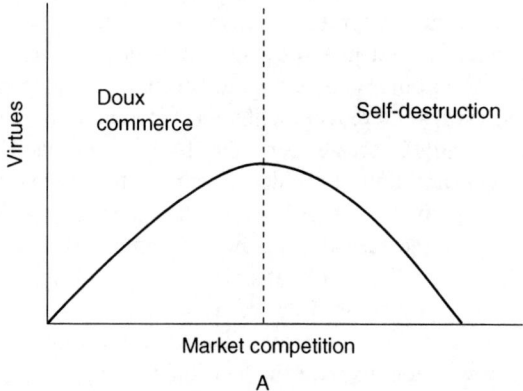

Figure 4.1 Curvilinear relationship between market competition and virtues.

stimulates the development of various virtues. Beyond this point, a further increase in competition tends to eliminate virtues and increase vices. Thus, whether the market economy will erode virtues (self-destruction) rather than reinforce them (doux commerce) depends (among others) on the degree of competition. To the left of point A, the doux commerce thesis holds, but to the right of point A self-destruction sets in.

An illustration of how markets may encourage virtuous behavioral patterns but subsequently overrule them can be found in literature on corporate social responsibility (CSR). Many researchers have found that CSR is profitable in the longer run (Orlitzky *et al.*, 2003). Competition (through the reputation mechanism) encourages companies with low CSR to emulate others that are experiencing great financial success because of their proactive CSR strategy. Companies shielded from competition may therefore lack an incentive to practice CSR. However, fierce competition may also exert downward pressure on CSR by reducing the set of potential CSR strategies available to firms (Ven and Jeurissen, 2005). A case in point is the textile sector during the late 1990s: increasing competition and a stagnating clothing market put considerable pressure on financial returns and triggered low-cost strategies. CSR suffered as a result. For example, in the 1990s C&A was the only clothing company that was certified for ISO14001 (Robins and Humphrey, 2000). However, in 2000 C&A abandoned its efforts for ISO14001 certification in several European countries due to the heavy administrative burden involved: the internal and external audits required for ISO certification were putting too much additional pressure on C&A staff, and so these tasks were reduced to a minimum (Graafland, 2002b).

There are several reasons why curvilinearity should also hold more generally. It is particularly implied by hypotheses 1, 2, and 8–10 in Table 4.6 and the interactions between the relevant virtues. First, as noted above, lack of competition discourages the development of courage. But, on the other hand, if competition becomes fierce, economic pressure becomes so strong that it elicits both fear and recklessness. If economic pressure becomes very strong, companies may feel greater temptation to resort to fraud, although the costs can be extremely high.

Similarly, curvilinearity may also be present in the relationship between market operation and temperance or prudence. Moving from a monopolistic situation, in which consumers have no other choice than to accept the product supplied by the monopolist, toward a more competitive environment in which consumers have more choice, results in greater consumer freedom and increases the satisfaction derived from consumption. It enables consumers to get what they want, and to be actively and effectively engaged. However, excess competition between numerous suppliers may increase the number of options available to consumers to such an extent that it reduces the satisfaction from and rationality of consumer choice for the reasons discussed above. Hence, beyond a certain level of consumer freedom, more competition provides an additional stimulus to intemperate behavior and narrows people's focus in decision making.

Fierce competition may also override justice. We have noticed that there are several reasons to believe that a free market system fosters trust and social capital. However, if competitive incentives grow very strong, it becomes tempting to realize economic benefits by opportunistic behavior. The keener the competition, the heavier the pressure to reduce costs, and the more pervasive corruption will be, resulting in a stronger decline in the virtue of honesty. When markets become more competitive, corruption will spread: the honest competitor will face a decline in output and will eventually have to choose between paying bribes too or going out of business. Hence, beyond a certain point of competitiveness, an increase in competition will erode truthfulness and justice. This is particularly true for institutional reforms that increase flexibility and competitiveness without improving the quality of the juridical system.[28]

Finally, up to a certain level of competition, market incentives have a healthy impact on diligence. But if the stakes are high and the threat from other competitors becomes fierce, the virtue of diligence may turn into overzealousness. This will also cause stress and put other virtues like temperance, self-possession, and prudence under pressure. The literature in the fields of occupational psychology, occupational health and safety, industrial relations, and work–family conflict empirically documents the adverse effects of long working hours on various aspects of worker welfare (Golden and Wiens-Tuers, 2006). The clearest negative effects of excessive work are on workers' ability to balance their competing work and family responsibilities. Major *et al.* (2002) found similar results. Working overtime and organizational expectations for time spent at work contribute to work–family conflict. Without leisure, social relationships deteriorate amid misunderstandings, feelings of abandonment, neglect, betrayal, and the like, eroding trust and loyalty, two virtues necessary for enduring relationships. Furthermore, if parents work full time and are not available for their children, this will frustrate the development of the children, because the basis for self-confidence and the capacity to learn is laid during the early years.

The hump-shaped relationship between competition and virtues seems perfectly in line with the basic concept of Aristotelian virtue ethics, namely that the extremes of too little and too much should be avoided: both the extremes of no competition and of fierce competition damage the development of virtues. Lack of competition frustrates the reputation mechanism and therefore prevents internalization of extrinsic motives for honesty, truthfulness, and prudence. But if competition is too fierce, courage turns to fearfulness and recklessness, honesty and loyalty to opportunism, and diligence to overzealousness with accumulating distortions of the other virtues like temperance, self-possession, and prudence.

4.4 A Christian view on the market and virtues

That competition may contribute to virtues was acknowledged by the apostle Paul. A good example is the metaphor of the race in 1 Corinthians 9: 24–7. Competition demands the continual exercise of the virtues of diligence, discipline, endurance, courage, self-control, and the faith that one is able to win the match.

Nevertheless, because of the mixed effects of competition on Christian virtues, Christians tend to be skeptical about unlimited competition. The reason is that the type of virtues that are encouraged by competition – diligence, self-control, courage, and faith – are not the only virtues or most important virtues in Christian life. The most important virtues are those related to love: "and the greatest of these is love" (1 Cor. 13:13). The analysis in the preceding section indicates that fierce competition may crowd out the virtue of love and related virtues such as mercifulness, humility, forgivingness and kind-heartedness.

This is particular true in the case of cut-throat competition and if the interests that are at stake become extremely important. In a mixed economy where the community guarantees minimal subsistence and human dignity for those who lose out in the competition with others, most people will experience some basic security. In this context, competition contributes to Christian virtues, because it encourages people to take responsibility. If competition becomes a matter of life or death, of eating or being eaten, the game becomes correspondingly tougher, leaving no room for mercy, humility, or patience with the weak. Paul does not use the metaphor of the race to indicate that only one person can be the winner in the spiritual game. If that were true, the spiritual struggle would be a merciless, hellish game, in opposition to the central message of the Gospel, which is God's love for those who are lost and weak. This is also evident from the context of the metaphor of the race. The purpose that Paul sets for himself is to save as many souls as possible. It is not about defeating others, but about serving them: "I make myself everybody's slave in order to win as many people as possible" (1 Cor. 9:19). Likewise, Jesus calls on his disciples to follow his example instead of that of the rulers of the world:

> If one of you wants to be great, he must be the servant of the rest ... like the Son of Man, who did not come to be served, but to serve and to give his life to redeem many people.
>
> (Matt. 20:26–8)

The market economy does not seem to foster this kind of attitude. Real altruism is relatively rare. Market players are motivated more by self-interest or reciprocity. In this context, encouraging competition will probably not encourage the Christian virtues. This does not imply a plea for an extensive welfare state. There is no proof that socialist societies are more virtuous than capitalist societies (Solomon, 1997). External coercion by the law can also erode solidarity with fellow humans and weaken the bonds of community. An extensive welfare state does not only have a fatal influence on typical capitalist virtues like diligence and courage, but also discourages typical Christian virtues such as compassion for others. In a society that organizes human solidarity by extensive, anonymous social security systems and makes the state responsible for the care of others, the need to give voluntary help to others diminishes.

4.5 Summary

4.5.1 The classical virtue ethics of Aristotle

A human being is happy if he or she performs spiritual activities that express excellence or virtue. Virtues are developed by habit formation. One cannot change overnight from a bad person into a good person.

Aristotle mentions several virtuous characteristics: courage, temperance, self-possession, righteous indignation, generosity, pride, friendliness, and justice. The common feature of these virtues is that they keep a middle ground between the vice of excess and the vice of parsimony in one's actions.

The various virtues are complementary and incommensurable. Which virtues deserve priority depends on the situation. Virtues are therefore context-dependent.

4.5.2 Christian virtues

Christian ethics is not only about ethical actions and institutions, but also about being a virtuous person.

Many virtues mentioned in the Bible are coherent with Aristotelian virtue ethics.

The Bible differs from Aristotelian virtue ethics in its core focus on the virtue of self-sacrificing love and related virtues such as humility and mercifulness.

The Christian virtues tend toward imitation of Christ and *consensus ad idem* with God.

Self-interest is only legitimate if it is in balance with the pursuit of the interests of others.

Self-sacrificing love is limited by justice and by the self-respect of the beloved.

Self-sacrificing love has a catalyst function. The beloved should seize upon the opportunity to change and develop a mature relationship of mutual love. If not, it is legitimate to take a step back.

4.5.3 The influence of the market on virtues

Since little research has been done on the impact of the market on virtues, the following results are only indicative.

The market nurtures courage. Under certain conditions, fierce competition may encourage recklessness and fear.

The market erodes temperance because it provides ample choices between alternatives, and gives companies a strong motive to advertise their products.

The market discourages inertia.

The market encourages envy, because it increases inequality.

The market discourages generosity through price incentives.

The market discourages humility and encourages pride or arrogance.

A good legal system and security of property rights encourage trustfulness; fierce competition and a high degree of flexibility encourage opportunism.

Fierce competition gives rise to fraud, but the reputation mechanism encourages honesty

The net effect of the market on prudence is ambiguous.

The market fosters diligence.

Fierce competition erodes self-sacrificing love.

Competition stimulates the virtues of faith and hope in God.

Christian virtues, like gratitude, benevolence, helpfulness, justice, forgivingness, truthfulness, endurance and faith in God, make people happier.

More market operation encourages the development of virtues up to a certain point. Lack of competition frustrates the reputation mechanism and therefore prevents internalization of extrinsic motives for honesty, truthfulness, justice, and prudence.

However, beyond a certain point, more competition tends to crowd out virtues and make room for vices. Courage turns to fearfulness or recklessness, honesty and loyalty to opportunism, and diligence to overzealousness with accumulating distortions of the other virtues like temperance, self-possession and prudence.

4.5.4 A Christian view on the market and virtues

Virtues that are encouraged by competition – diligence, self-reliance, courage, and faith – are not the most important virtues in Christian life. The most important virtues are those related to love. Since fierce competition may erode the virtue of love and related virtues such as mercifulness, humility, forgivingness and kind-heartedness, Christian ethics should be skeptical about unbridled competition.

5   Integration and application

In Chapters 2–4 we evaluated market operation from the perspective of welfare, justice, and virtue. In this chapter we connect the three perspectives and develop an integrated view on the market . This view is necessarily generic. Application to concrete market policies in particular sectors demands an accurate analysis of the specific context. An example is economic policy that aims at a more market-based energy sector. According to Armstrong and Sappington (2006: 326), even a comparatively simple choice between regulated monopoly and unregulated competition

> can be intricate and complex in practice. The decision to introduce competition into an industry is only the beginning of a journey down a long and winding road that can present many obstacles and detours. The best route from monopoly to competition can differ substantially in different settings. Therefore, there is no single set of directions that can guide the challenging journey from monopoly to competition in all settings.

Armstrong and Sappington conclude that in practice the question is not whether liberalization policies per se are desirable or undesirable, but which benefits and costs specific liberalization policies generate. There is a wide variety of liberalization policies and their merits vary considerably.

Concrete application of various standards of economic ethics often leads to different conclusions. Where outcomes conflict, a final judgment must include an account of the priorities in the different moral standards used. The purpose of this chapter is therefore twofold. First, we compare the outcomes of the partial evaluations of the market in Chapters 2–4 and form an integrated picture. In an excursus we illustrate these findings with an interpretation of the causes and cures of the credit crisis. Second, we discuss the hierarchy between the various ethical standards and, third, develop a practical method for applying Christian economic ethics to concrete economic policies. Section 4 presents a case study illustrating the application of the method proposed. In particular, we evaluate replacing a progressive tax system by a flat income tax system, which (under certain conditions) can be interpreted as a step toward a freer market.

5.1 Connecting three perspectives: welfare, justice, and virtue

Table 5.1 presents the most important conclusions of Chapters 2–4. Comparison of the findings provides a fairly coherent picture.

All three perspectives legitimate the market. From a welfare perspective, the market is positive because it fosters economic growth, which is deemed necessary for alleviating absolute poverty. No other economic system has been as productive as capitalism or has provided ordinary people with so much freedom and deliverance from poverty. If one cares about the poor, one should accept the market as an important and useful instrument to improve their situation. Without economic growth it would be impossible to improve the welfare of the poor. The rights and justice ethics legitimate the market because of respect for negative rights to freedom and because of the capitalist principle of justice (rendering to each his or her due). Virtue ethics also legitimates market competition, because it makes people responsible for their acts and has a positive influence on various virtues.

At the same time, all three perspectives recognize the need for limitations on the free market. Fostering human happiness requires that free markets are regulated in order to fight market imperfections. Furthermore, respect for human

Table 5.1 Overview of conclusions

Welfare and happiness
The market fosters economic growth. Economic growth is legitimate, but should be selective and targeted at the fulfillment of the needs of the poor, preservation of creation and flourishing of community bonds, rest and spiritual well-being. Notwithstanding substantial limits on the government and the growing importance of socially responsible behavior by private parties, a strong state is still necessary to reduce market imperfections and to make economic growth subservient to the Christian priorities mentioned above.

Rights and justice
The economic order should be structured such that positive basic rights are secure. As far as possible, institutions should respect the negative rights to freedom of citizens. But, if necessary, negative rights to freedom may be violated to guarantee positive basic rights to freedom, such as the right to subsistence, by a proper tax- and social security system. The Christian ideal of the economic order is not limited to securing positive basic rights. Income distribution should be reasonable as well, so that everybody can be more or less equally happy. Ideally, this situation is realized by respecting negative rights to freedom and the principle of moral merit and by voluntary solidarity and mutual insurance against disaster. However, it is an illusion to expect this to be sufficient. Therefore, we also need additional government redistribution policies. The degree of redistribution depends on its effectiveness to realizing equality and on the social preferences of citizens.

Virtues
Market competition is not incompatible with Christian virtue ethics. But the extremes of too little and too much competition should be prevented. Unlimited competition harms the virtues of temperance, benevolence, justice, solidarity, modesty, and love. It makes people too diligent. Too little competition, however, discourages the development of the virtues of honesty, trustfulness, justice, prudence, courage, diligence, faith, and hope.

---

rights demands that the outcomes of the free market be corrected by government redistribution policies in order to secure a fair income distribution and positive rights to freedom. Third, the market should be limited in order to prevent intense competition eroding important Christian virtues.

So the question that we must ask ourselves is not whether capitalism should be preferred to socialism, but rather how we can diminish the harmful consequences of the capitalist system. We should not replace the market system by some other coordination mechanism, but rather adjust it to reduce its imperfections. For that purpose, we need a strong state that is not guided by commercial interests, but effectively controls market structures and corrects the market in order to prevent substantial abuse of market power. A strong state is necessary to protect justice in the market. Therefore, politics, the media, and science must remain independent of the commercial interests of companies.

On the other hand, one should also be cautious about putting too much hope in the government. Complete justice is unattainable and striving for it creates a high degree of inflexibility. One needs a large amount of information about the causes of social evils and a highly committed and honest government to create a more just situation. This cannot be taken for granted. One should therefore always ask oneself whether a policy that aims to fight a certain social evil will prove effective and will not cause other injustices of even greater magnitude (Hill, 1994). Too much government regulation erodes the freedom and responsibility of individuals and their representative organizations. Therefore, it is equally important that strong states should be supplemented by strong, non-commercial communities that contribute to the development of virtues and a social atmosphere of mutual trust and solidarity that enhances efficient and just market outcomes.

5.1.1 Excursus: The credit crunch

In 2007 I published a more elaborate version of this book in Dutch. Since its publication, we have witnessed one of the severest crises of capitalism since the great depression of the 1930s. Like many economists, I had never expected such a worldwide and deep recession in modern times. In the Netherlands, several people have asked me how the credit crunch relates to the conclusions of my book. Now that more information has become available about the causes and possible cures of the credit crisis, I believe that my book contains many elements that are relevant for explaining how it happened as well as reducing the probability of such a crisis in the future. In this excursus, I will argue why.

For this purpose, I first briefly summarize the main causes of the credit crisis and the major players that have been responsible. Then I interpret the crisis in light of the main conclusions summarized above. I conclude that several elements of the credit crisis are inherent to a free capitalist system; however, the crisis should be overcome not by abandoning the capitalist model, but rather by making further improvements in market regulation as well as giving a larger role to virtue ethics.

5.1.2 Causes of the credit crisis

Although the credit crisis still needs a lot of analysis, the public debate suggests that some of the following main causes and players were responsible.

First, government institutions failed in various respects. In particular, the US government can be blamed for implicitly subsidizing the credit expansion in the US property market through the government-sponsored enterprises Fannie Mae and Freddie Mac. Although risk managers working at Fannie Mae and Freddie Mac sounded alarm bells, political pressure induced senior management to deliberately continue buying large amounts of Alt-A and subprime loans. They did so because they wanted to meet certain goals set by the Department of Housing and Urban Development (Calomiris, 2008). By shaping the market for mortgage loans, they encouraged private investors to enter as well. The securitized mortgages had no fixed interest rate and so when interest rates rose, many homeowners were unable to meet their obligations to the bank and consequently house prices slumped. US policy makers also failed in monetary policy. To sustain economic growth, the Federal Reserve systematically lowered the price of money. The resulting excess liquidity was invested in housing, causing the housing bubble. A third failure (already discussed in Chapter 2 above) concerns the lack of proper supervision and regulation of financial markets, both in the US and in other countries. This promoted lax underwriting standards by loan originators and failed to correct market imperfections in the trade in financial products elsewhere in the financial chain. Another major shortcoming in regulation concerns the lack of macro prudential supervision on a multi-country level. Supervision in Europe as well as on the global level focused too much on individual firms, primarily on banks. Moreover, observation of significant risks did not result in appropriate action (De Larosière Group, 2009). Due to severe competition with other countries, managers feared that tighter supervision would harm their competitive position. A lot of national managers were not willing to openly discuss the fragility of their financial institutions. Moreover, there were significant differences in management policies.

The second major group of players comprises the commercial banks that sold mortgages to subprime borrowers. They neglected to check the credit history, income, and other relevant details of borrowers because the subprime loans were being sold in the secondary loan market within a year of origination. The credit risk was thus passed on to the buyers of these secured mortgages (Mian and Sufi, 2008). Their self-interest was therefore promoted by selling as many mortgages as possible and leaving the risk to others.

The third major group that contributed to the credit crisis are the investment banks that transformed the mortgages into mortgage-backed securities and collateralized debt obligations. As such, these new innovative instruments for risk sharing can be beneficial. On the other hand, because of their complexity, they also create more opportunities for asymmetric information that can be used to conceal risk, to the detriment of the buyers of these products.

This leads us to the fourth major actor, the credit rating agencies. Competition between these agencies through rating shopping resulted in rating inflation.

Empirical evidence suggests that the more complex the security, the higher the rating bias produced by rating agencies (Skreta and Veldkam, 2009).

The fifth type of player is the buyers of derivatives, whose behavior was influenced by two factors. On the one hand, they did not have sufficient insight into the risks of the derivatives, because of the complexity of these products and because the models used to evaluate their risk profiles turned out to be inappropriate. Furthermore, the appetite for risk resulted from a strong focus on short-run financial success, which was encouraged by bonus systems that rewarded profitability in the short term.

Finally, the shareholders of banks were a factor behind the strong focus on short-term profitability. As already stated in Chapter 4 above, the average holding period for stocks has fallen substantially during recent decades and is now less than a year in professionally managed funds. Aggressive shareholders like hedge funds induced banks to take a short-term focus on maximizing stock value.

5.1.3 Interpretation

In light of this analysis of the causes of the credit crisis, Chapters 2 and 4 above have indicated several relevant points.

First, the crisis clearly shows the importance of good government regulation. Blind trust in the working of the market is unwarranted. The Chairman of the Federal Reserve Bank Greenspan admitted to a committee of the American House of Representatives that he had made a mistake in presuming that the self-interest of organizations, specifically banks and others, made them best able to protect their own shareholders and equity holdings.

The persistence of market imperfections is also illustrated by the lack of understanding of risks shown by investment banks when buying derivatives. The free market ideology assumes that market actors are rational. But use of the wrong risk models by portfolio managers of banks reflects bounded rationality. Only a few financial institutions used more appropriate risk models and foresaw the problems connected with securitized products (Bervas, 2006). Following this line of reasoning, we can blame neoliberal capitalism for contributing to the crisis by allowing too complex products that facilitated asymmetric information. In the Keynesian vision of the market, the government has the obligation to protect citizens against bounded rationality.

The credit crisis also illustrates the thesis of Chapter 4 above that too much competition may erode virtue and the moral basis of the free market. The hazardous selling of mortgages to subprime borrowers with insufficient collateral or financial strength was motivated by a short-term focus on self-interest without consideration that continuous accumulation of credit risk could severely harm other market actors. It seems reasonable to assume that these banks were aware of the weak financial status of their borrowers and the high risks involved. That did not stop them from large-scale selling of this type of mortgage and shifting the risks to other investment parties. This indicates the vices of injustice and greed.

Furthermore, competition between various regulators of the banking sector (in the US between the Federal Deposits Insurance Corporation, the Office of the Controller of the Currency and the Federal Reserve Board, and in Europe between the various national regulators) overwhelmed the professional regulation standards designed to keep the financial sector healthy. Competition between rating agencies caused a drop in professional standards, because it was profitable for them to give a somewhat inflated rating to securities to make them acceptable to their customers.

The credit crisis also illustrates the possibility that competition generates a short-term focus and erodes the virtue of prudence. This failure of investment banks to consider long-term consequences was not an isolated occurrence but a direct consequence of the short-term focus of shareholders. Society has allowed shareholder interests to become the only issue that counts. Banks that tried to fight the dominant position of shareholders lost. This made it extremely difficult for banks to take on their responsibility for focusing on the long term. And, as discussed in Chapter 4, the short-term focus of shareholders is inherent in the Anglo-Saxon model of capitalism.

The hazardous effects of vices can also be illustrated by the deplorable effects of exorbitant bonus systems. Hunger for money obscured the bank investors' ability to exercise sound risk judgment. Even now, when many banks have received government assistance to continue their business, many bank managers still want huge bonuses. A report by Andrew Cuomo showed that the nine big American banks that received $165 billion in government help paid 5000 employees a bonus of more than $1 million in 2008. It makes one wonder how this type of greed can ever be stopped: if not now, when?

A final application of virtue ethics to the credit crisis concerns the virtue of temperance. The credit crisis gathered momentum partly because of the vulnerable financial situation of the US. Both on the micro and the government level, debt has substantially increased. Total private and public debt rose from 155 percent of GDP in the early 1980s to 342 percent of GDP in mid-2008 (Ferguson, 2009). Taking into account that the US is one of the world's richest countries, this indicates that the American lifestyle is extremely materialistic and can be characterized as overconsumption. Because of the huge debt, the capacity for absorbing the reduction in wealth caused by the decline in house prices is very small. This has eroded the market's trust in government policy and is one of the reasons why the credit crisis has been so serious.

5.1.4 Conclusion

The preceding sections have shown that the Anglo-Saxon model of neoliberal capitalism has several weaknesses that contributed to the credit crisis. Government reluctance to regulate free market actors has proven extremely harmful. Policy makers therefore rightly conclude that the regulation of the financial sector should be improved and various national and multinational committees have made proposals on how to do so. For example, to improve supervision at the European level, the De Larosière Group proposed the founding of a European Systemic Risk Council, tasked to pool and analyze all risks that might impact financial stability. An effective early warning system should be imposed so that if turmoil threatens the financial markets, corrective action can be taken. In addition, the De Larosière Group proposed a new body for supervision at the micro level, the so-called European System of Financial Supervision, which would be responsible for the supervision of banks, insurance companies, and stock markets at the national level.

Nevertheless, one should be aware of the danger of overregulation. One should also acknowledge that the origin of the crisis lies in failures of government policy. Had the US government sought for ways to provide poor people with their own home other than by risky mortgages on the capital market (for example by rent subsidies or other forms of direct assistance), the credit crisis would not have occurred. From a virtue point of view, too much regulation may be counter-effective, because leaving too little responsibility to private companies may be detrimental to the development of intrinsic motivations to honesty, temperance, and prudence. Financial companies must be able to learn from the crisis. We are all now aware that banks can go bankrupt and this will have a decisive impact on the collective memory for the next decade. I therefore expect banks to adjust their balances voluntarily and this may prove to be much more important than government regulation. Governments should not frustrate this process by too much regulation. Instead of increasing regulation, the focus should be on reorganizing it from a national to an international level and on increasing its efficiency without making it more burdensome. Too much regulation will not only prove costly to society, but, from a moral point of view, also incurs the risk of lack of respect for the freedom of private firms.

5.2 Is there a hierarchy in values?

Although the summary of conclusions and the underlying analysis in Chapters 2–4 provide an important starting point for Christian economic policy, they do not give sufficient guidance for an evaluation of concrete policy proposals concerning economic institutions. An example is subsidizing child care for working parents. This kind of subsidy encourages women's participation in the labor market.[1] It can be defended on the principle of equal opportunities and also on the utilitarian principle of increasing overall welfare, particularly in Europe where there is an aging population. On the other hand, subsidizing child care for working parents violates the negative right to property of the working population who are faced with higher taxes to finance the subsidy. It is a compulsory redistribution of income from non-parents to parents. Parents who prefer to care for their children themselves also have to pay this tax, even though they do not benefit themselves from the subsidies. Hence, we are faced with a dilemma between promoting equal labor opportunities between men and women and respecting property rights. Which of these principles should take priority?

Ethical theory does not provide us with an unambiguous hierarchy of principles. There is no objective or even intersubjective answer to the question which moral standard should take precedence over others. Most philosophers take their own point of view. For example, John Stuart Mill (1871) argues that utilitarianism has priority over all other standards. Other ethical standards should only be supported as long as they contribute to the overall utility or happiness. According to Mill, deontological principles and virtues derive their moral worth because they foster happiness. Respect for rights and justice are after all important conditions for guaranteeing security and peace and, thus, happiness.

Although Mill considers utilitarianism to be coherent with the Christian belief that God wants the happiness of all, Chapter 2 above has shown that maximizing overall utility cannot be the only valid, final principle from a Christian point of view. People's individuality should not be disregarded if this raises total utility. Christian ethics must also take account of the Kantian notion that the moral value of an act depends on the intention of the actor. Furthermore, individual preferences cannot provide the sole ground for determining the moral value of a certain policy or institution. Because of the sinful nature of human beings, the preferences that they happen to have are not beyond criticism. Furthermore, future generations and non-human reality should also be respected and not instrumentalized to serve the interests of present generations. Basing morality on the satisfaction of individual preferences also disregards communitarian values that cannot be taken as equivalent to the sum of the personal preferences of all individuals belonging to the community. Finally, aggregation of utilities of individuals may violate the Christian priority of the poor.

If a certain set of choices does not allow a complete ordering of alternatives on the basis of the various ethical principles, one should balance these standards by specifying a weighting procedure for different criteria (Sen, 1981). The literature provides several examples. Often the various alternative criteria are weighted in lexicographic form with no trade-offs. An example is the rule of thumb whereby protection of individual rights has greater weight than distributive justice and distributive justice has greater weight than maximization of aggregate utility (Velasquez, 1998). The reason for this is that moral rights identify areas of personal life in which other people may not interfere even if to do so would create greater benefits from an overall welfare perspective. Likewise, maximization of total utility is unacceptable if it leads to a highly unequal income distribution. Distributional justice therefore generally take precedence over utilitarianism.

This rule of thumb only ranks the various liberal standards.[2] In Chapter 4 above we argued that Christian ethics also stresses the importance of virtues. In the New Testament, commands and virtues are often closely interconnected. The law of love is the summary and fulfillment of the law. Whoever loves one another obeys the law (Matt. 22:37–40; Rom. 13:8–10; Gal. 5:14). Nevertheless, there are several reasons to give priority to the commandment of God. Although virtues are necessary to put the law of God into practice, we need moral norms that determine which values should be promoted and which acts are just. Terrorists can be as brave as soldiers who fight for a good cause. The Bible gives greater priority to the commandments of God than to virtue (Loonstra, 2000). In the New Testament the focus on developing virtues is less marked than in Greek philosophy.

Another possible tension between the liberal ethical standards of utilitarianism and rights and justice theories on the one hand and Christian ethics on the other concerns the legitimacy of communitarian values. As argued in Chapter 3 above, Christian ethics acknowledges the communitarian idea that members of one's own community deserve a higher priority than members of other communities. This creates a certain tension with the principle of impartiality. It is difficult to present an unambiguous rule that regulates this tension. In each case one should consider whether community bonds or the principle of equality should prevail. Only in cases where basic human rights are violated should the principle of justice be given priority.

5.3 Applying Christian ethics to economic policy: a method

In the economic policy-making process, politicians have to face all kinds of dilemmas. A moral dilemma arises if two moral standards are in conflict (Graafland *et al.*, 2006).[3] What method can be applied to arrive at a responsible decision when one faces such a difficult dilemma?

The literature presents several practical methods for handling moral dilemmas. Examples are the eight-step plan of Trevino and Nelson (2004) (which is more or less similar to the method of van Luijk (1993)) and the dilemma-analysis scheme of Graafland and Mazereeuw (2005). Below I present a seven-step plan that combines several elements of these methods:

1   Gather the facts behind the issue. How did the situation occur?
2   Identify the policy options.
3   Identify the affected parties.
4   Identify the consequences of each option for each of the affected parties.
5   Identify the moral standards that are met or violated by the options or their consequences.
6   If various moral standards are involved and the different options cannot be completely ordered, determine the hierarchy of moral standards that should prevail and identify the option that optimally meets this hierarchy.
7   Check the outcome:

   a   Think again creatively about potential options that could possibly meet the conflicting standards involved.
   b   Check your intuition. The emphasis in the preceding steps has been on a highly rational fact-gathering and evaluation process. But that does not insure that you derive a conclusion that fits your intuition. If you feel uncomfortable about the finally selected option, give the preceding steps more thought and try to identify which step causes the problem.
   c   Use the model of the methodological assumption to determine whether the outcome is defensible to others (see p. 148).

5.3.1 *Clarification of step 6: a rule of thumb for weighting moral standards*

Step 6 demands an assessment of the moral standards involved. As discussed above, ethical theory does not provide an unambiguous key to determine the hierarchy between various ethical standards. Nevertheless, based on the arguments in section 5.2, I propose a certain rule of thumb that can help us identify the relative importance of the different ethical standards.

In particular, if an economic policy decision allows a set of options that generates a dilemma between various moral standards, one should make the following deliberations to determine which option is morally obligatory:

1   Select the alternatives that respect positive basic rights.
2   Of these selected alternatives, reject those that (substantially) violate negative economic rights or principles of moral desert and equal opportunities. Also reject alternatives that discourage Christian virtues (particularly the virtue of love) and encourage vices. If these standards conflict, one should intuit which principle should be preferred.
3   Of the alternatives that remain after the second test, prefer the alternative that meets Rawls' difference principle or some similar principle (such as the weighted priority view).

This proposal is only a crude rule of thumb. The application of this method always depends on the context. An objective sequence that can be applied to all situations does not exist. Specific cases always require careful consideration of all the moral standards involved.

5.3.2 *Clarification of step 7c: the model of methodological assumption*

For the final choice, Manenschijn (1982) proposes applying the model of methodological assumption. After one has identified the best option by going through steps 1–7b, the choice is methodologically tested by being confronted with contra-indications. This means that the conclusion is put forward as a provisional decision that can be contested by others (often informed by practical experience). Often this confrontation takes place in an exchange of viewpoints with others. But if communication with others is not possible, one can also try to reconstruct the debate by putting oneself in the position of others. One should try to develop the strongest contra-arguments, both those that relate to relevant facts (about the consequences of the option) and those relating to principles. The advantage of confronting the provisional decision with the strongest contra-argument is that, if the provisional decision remains valid, one can disregard other weaker contra-arguments. If the contra-argument proves to be more convincing than the provisional decision, however, one should adapt it accordingly.

5.3.3 What is Christian about the proposed seven-step method?

The dilemma analysis scheme proposed above can be applied independently of the religious background of the decision maker. An exception is step 6, however, because different philosophies often give different answers as to which moral standards should be preferred. Still, readers may question what is particularly Christian about the rule of thumb proposed above, because there are obvious similarities with other rules of thumb, such as the one proposed by Velasquez (1998) (rights > justice > utilitarianism). Indeed, the differences are relatively small. Still, the rule of thumb that I propose contains several elements that are typical of Christian ethics.

First, in contrast to liberal ethics, the rule of thumb gives a relatively high priority to Christian virtues. As discussed in Chapters 1 and 4, Christian ethics features many communitarian characteristics. Communitarian values and encouragement of community bonds have a high priority in Christian ethics. In liberal ethics, virtues are relatively less important. Moreover, the virtue ethics that should be acknowledged in the second phase of step 6 deviates from secular virtue ethics because of a specific Christian stress on the virtue of love (and related virtues such as humility and mercifulness) and the spiritual virtues of faith and hope in God. The rule of thumb thus fits quite well with rules of thumb of other Christian ethicists based on biblical principles. For example, Loonstra (2000) argues for priority to love. This fits the Jongeneel's (1996) characterization of the biblical economy as the economy of mercy, or Haan's (1985) as the economy of reverence (by which he means an economy of serving God by serving others).

A second Christian element of this rule of thumb is the high priority given to positive basic rights. This fits the needs principle of justice which acknowledges that the poor have a basic right to minimal subsistence if they are not able to earn a sufficient income by themselves. As discussed in Chapter 3 above, respecting positive basic rights should take precedence over respecting negative rights to freedom; therefore government redistribution policies to prevent absolute poverty are legitimate. In this respect, the rule of thumb clearly diverges from libertarian ethics that only acknowledges the protection of negative rights. In poor countries where governments are not able to guarantee positive basic rights, economic growth should go hand in hand with human development.

A third Christian characteristic of the proposed rule of thumb is the relatively low priority given to the standard of overall welfare. In the third test of the rule of thumb, priority is given to improving the position of the least advantaged or some other principle that attaches a relatively high weight to the poor, such as the weighted priority principle. The decision to put some modest egalitarianism above utilitarianism is motivated by the Christian ideal of a society where everybody is more or less equally happy. A society with relatively low income inequality probably approaches this ideal more than a society that maximizes total welfare. The extent of redistribution depends, however, on its effectiveness and on the preferences of the population. If redistribution does not improve the quality of life of the least advantaged at all, an economic order that merely secures positive basic rights is legitimate. European history shows, however, that it is possible to improve the position of the least advantaged by additional redistribution without harming overall productivity. Nevertheless, the second test in the rule of thumb requires that negative rights should be respected as much as possible.

5.4 Case study: flat income tax system

The societal debate about market liberalization relates to many different markets with very specific characteristics, such as telecommunications, the labor market (protection against redundancy, minimum wage, etc.), the health sector, the residential property market, public transport, higher education, the energy market, and the capital market. Whether and how market competition can be fostered and whether government regulation can be reduced depends on the specific context of each market.

In Graafland (2007a) I evaluate several specific cases by applying ethical theory, such as policies that aim at more labor market participation by women; reforms of the pension system (because of aging in Europe); the free market in cosmetic surgery; the regulation of working hours on collective holidays (including Sundays). I also evaluate the case of correcting international income distribution by development aid.

In this section I present only one case study to illustrate the operation of the seven-step method proposed in section 5.3. For this purpose, I selected the case of replacing a progressive income tax system by a flat income tax system. This policy has been implemented in several East European countries and has also recently been discussed in some West European countries such as the Netherlands. One can interpret this policy as a reduction of the distortion of the operation of the free market by government redistribution and, thus, as a step in the direction of the free market. I base the case study on a recent Dutch report on proposals for a flat tax system in the Netherlands, because of the practical advantage that I am relatively well informed about the perceived consequences of the proposals.[4]

5.4.1 Step 1: Background information

A flat tax system is a system that annually taxes an income base with one fixed tariff (Kam and Ros, 2006a). In contrast, the progressive tax system applies different and rising tax rates as income increases. Most West European countries, but also the US, Japan, Canada, and Australia, use a progressive tax income tax system. Only the two islands of Guernsey and Jersey have had a flat income tax system (of 20 percent) for many years. Recently, the popularity of the flat tax system has increased. East European countries like Estonia, Latvia, Lithuania, Russia, Slovakia, Serbia, Georgia, and Romania have all introduced a flat income tax system during the last twelve years.

Various forms of flat income tax have recently been discussed in the Netherlands. In 2001 the scientific bureau of the Christian Democratic Party (CDA) published a report presenting a flat tax system with a 35 percent tax rate. In 2005 the Conservative Liberal Party (VVD) also proposed a flat income tax. Economists like Bovenberg and Teulings (2006) developed a flat income tax system with a tax rate of 38 percent. In November 2008, Prime Minister Balkenende expressed serious interest in such a proposal.

5.4.2 Step 2: Identify the policy options

Normally, a flat tax system is perceived as combining a broad tax base with a low tax rate. In Estonia the tax rate is 24 percent, in Russia 13 percent, and in Serbia as little as 10 percent (Kam and Pen, 2006). It is obvious that this kind of tax system particularly benefits the rich income groups and do little to correct the primary income distribution. There are, however, many alternative flat tax systems and the implications for the net income distribution crucially depend on the specific characteristics of each. Table 5.2 only presents two concrete proposals for the Netherlands.

In proposal one, the current tax brackets are replaced by a single tax bracket. Incomes are taxed at a rate of 37.5 percent. In proposal two, the tax credit (tax-free personal allowance) is raised by 1400 euro. This is financed by increasing the tax rate from 37.5 percent to 43.5 percent.[5]

5.4.3 Step 3: Identify the affected parties

Replacing a progressive tax system by a flat tax system affects all income earners. Economic analyses often distinguish between household types, such as single persons, breadwinners (sole earners in households with at least one dependent adult or children), two-income households, recipients of unemployment

Table 5.2 Two examples of a flat tax system for the Netherlands

	Current progressive tax system		*Two alternative flat tax systems (Jacobs et al., 2006)*	
			Proposal 1	*Proposal 2*
Tax credit	1900[a]		1900	3300
Tax rates	Tax rates	Income bracket starting at:[b]	37.5%	43.5%
	34.15%	0		
	41.45%	17,000		
	42%	30,600		
	52%	52,200		

Notes
a In addition to a labor income credit of 1300 euro. Capital income is taxed by a separate regime with a flat tax rate of 30%.
b Thousands of euros.

assistance and the retired elderly. Micro-simulations are used to determine how the various income groups within these household types will be affected. In our analysis, we distinguish low-, medium-, high-, and top-income groups.

5.4.4 Step 4: Identify the consequences of each option for each of the affected parties

The possible advantages and disadvantages of the flat tax system are summarized in Table 5.3.

The first advantage is that opportunities for tax avoidance diminish (Bovenberg and Teulings, 2006). Since the rich are better able to afford tax experts, the simplification of the tax system benefits the low- and medium-income groups. However, this advantage is particularly relevant if tax exemptions are eliminated. In the two proposals under review, the tax base is not changed. The argument that a flat tax system reduces the opportunities for tax fraud is only relevant if the number of tax exemptions is decreased. It is the complexity of the tax exemptions, not the difference in tax rates, that gives rise to tax fraud.[6]

One of the disadvantages of the flat tax system is that it directly benefits the higher income groups. However, as already stated, the precise effects depend on the exact specification of the tax system. This is illustrated by Table 5.4.

The table shows that the effects on income are highly diverse. Nevertheless, there are some general tendencies. First, in both flat tax systems the retired people face a reduction in income. Second, the highest income groups benefit. Unfortunately, I could only get indirect information about the income effects of the highest income groups. For example, Kam and Pen (2006) show that the income of top managers like the CEO of Shell will increase by 8 percent in proposal one. Finally, an important difference between proposals one and two is that the least advantaged groups benefit more from proposal two, due to the increase in the tax credit.

The effects on income presented in Table 5.4 do not take into account the behavioral effects of replacing a progressive tax system with a flat tax system. It is often assumed that a flat tax system encourages labor supply because the marginal tax rate declines. The impact on labor supply depends, however, on the

Table 5.3 Advantages and disadvantages of flat tax system

Advantages	Disadvantages
Rich benefit less from tax avoidance	More unequal income distribution
More labor supply	Less labor supply
Government is more predictable	Less possibilities for fine-tuning of income distribution by government
Less fiscal arbitrage and tax fraud	
Simplification and lower administrative costs of employers	
More transparency for citizens	

Table 5.4 Effects of flat tax system on income[a]

Household types	Income group	Flat tax 37.5%	Flat tax 43.5%
Single employees	Low	−2.5	−1.5
	Medium	−0.5	−2.25
	High	3.25	−1.75
	Very high	?	?
Breadwinners	Low	−2	−1.5
	Medium	−0.5	−2
	High	4.25	−0.75
	Very high	8	?
Two-earner households	Low	−2	1.25
	Medium	−2	1.25
	High	0.25	−1.25
	Very high	?	?
Unemployment assistance	Low	−3.75	1.25
	Medium	−1.5	−2.25
Retired	Low	−3.5	−1.5
	Medium	−1.5	−4

Note
a % growth compared to current tax system. Source: Jacobs *et al.* (2006; Table 5.1, 5.2).

exact profile of the marginal tax structure. Using the MIMIC model (Graafland *et al.*, 2001), Jacobs *et al.* (2006) estimate that proposal one decreases the participation rate of women (see Table 5.5), because the new tax rate of 37.5 percent is higher than the current tax rate of the first tax bracket (34.15 percent). The total number of hours worked increases, however, because the marginal tax rate for most other income groups declines. Investment in human capital through education improves. Proposal two causes a decline in the total number of hours worked.[7] Labor supply research shows that part-time and low-income workers respond relatively more to financial incentives than high-income groups. For these groups, the marginal income tax rate increases, causing negative substitution effects. Although the marginal income tax rate declines for high-income groups, these groups are fairly insensitive to economic incentives and therefore hardly raise their labor effort.

This illustrates the lessons from optimal tax literature showing that the optimal tax structure depends on four factors (Jacobs *et al.*, 2006: 94): (1) income inequality before taxation; (2) the society's aversion to income inequality; (3) the impact of monetary incentives on labor supply; (4) the density of income distribution. If a society is averse to income inequality, the optimal marginal tax structure will have a U shape: low income groups will receive high income tax credits and pay low taxes. In order for sufficient taxation to be collected, medium- and high-income groups will have to pay substantially more tax and this requires that the marginal tax rate between low- and medium-income

Table 5.5 Economic effects of a flat tax system[a]

	Flat tax 37.5%	Flat tax 43.5%
Theil coefficient	6.50	−3.00
Marginal tax rate (absolute change)	−3.0	0.25
Participation rate of women	−1.75	1.50
Labor supply in hours	1.00	−0.25
Breadwinners	1.25	0.00
Two-earner	0.00	−0.25
Single person	1.00	−1.00
Share high skilled in labor supply	0.75	0.00
Employment	1.50	−0.25
Low skilled	−2.00	−0.50
High skilled	2.50	−0.25
Unemployment rate	0.00	0.00

Note
a % growth compared to current tax system. Source: Jacobs *et al.* (2006: Table 5.3).

groups is relatively high (A in Figure 5.1). However, for medium-income groups high marginal tax rates have a large disincentive effect on labor supply. This explains why marginal tax rates should be lower for medium-income groups than for the lowest-income groups (B in Figure 5.1). The labor supply of high-income groups is less sensitive to economic incentives. Hence, for high-income groups marginal tax rates have to increase again in order to realize additional income redistribution (C in Figure 5.1). These lessons imply that a flat tax system will not be efficient in general.

A third advantage mentioned by proponents of a flat tax system is a more reliable government. If the tax system only consists of a tax credit and one tax rate,

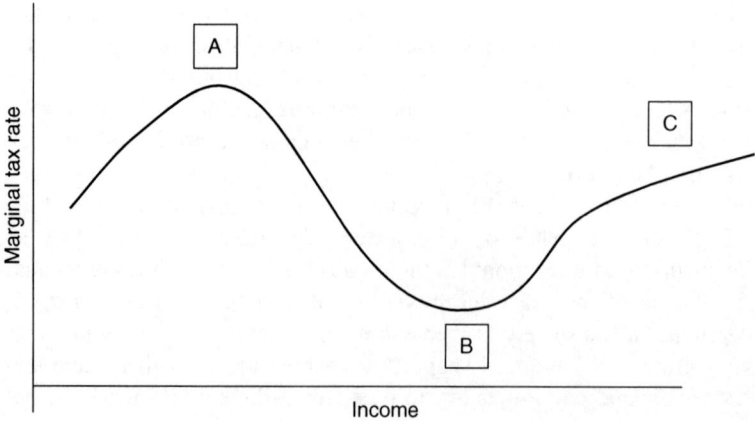

Figure 5.1 Optimal marginal tax structure according to optimal tax literature.

the government has fewer opportunities for intervening in the market and therefore becomes more predictable. This advantage entails the obvious disadvantage that the simplified tax structure leaves the government with fewer possibilities for correcting income distribution. The debate about the incomes of top executives shows that the government also runs a risk of losing credibility if it cannot intervene when top executives earn salaries that a majority of citizens regard as exorbitant.

Another advantage of a flat income tax is a reduction of opportunities for tax arbitrage. If different tax bases (for example of labor income and capital income) are taxed at significantly different rates, people will try to reallocate income toward the tax base with the lowest rate. Jacobs *et al.* (2006) argue, however, that a flat tax system is not necessary to reduce tax arbitrage. One can also redefine tax bases in a way that precludes or hinders tax arbitrage, for example by sampling all types of income in one base (without using one tariff) (Kam and Ros, 2006b).

Other advantages of the flat tax system are a reduction in the administrative costs of employers and more transparency for citizens (Bovenberg and Teulings, 2006). This contributes to the flexibility of the labor market. Kam and Ros (2006b) doubt, however, the empirical relevance of these effects, since other parts of the social security system still require companies to provide the type of information that a flat tax system would render unnecessary.

5.4.5 Step 5: Identify the moral standards that are met or violated by the option or its consequences

Table 5.6 presents an overview of the values that are involved in the two variants.

First, one may doubt whether the two flat tax systems really improve efficiency and welfare. The theoretical analysis of Jacobs *et al.* (2006) indicates that a simple flat tax system is less efficient than a progressive tax system that takes account of the variation in the incentive effects of taxes for different income groups. If one also considers the negative external effects of positional competition (which is not taken into account by Jacobs *et al.*), the efficiency effects become even more doubtful. In Chapter 2 we referred to analyses that show that internalization of the negative externalities caused by positional competition and habit formation requires tax rates of 50 percent or more. Furthermore, the

Table 5.6 Qualitative effects of a flat tax system on values

	Flat tax 37.5%	*Flat tax 43.5%*
Welfare/efficiency	?	?
Egalitarian justice	–	+
Capitalist justice	+	–
Virtues	?	0

efficiency gains from less tax arbitrage, less tax fraud, lower administration costs, and more transparency remain modest as long as the tax base is not substantially broadened and simplified. Therefore, I expect the overall impact on welfare and efficiency to be relatively small.

The second principle that we consider is egalitarian distributive justice. Proposal one decreases the income of all low-income groups, whereas the higher-income groups all benefit. The Theil coefficient – an aggregate standard for income inequality – increases by 6.5 percent. In the second variant inequality decreases: the Theil coefficient declines by 3 percent, because the low-income groups benefit from the higher tax credit. From this we conclude that the first variant should be rejected and the second accepted from the perspective of egalitarian justice.

A reverse evaluation is obtained when applying capitalist justice. Whereas the first variant increases the link between net income and gross income (which can be interpreted as an indicator of marginal productivity) by lowering marginal tax rates, the second variant increases the marginal tax rate on average. Note that even a flat tax system is not just from a strictly capitalist point of view, because it still implies that the rich pay more taxes than the poor. From a capitalist point of view, this is only fair if the rich also benefit more from public expenditure than the poor (which they probably do, but the extent is uncertain).

The final principle that we apply is virtue ethics. As described in Chapter 4, the impact of the market on virtue is highly variable. Since proposal one restructures the tax system in a way that renders net incomes more in line with market outcomes, one would expect more or less similar effects, as discussed in Chapter 4. Kam and Pen (2006) argue that the large increase in the incomes of very high-income groups will elicit negative effects on tax morality, because people will consider these effects unfair. On the other hand, a flat income tax may encourage the virtue of diligence, because it creates an incentive to work harder and invest in human capital. It is not possible to determine empirically the net effects of both variants on the different virtues, or to derive an overall judgment. The effects of proposal two are probably too marginal to imply any substantial impact on virtues.

5.4.6 Step 6: If various moral standards are involved and the different options cannot be completely ordered, determine the hierarchy of the moral standards that should prevail and identify the option that optimally meets this hierarchy

In order to derive a final evaluation, we have to weigh the various moral standards listed in Table 5.6. Whereas the effects on efficiency and virtue are ambiguous, proposal one scores better in terms of capitalist justice and proposal two in terms of egalitarian justice. This renders an ordering satisfactory to both impossible. A final judgment therefore requires a hierarchy between, in this case, egalitarian and capitalist justice. Figure 5.2 represents the choice-making process implied by the rule of thumb proposed in section 5.3. First, in all cases – the

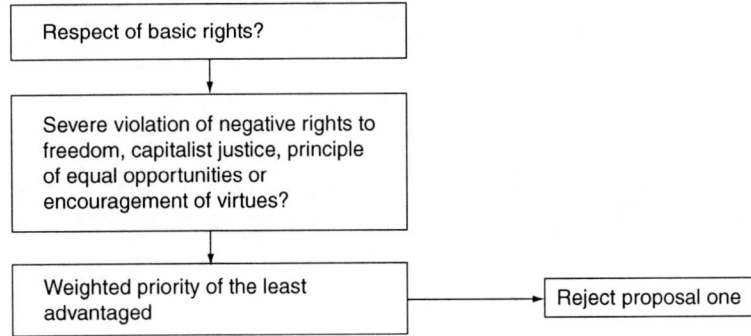

Figure 5.2 Application of the rule of thumb.

current tax system, proposal one, and proposal two – no positive basic rights are violated. That implies that all three tax systems pass the first test.

In the second test all variants that cause a severe violation of negative rights to freedom, of the principle of rendering to each his or her due, of equality of opportunities or of encouragement of vices are rejected. Again, there is no ground to reject any of the three tax systems. Although the current tax system and proposal two confront citizens with a higher (marginal) tax burden, the violation of their property rights is too limited for these alternatives to be rejected on ground of the second test.

That implies that the choice should be determined by the last test of the rule of thumb. In this test, proposal one is rejected because it worsens the position of all low-income groups and increases income inequality. Whereas proposal two benefits the low-income groups receiving unemployment benefits, it reduces the income of other low income groups (see Table 5.4). Overall, proposal two increases income equality, however. This test therefore points at a slight preference for proposal two.

5.4.7 Step 7: Check the outcome once again

The evaluation of the flat income tax system above is just a finger exercise that illustrates the application of the seven-step model presented in section 5.3. Based on the theoretical analysis of Jacobs *et al.* (2006), I do not regard proposal two as the optimal tax system. For example, a tax system with two brackets that taxes higher income groups progressively (as proposed by Kam and Pen, 2006) is probably both more efficient and more just. One can think of innumerable other variants of tax systems that vary in terms of tax credit, number of tax brackets, length of tax brackets and tariffs per tax bracket. Furthermore, one should also consider changes in the tax base, which we have left out in this section (for purposes of clarity). It is up to the creativity of policy makers to construe attractive alternatives and to evaluate them on the basis of the moral standards that have been described in this book.

Notes

1 Introduction

1 For the text of the declaration, see http://warc.jalb.de/warcajsp/side.jsp?news_id=1157 &navi=45.
2 Since the meaning of this political concept is not unambiguous, I will not use it but, instead, refer to a free market system in which the government's only task is to safe-guard private property rights.
3 Earlier, in 2003, the Lutheran World Federation addressed the international economic system in very similar terms by stating that

> this false ideology [neoliberalism] is grounded in the assumption that the market, built on private property, unrestrained competition, and the centrality of contracts is the absolute law governing human life.... This is idolatry, and leads to the systematic exclusion of those who own no property, the destruction of cul-tural diversity, the dismantling of fragile democracies and the destruction of the earth.
>
> (cited in Atherton 2008: 61)

4 Official church documents show that there is a considerable convergence of underlying economic principles. There are, however, also differences in emphasis that resemble the distinction between liberalism and communitarianism. For an overview of convergence and divergence between church documents on the economy, see Graafland (2008).
5 Hence, distributional concerns are postponed until Chapter 3. This division allows me to concentrate in Chapter 2 on the many topics that can be discussed without elaborat-ing on distributive justice and to concentrate in Chapter 3 on justice and distribution.

2 The market and welfare

1 Research shows that the happiness that people report closely corresponds to activity in the brain. According to Layard (2003), this means that happiness corresponds to an objective reality and is not a vague concept.
2 Welfare theory therefore also developed a second theorem that provides a solution to this moral criticism. This second welfare theorem states that every Pareto optimum can be obtained as a competitive general equilibrium, given some distribution of initial endowments to economic agents. However, in practice changes in the initial endow-ments to meet standards of distributive justice are very difficult to identify, because information about the distribution of initial endowments is very hard to get (Sen, 1984).
3 In Genesis 9: 10 the animals are explicitly included in the covenant that God makes with Noah and his descendants:

> God said to Noah and his sons: I am now making my covenant with you and with

your descendants, and with all living beings, all birds and all animals, everything that came out of the boat with you.

Just as the animals had shared in the curse of the flood, they should share in the blessing after the flood.

4 Another reason why unconditional protection of existing nature is problematic is that nature itself is subject to the force of evil and sometimes threatens human life. In the Bible some animals, like dogs, are even considered impure (Matt. 7:6, Luke 16:21) or dangerous (Ps. 22:17).

5 For this reason Carter (2005) addresses the problem that abundance destroys generosity. He then argues that the act of giving in a situation of abundance is a purer form of generosity that any other, since it brings no feeling of any need for reciprocation. But it is still difficult to see why a gift is a sign of love if it involves no sacrifice by the giver.

6 However, one may wonder whether in an ideal society ruled by the value of love justice is still necessary. In this respect a heavenly society may differ fundamentally from the just society that John Rawls (1999a) assumed in his well-known ideal theory of justice. In this theory, people act out of well-understood self-interest. Moderate scarcity motivates self-interested individuals to cooperate. The rich will realize that they need the cooperation of the poor to fulfill their own plans and will therefore respect Rawls' principles of justice.

7 According to Atherton (1992) there is no need of a market economy in paradise, because a market is only useful in case of scarcity.

8 Recently so-called creative capital was also recognized as one of the determinants of competitive power. According to research by Florida (2002), cities with a large proportion of creative people perform better than other cities. The core of the creative class consists of people who work in science and engineering, computer and mathematics, education, arts, design, or entertainment.

9 In order to prevent simultaneity bias, Blume and Voigt (2006) use a lag of three years between the data of the various indices and the data of economic growth.

10 Cited in Rodrik (2002).

11 Just as for economic freedom, it is difficult to provide reliable measures of the openness of a country. Empirical studies of the relationship between free trade and economic growth therefore remain merely indicative. Interpretation of this kind of research is further complicated by possible simultaneity bias, because the inverse causality that rich countries can be more competitive on the world market and are therefore more open is also plausible.

12 As a result, income distribution is much more equal in South Korea than in countries with low collective social expenditure such as Brazil. In South Korea the income of the richest 20 percent is on average seven times higher than the income of the poorest 20 percent; in Brazil this ratio is 30:1 (Sider, 1997).

13 Other researches confirming the positive relationship between income equality and economic growth are Alesina and Rodrik (1994) and Persson and Tabellini (1994).

14 For references, see Ranis and Stewart (2005).

15 For references, see Ranis and Stewart (2005).

16 Book IV, chapter VI, cited in Brekke and Howarth (2002: 2).

17 However, if well-being is measured by life satisfaction rather than by happiness, the relationship becomes less marked, with satisfaction and GDP per capita moving in the same direction in only forty-six of ninety countries.

18 This implies that Atherton's analysis, which is based on previous research that showed that beyond some minimum level increasing income is at best weakly correlated with improvements of welfare, is slightly outdated by these new findings.

19 Atherton (2008) observes that, nevertheless, the proponents of happiness are rarely heard actually promoting marriage and religious faith. There is apparently a big gap between research findings and the policy implications that modern societies derive from them.

20 But, as Atherton (2008) rightly acknowledges, Christian morality cannot be reduced to happiness. Christian ethics aims not only at individual happiness but also at fostering the common good (to be discussed in Chapter 4) and emphasizes the importance of justice (to be discussed in Chapter 3).

21 Similarly, Sider (1997: 128) defends a theology of sufficiency. Western countries should develop models of simpler lifestyles and corporate policies that permit people to choose parenting, leisure, and community service over maximizing income, and macroeconomic policies that discourage overconsumption. Western countries should consume and pollute less. At the same time he points to various complications, because the poor are the first to be hit by rising unemployment caused by falling growth and by higher consumer prices, whereas the wealthier classes benefit from the cleaner environment.

22 The Oxford Declaration on Christian Faith and Economics (Schlossberg *et al.*, 1994: 16) states at the same time, however, that work should also not be overvalued. The essence of human beings is that they are made in the image of God. The ultimate, though not exclusive, source of meaning and identity lies not in work, but in becoming children of God.

23 It should be acknowledged that the economics of sufficiency, as proposed by Goudzwaard and de Lange (1995), can be interpreted in this way, because their criticism of the traditional goal of economic growth focuses on the material component (the use of energy and resources and the pressure on the ecological system). The purpose of an economics of sufficiency would then not be a stationary economy but a sustainable economy.

24 In reality, the freedom of prostitutes is often very limited. In the Netherlands many prostitutes are victims of a slave trade or are forced into prostitution by pimps.

25 Storkey (2006) makes a similar point in relation to the weapons industry. After the cold war the output of the weapons industry was halved, but without seriously harming the market economy. The market proved able to adjust smoothly to the changes in the demand for goods.

26 For example, by subsidizing child care. Graafland (2000) shows that this kind of policy can be very effective in stimulating labor supply and economic growth.

27 CPB (1995) predicts that an 8 percent increase in the opening hours of shops raises the output of the retail sector by only 0.2 percent.

3 The market and justice

1 The literature distinguishes between a weak and strong variant of the difference principle. In the strong variant the difference principle rules out any inequality that does not improve the position of the worst-off: an inequality that does not maximally improve the prospects of the worst-off is unjust. One of the objections to the strong difference principle is that it does not allow improvements for the better-off that do not harm the least well-off (Parfit, 1998). In the quest for equality, it is thought preferably to dispense altogether with goods that cannot be equally shared than to let some have more than others. Some philosophers consider this highly counterintuitive (Murphy, 1998; Arneson, 2002; Crisp, 2003). In the weak variant, the difference principle rules out any inequality that worsens the position of the worst-off. An inequality that does not worsen the prospects of the worst-off can be just. The weak variant is consistent with the lexical difference principle. The lexical difference principle directs us to maximize the prospects of the worst-off group, and then, subject to this constraint, maximize the prospects of the next worst-off group, and so on until the prospects of the best-off group are maximized. So inequalities are fine as long as they do not hurt the worst-off or, if the worst-off category is unaffected, the worst-off category but one etc. It is also consistent with the absolute priority view and the so-called principle of personal good. The absolute priority view states that when benefiting

others, the worst-off are to be given absolute priority over the better-off (Crisp, 2003). The principle of personal good states that for all alternatives z and y, if everyone is at least as well off in z as in y and z is better for at least some people, then this outcome is better than alternative y (McKerlie, 2003; Tungodden, 2003). Shaw (1992) argues, however, that the difference between the weak and the strong variant is not very relevant in the economic sphere, because material resources are easily transferable.

2 Sen (1984: 320) thinks that there are good reasons to assume that Rawls also – contrary to what Rawls states – is really after something like capabilities instead of primary social goods, because Rawls motivates the focus on primary goods by discussing what these goods enable people to do.

3 The capitalist and libertarian standards of justice are also known as commutative justice. Commutative justice holds for voluntary exchange of value for value in trade among individuals. Nevertheless, they can also be classified as standards of distributive justice, because these standards also have implications for the distribution of income outside the market. Distributive justice is a generalization of commutative justice.

4 The principle of equal opportunities takes an intermediate position. How far this principle is egalitarian depends on its exact formulation.

5 Whether the Bible rejects taxation for social purposes cannot be derived from these texts. In the New Testament, Paul calls on believers to pay taxes to the government, but in his day the primary function of the state was to maintain law and order and protect private property, infrastructure and safety, which is also allowed in the libertarian view on taxes. Nor did Jesus seem to reject taxation (Matt. 22:17; Mark 12:14; Luke 20:22). In Matthew 17:24–7 his attitude is, however, more ambivalent. He uses the argument that Roman citizens need not pay taxes to argue that he does not have to pay taxes either. Still, he orders Peter to pay the tax, merely for the sake of not offending others.

6 The law prohibiting interest did not apply to borrowing by strangers (Deut. 23:20), partly because they usually borrowed for business reasons, not because of poverty. Calvin argues that interest is not generally forbidden. He refers to Matthew 25:27 and Luke 19:23 that implicitly indicate that Jesus accepted the practice of interest.

7 Calvin argues, however, that the principle of justice reflected in this story does not apply to our society. Since manna was given every day to the Israelites without tillage or labor, it is not surprising that God commanded that each one of the people should partake of it equally. According to Calvin, the logic of ordinary production is different. For that it is necessary that each should be able to increase his resources in proportion to his diligence, strength, dexterity, or other means. It would be absurd to apply to our ordinary needs the law which is laid down for manna (Bieler, 2005; Calvin's commentary on Ex. 16:13–18).

8 Taken literally, priority to the principle of equal opportunity may not leave any resources for the difference principle (Parijs, 2003). To illustrate, even if much has been done to implement equal opportunity, Rawls demands that additional expenditure should be put into extra education if that would marginally improve equal opportunities rather than being put into helping the disadvantaged according to the difference principle.

9 For a discussion of the relationship between Matthew 5:3 and Luke 6:20 and the question of whether these texts should be understood in a spiritual or economic sense, see, for example, Santa Ana (1977). Lindijer (1981) believes that Luke 6 is the more authentic text and that "spiritually" has been added as a clarification. However, the difference in interpretations become less significant if one realizes that the pious and the poor were often the same people: their miserable circumstances would have contributed to a sense of dependence on God.

10 This reasoning is also reflected in Calvin's commentary on Exodus 31:2, where he states that people are not able to perform the simplest type of work if God's spirit does not enable them to do so. Therefore, people cannot claim any reward before God. Any reward is due to God's free love.

11 The parable also implicitly shows that Jesus acknowledges that people have different abilities: although all the servants received one gold coin, the profitability of their dealings differed substantially. Another implication of this parable is that Jesus seems to accept the practice of interest for business dealings.

12 For a definition of these indicators, see CPB (2007).

13 The poverty elasticity estimates the percentage change in the number of people in poverty for each 1 percent growth in average income for each region in the world.

14 Atherton (2008) presents conclusions from Wolf's *Why globalization works: The case for the global market economy* (Yale University Press, 2004) which shows that globalization has not made the poor worse off in terms of a wide range of indicators of human welfare, such as life expectancy, infant mortality, literacy, hunger, fertility, and the incidence of child labor.

15 The experience of developing countries that globalized during the 1980s and 1990s (Mexico, Colombia, Argentina, Brazil, Chile, India, and Hong Kong) contrasts with the experience of several Southeast Asian countries (South Korea, Taiwan, Singapore) that underwent trade reforms in the 1960s and 1970s and exhibited a decline in inequality as they opened their economies to foreign markets.

16 Sahoo (2008) also finds that more competition in India caused more efficiency and less poverty, but increased income inequality in the short and medium term. In the long run, the effects on income equality are, however, positive.

17 To illustrate how outsourcing of industrial activities from the US to China particularly hit the middle class of workers, Kynge (2006) gives the example of Rockford, Illinois, an industrial area in decay. The example shows how globalization can induce polarization of the labor market. Statistics from the US Census Bureau show that the number of middle-income employees has declined compared to employees with an income lower than $25,000 or higher than $75,000.

4 The market and virtues

1 Although trust is, strictly speaking, not a virtue, it is obviously closely related to the virtue of trustfulness: if people can be trusted, one is inclined to trust others.

2 Aristotle does not distinguish moral virtues from non-moral virtues. He used the word "moral" simply to mean "practical" (Solomon, 1992). According to Solomon (1992) we should not draw a sharp distinction between moral virtues (such as honesty) and non-moral virtues (such as wit), because many virtues seem ambiguous in moral terms.

3 Besides education, habit formation, and natural inclination, Aristotle also acknowledges the value of external pressure from good and reasonable laws to induce people to good behavior.

4 Related concepts are common sense, rationality, self-interest, caution, foresight, calculation.

5 Other vices may also lead to poverty. Strangers will take the wealth of adulterous men (Prov. 5:10), prostitutes' clients (Prov. 29:3) drunkards (Prov. 23:21), and conceited people (Prov. 13:18). Wealth is connected to a diligent, virtuous, and pious life (Prov. 22:4). However, the wisdom writers are also aware that wealth and effort are not always correlated (Eccl. 9:11). They realize that hard work without the blessing of God can be fruitless (Ps. 127:2).

6 Some other biblical virtues, like firmness and dedication, show parallels with the virtues of courage (because these virtues are necessary to maintain one's conviction, even in the event of danger), self-control, and prudence. A self-controlled person sticks to the conclusion of his deliberations. In the New Testament the word "firmness" (*hupomone*) is also translated as "endurance." In combination with ordeals and oppression, endurance suggests resignation. But often endurance is connected to hope (Rom. 8:25). It demands an active effort by the believer to keep hoping for salvation.

7 The justification of self-interest is also confirmed by the defense of private property

(see Chapter 3). Private property is a means that helps people to determine their own responsibility, by securing juridical competences. It enables them to take decisions for which they can be held responsible.

8 When reworking Part IV of the Dutch version *Het oog van de naald* in this section, I benefited from some additional literature suggestions from the Master's thesis of Tim Wiegant (titled "The market, virtues, and happiness: an Aristotelian view on the market economy," Tilburg University, 2008.).

9 Badhwar (2008) also argues that free markets are the most powerful force for deobjectifying people and relationships and that the market society creates a more secure environment for civic and personal friendship than any other form of developed society. He responds to the well-known criticism that markets commodify human relationships by showing that market relations are not entirely instrumental (and non-market relations not entirely non-instrumental).

10 A full reading of MacIntyre indicates that the tension he observes – that practices are vulnerable to the competitiveness of the institution (of the market) – may not be as destructive as he suggests, because no practice can survive unless it is sustained by institutions and external goods. Moreover, external goods also provide indications of the achievement of internal goods by practice. Only if business becomes completely focused on external goods may it fail to support the practice on which it is founded.

11 Another possible escape from the need for longitudinal studies is cross-country analysis. However, identifying the influence of the market on virtues is then complicated by differences in cultural contexts, which typically are much more varied between countries than within countries.

12 To illustrate, Glaeser *et al.* (2004) found that political institutions are influenced by economic growth rather than the other way around. Their findings are consistent with the view that the set of institutional opportunities that each community faces is largely determined by the human and social capital of its population.

13 McCloskey (2006: 361) gives the following examples: love and faith yield loyalty; courage and prudence yield enterprise. Aquinas considered the seven cardinal virtues to be primary virtues on which the other virtues are based.

14 Another problem concerns the embedding of virtues in the culture of a community. Whereas communities are collective, virtues are characteristics of individuals. However, both are highly intertwined. As Solomon (1992) argues, what is best in us – our virtues – is in turn defined by the larger community. Market operation may influence the community by affecting the character traits of (groups of) individuals, but communities may also resist these influences if certain values are strongly anchored in a culture. Some sub-communities, such as that of the Quakers, are hardly influenced by the commercial values of the market economy. In my analysis, I disregard this kind of interactions between virtues and cultures.

15 It should be noted, however, that in 1997 the percentage of people believing that job security was declining was more or less similar. The answers may therefore reflect not only an assessment of current conditions but also an inherent human tendency to view the past through rose-colored spectacles (Pew Research Center, 2006: 6).

16 In the US, the average adult watches five hours of TV a day. That means watching 21,000 commercials a year (Sider, 1997).

17 There are currently one billion obese people. Obesity is caused by various factors, such as increased labor market participation of women, more use of cars and more TV watching or computer use. Industry is responding very slowly to this societal problem.

18 They also tested whether the decline in support could be explained by strategic behavior (understating willingness in order to increase compensation) or signaling (offering generous compensation is interpreted as an indication that the facility is more dangerous had previously been thought), but both hypotheses were rejected.

19 However, it should be noted that Aristotle also states that we sometimes honor a non-ambitious person for his or her simplicity and modesty (EN: 1125b15).

20 Here we also include friendship as discussed in chapter eight of EN.

21 Florida (2002) admits that capitalism may weaken traditional bonds, but considers the numerous weak ties of the modern network economy to have greater strength. Modern people prefer weaker ties, because they allow them to mobilize more resources and more possibilities.

22 Atherton (2008: 90) also refers in this context to G. Himmelfarb (*The de-moralization of society: From Victorian virtues to modern values*, London: IEA Health and Welfare Unit, 1995) who uses longitudinal research on crime indices. She shows that indictable offences in Britain had increased from 480 per 100,000 people in 1857 to 10,000 by 1991.

23 Berggren and Jordahl (2006) also found that education has positive effects on trust, but regard the estimated parameter as insignificant.

24 In *Lectures on jurisprudence*, eds. R.L. Meek, D.D. Raphael, and P.G. Stein (Oxford: Clarendon Press, 1978). Cited in Maitland (1997: 22).

25 Grant and Visconti (2006) report several empirical studies that found a link between executive compensation and companies' restatement of revenues and earnings.

26 S. Messner and R. Rosenfeld (1994) *Crime and the American dream* (Belmont: Wadsworth).

27 In Sweden, a reverse trend is found: young people are more inclined to trust others than elders. See Berggren and Jordahl (2006: 151).

28 To illustrate, in the Scandinavian countries the rule of law index is on average 1.95, which is substantially higher than in the US (1.70). The index of economic freedom is, however, lower in the Scandinavian countries, namely 7.5 versus 8.2 in the US. As described above, the rule of law index is particularly important for creating trust, whereas the other elements of the index of economic freedom are not.

5 Integration and application

1 For an economic analysis, see Graafland (2000). For a more extensive moral analysis of economic policies that foster labor market participation by parents, see Graafland (2007a).

2 For a more extensive discussion of methods of weighting, see Graafland (2007a: section 11.3).

3 In contrast, a dilemma that arises from a conflict between a moral standard and a practical standard is classified as a motivational dilemma. This dilemma confronts an individual with the problem of moral motivation: What motivates people to act in accordance with their moral standards (Crisp, 1998)?

4 The analyses of the economic consequences of various flat tax systems have been carried out with the so-called MIMIC model. I myself was very much involved with the development of this applied general equilibrium model for the Netherlands and the type of analyses studied in this section (Graafland *et al.*, 2001).

5 The capital tax system and the structure of tax exemptions are not changed. In Graafland (2007b) I also discuss a third proposal that enlarges the tax base by cancelling various major tax exemptions and lowers the tax rate to 25.5 percent. The economic effects of the abolition of tax exemptions are, however, very complex and largely unknown. For presentational purposes, I disregard this option here.

6 An additional disadvantage of the flat tax system is that it reduces the damping effect of the tax system on economic fluctuations.

7 Women's participation rate increases because the additional tax credit in this proposal only applies to those receiving a personal income. This encourages non-working partners to accept a small part-time job.

References

Achterhuis, H. (1988) *Het rijk van de schaarste van Hobbes tot Foucault*, fifth edition, Amsterdam: Ambo.

Ackerman, F. (2005) "The shrinking gains from trade. A critical assessment of Doha round projections," Global Development and Environment Institute, Tufts University, Working paper No. 05–01.

Alesina, A. and Rodrik, D. (1994) "Distributive politics and economic growth," *Quarterly Journal of Economics*, 109: 465–90.

Alesina, A. and La Ferrare, E. (2002) "Who trusts others?," *Journal of Public Economics*, 85: 207–34.

Alessie, R. and Kapteyn, A. (1991) "Habit formation, interdependent preferences and demographic effects in the almost ideal demand system," *The Economic Journal*, 101: 404–19.

Alpizar, F., Carsson, F., and Johansson-Stenman, O. (2005) "How much do we care about absolute versus relative income consumption?," *Journal of Economic Behaviour & Organization*, 56: 405–21.

Anderson, D.M. (1998) "Communitarian approaches to the economy," in H. Giersch (ed.), *Merits and limits of the market*, Berlin: Springer.

Anderson, E. (1993) *Value in ethics and economics*, Cambridge/London: Harvard University Press.

Anderson, E.S. (1999) "What is the point of equality?," *Ethics*, 109: 287–337.

Aristotle, *Ethica Nicomachea*, Groningen: Historische Uitgeverij.

Aristotle, *Politics*, book I and II, Oxford: Clarendon Press.

Armstrong, M. and Sappington, D.E.M. (2006) "Regulation, competition, and liberalization," *Journal of Economic Literature*, XLIV: 325–66.

Arneson, R.J. (1999) "Against Rawlsian equality of opportunity," *Philosophical Studies*, 93: 77–112.

Arneson, R.J. (2000) "Luck egalitarianism and prioritarianism," *Ethics*, 110: 339–49.

Arneson, R.J. (2002) "Why justice requires transfers to offset income and wealth inequalities," *Social Philosophy and Policy Foundation*, 19: 172–200.

Arrow, K. (1972) "Gifts and exchange," *Philosophy and Public Affairs*, I: 343–62.

Atherton, J. (1992) *Christianity and the market: Christian social thought for our times*, London: SPCK.

Atherton, J. (2008) *Transfiguring capitalism. An enquiry into religion and global change*, London: SCM Press.

Auger, P., Burke, P. Devinney, T.M., and Louviere, J.J. (2003) "What will consumers pay for social product features?," *Journal of Business Ethics*, 42: 281–304.

Badhwar, N.K. (2008) "Friendship and commercial societies," *Politics, Philosophy & Economics*, 7: 301–26.

Barro, R.J. (1999) "Determinants of democracy," *Journal of Political Economy*, 107: s158–83.

Baumeister, R. and Vohs, K. (2003) "Willpower, choice and self-control," in G. Loewenstein, D. Read, and R. (eds.), *Time and decision: Economic and psychological perspectives on intertemporal choice*, New York: Russell Sage Foundation.

Beauchamp, T.L. (1982) *Philosophical ethics: an introduction to moral philosophy*, New York: McGraw-Hill.

Bebchuk, L.A. and Fried, J.M. (2005) "Pay without performance: Overview of the issues," *Journal of Applied Corporate Finance*, 17: 8–22.

Beisner, E.C. (1994) "Justice and poverty: Two views contrasted," in H. Schlossberg, V. Samuel, and R.J. Sider (eds.), *Christianity and economics in the post-cold war era. The Oxford declaration and beyond*, Grand Rapids, Mich.: William B. Eerdmans.

Berggren, N. (1999) "Economic freedom and equality: Friends or foes?," *Public Choice*, 100: 203–23.

Berggren, N. and Jordahl, H. (2006) "Free to trust: Economic freedom and social capital," *Kyklos*, 59: 141–69.

Bervas, A. (2006) "Market liquidity and its incorporation into risk management," *Financial Stability Review*, No. 8, Banque de France, May.

Beugelsdijk, S., de Groot, H.L.F., and van Schaik, A.B.T.M. (2004) "Trust and economic growth: A robustness analysis," *Oxford Economic Papers*, 56: 118–34.

Bieler, A. (2005) *Calvin's economic and social thought*, ed. E. Dommen, Geneva: World Alliance of Reformed Churches/World Council of Churches.

Biermans, M. (2005) "The political economy of dignity. Monitoring the advancement of socio-economic human rights in a globalized economy," Discussion Paper 43, SEO Economisch Onderzoek, Amsterdam.

Bizjak, J.M., Brickley, J.A., and Coles, J.L. (1993) "Stock-based incentive compensation and investment behavior," *Journal of Accounting and Economics*, 16: 349–72.

Bjørnskov, C. (2005) "Investigations in the economics of social capital," dissertation, Aarhuis School of Business.

Blaug, M. (1978) *Economic theory in retrospect*, third edition, Cambridge: Cambridge University Press.

Blok, M. and Graafland, J. (2004) "Subsidiariteit, soevereiniteit in eigen kring en de bouwfraude," *Philosophia Reformatica*, 69: 2–13.

Bloom, M. (1999) "The performance effects of pay dispersion on individuals and organizations," *The Academy of Management Journal*, 42: 25–45.

Bloom, M. and Michel, J.G. (2002) "The relationships among organizational context, pay dispersion and managerial turnover," *Academy of Management Journal*, 45: 33–42.

Blume, L. and Voigt, S. (2006) "The economic effects of human rights," mimeo, Universiteit van Kassel.

Bovenberg, A.L. (2000) "On the cutting edge between policy and academia: challenges for public economists," *De Economist*, 148: 295–329.

Bovenberg, A.L. (2002) "Norms, values and technological change," *De Economist*, 150: 521–53.

Bovenberg, A.L. (2007) "Bespreking van Johan J. Graafland, Het oog van de naald. Over de markt, geluk en solidariteit," *Christen Democratische Verkenningen*, herfst 2007: 166–70.

Bovenberg, A.L. and Teulings, C.N. (2006) "Vlaktaks: haken en ogen," in C.A. de Kam and A.P. Ros (eds.), *De vlaktaks. Naar een inkomstenbelasting met een uniform tarief?*, Willem Drees Stichting voor Openbare Financiën, The Hague: Van Deventer.

Bowles, S. (1998) "Endogenous preferences: The cultural consequences of markets and other economic institutions," *Journal of Economic Literature*, XXXVI: 75–111.

Brekke, K.A. and Howarth, R.B. (2002) *Status, growth and the environment; Goods as symbols in applied welfare economics*, Cheltenham: Edward Elgar.

Brown, L.D. and Higgins, H.N. (2001) "Managing earnings surprises in the US versus 12 other countries," *Journal of Accounting and Public Policy*, 20: 373–98.

Brümmer, V. (1993) *Liefde van God en mens*, Kampen: Kok Agora.

Bruni, L. and Stanca, L. (2006) "Income aspirations, television and happiness: Evidence from the World Values Studies," *Kyklos*, 59: 209–25.

Calderón, C., Loayza, N., and Schmidt-Hebbel, K. (2005) "Does openness imply greater exposure?," World Bank Policy Research, Working Paper 3733, Washington DC: World Bank.

Calomiris, C.W. (2008) "The subprime turmoil; What's old, what's new, and what's next?," NBER working papers, August.

Cappelen, A. and Tungodden, B. (2006) "A liberal egalitarian paradox," *Economics and Philosophy*, 22: 393–408.

Carlsson, F., Johansson-Stenman, O., and Martinsson, P. (2003) "Do you enjoy having more than others? Survey evidence on positional goods," Goteborg University, Working Papers in Economics, 100.

Carmon, Z., Wertenbroch, K., and Zeelenberg, M. (2003) "Option attachment: When deliberating makes choosing feel like losing," *Journal of Consumer Research*, 30: 15–29.

Carter, E.J. (2005) "Resurrection and economics," *Association of Christian Economists Journal*, 35: 1–10.

Choo, F. and Tan, K. (2007) "An American dream theory of corporate executive fraud," *Accounting Forum*, 31: 203–15.

Christman, J. (1998) "Property rights," in *Encyclopedia of applied ethics*, 3, San Diego: Academic Press: 683–92.

Chryssides, G.D. and Kaler, J.H. (1993) *An introduction to business ethics*, London: Chapman & Hall.

Clark, A.E. (1999) "Are wages habit-forming? Evidence from micro data," *Journal of Economic Behavior & Organization*, 39: 179–200.

Conlisk, J. (1996) "Why bounded rationality?," *Journal of Economic Literature*, XXXIV: 669–700.

Cornia, G.A. (ed.) (2004) *Inequality, growth and poverty in an era of liberalization and globalization*, Oxford: Oxford University Press.

CPB (Centraal Planbureau) (1992) *Scanning the future. A long-term scenario study of the world economy 1990–2015*, The Hague: Sdu Publishers.

CPB (Centraal Planbureau) (1995) "Economische effecten van liberalisering van winkel-tijden in Nederland," The Hague: Working Paper 74.

CPB (Centraal Planbureau) (2007) "Measuring competition in the Netherlands," Research Memorandum 163, The Hague.

Crisp, R. (ed.) (1998) J.S. Mill, *Utilitarianism*, Oxford: Oxford University Press.

Crisp, R. (2003) "Equality, priority and compassion," *Ethics*, 113: 745–63.

Davies, E.W. (1989) "Lands; its rights and privileges," in R.E. Clements (ed.), *The world of ancient Israel: Sociological, anthropological and political perspectives*, Cambridge: Cambridge University Press.

Dawson, J.W. (1998) "Institutions, investment, and growth: New cross-country and panel data evidence," *Economic Inquiry*, XXXVI: 603–19.

Deaton, A. (2008) "Income, health and well being around the world. Evidence from the Gallup World Poll," *Journal of Economic Perspectives*, 22: 53–72.

De Larosière Group (2009) *The High-Level Group on Financial Supervision in the EU*, report, February.

Desjardins, J.R. (1984) "Virtues and business ethics," in M. Hoffman (ed.), *Corporate governance and institutionalized ethics*, Lexington, Mass.: D.C. Heath.

DeWitt, C.B. (1998) *Caring for creation. Responsible stewardship of God's handiwork*, Grand Rapids, Mich.: Baker Books.

Diener, E. and Diener, C. (1995) "The wealth of nations revisited: Income and the quality of life," *Social Indicators Research*, 36: 565–91.

Dowrick, S. and Colley, J. (2004) "Trade openness and growth: Who benefits?," *Oxford Review of Economic Policy*, 20: 38–56.

Duchrow, U. (1987) *Global economy: A confessional issue for the churches?*, Geneva: WCC.

Duffhues, P.J.W. and Jobson, M.A. (2006) "Imperfecties op de arbeidsmarkt voor topbestuurders," *Economisch Statistische Berichten*, 91: 552–5.

Easterlin, R. (1974) "Does economic growth improve the human lot?," in P. David and M. Reder (eds.), *Nations and households in economic growth: Essays in honor of Moses Abramowitz*, New York: Academic Press.

Easton, S.T. and Walker, M.A. (1997) "Income, growth, and economic freedom," *American Economic Review*, 87: 328–32.

Etzioni, A. (1988) *The moral dimension. Towards a new economics*, New York: The Free Press.

Fehr, E. and Gächter, S. (1999) "Reciprocity and economics: Implications of reciprocal behavior for labor markets," Paper presented at the Annual Conference EALE, September 23–26, 1999, Regensburg, Germany.

Ferguson, N. (2009) "The age of obligation," www.niallferguson.com/site/FERG/Templates/ArticleItem.aspx?pageid=200, accessed March 2009.

Florida, R. (2002) *The rise of the creative class. And how it's transforming work, leisure, community and everyday life*, New York: Basic Books.

Frank, R.H. (2004) *What price the moral high ground*, Princeton, NJ: Princeton University Press.

Frey, B. (1998) *Not just for the money: An economic theory of personal motivation*, Cheltenham: Edward Elgar.

Frey, B.S. and Oberholzer-Gee, R. (1997) "The costs of price incentives: An empirical analysis of motivation crowding out," *American Economic Review*, 87: 746–55.

Frey, B.S. and Jegen, R. (2001) "Motivation crowding theory," *Journal of Economic Surveys*, 15: 589–611.

Frey, B.S., Benesch, C., and Stutzer, A. (2005) "Does watching TV make us happy?," Institute for Empirical Research in Economics, University of Zurich, Working Paper 241.

Frick, F.S. (1989) "Ecology, agriculture and patterns of settlement," in R.E. Clements (ed.), *The world of ancient Israel: Sociological, anthropological and political perspectives*, Cambridge: Cambridge University Press.

Friedman, M. (1953) *Essays in positive economics*, Chicago: University of Chicago Press.

Gächter, S. and Fehr, E. (1999) "Collective action as a social exchange," *Journal of Economic Behavior & Organization*, 39: 341–69.

Galbraith, J.K. (1958) *The Affluent Society*, Boston: Houghton Mifflin.

Gay, C.M. (2003) *Cash values. Money and the erosion of meaning in today's society*, Grand Rapids, Mich.: William B. Eerdmans.

Gimlin, D. (2000) "Cosmetic surgery: Beauty as commodity," *Qualitative Sociology*, 23: 77–98.

Glaeser, E.L. (2005) "Inequality," Harvard Institute of Economic Research, Discussion Paper 2078.

Glaeser, E.L. and DiPasquale, D. (1999) "Incentives and social capital: Are homeowners better citizens?," *Journal of Urban Economics*, 45: 354–84.

Glaeser, E.L., LaPorta, R., Lopez de Silanes F., and Shleifer, A. (2004) "Do institutions cause growth?," NBER Working Paper 10568, Cambridge, Mass.: NBER.

Gneezy, U. and Rustichini, A. (2000) "Pay enough, or don't pay at all," *Quarterly Journal of Economics*, 115: 791–810.

Goette, L. and Lienhard, M. (2006) "Productivity and well-being under fixed wages and piece rates," www.isu.uzh.ch/emap/docs/2006/poek/LienhardGoette.pdf.

Goldberg, P.K. and Pavcnik, N. (2007) "Distributional effects of globalization in developing countries," *Journal of Economic Literature*, XLV: 39–82.

Golden, L. and Wiens-Tuers, B. (2005) "To your happiness? Extra hours of labour supply and worker well being," *The Journal of Socio-Economics*, 35: 382–97.

Gorringe, T.J. (1994) *Capital and the Kingdom: Theological ethics and economic order*, London: Orbis Books and SPCK.

Goudzwaard, B. (1976) *Kapitalisme en vooruitgang. Een eigentijdse maatschappijkritiek*, Assen/Amsterdam: Van Gorcum.

Goudzwaard, B. (1982) "Economische waarde en de doeleinden en instrumenten van economisch beleid," in B. de Gaay Fortman (ed.), *Economie en waarde*, Alphen aan den Rijn/Brussels: Samson Uitgeverij.

Goudzwaard, B. and de Lange, H. (1995) *Beyond poverty and affluence. Toward an economy of care*, Grand Rapids, Mich.: William B. Eerdmans.

Graafland, J.J. (1990) *Persistent unemployment, wages and hysteresis*, Helmond: Wibro dissertatiedrukkerij.

Graafland, J.J. (2000) "Child care subsidies, labor supply and government finance," *Economic Modelling*, 17: 209–46.

Graafland, J.J. (2001) "Social and economic aspects in the Old Testament," in H. Klok, T. van Schaik, and S. Smulders (eds.), *Economologues. Liber amicorum voor Theo van de Klundert*, Tilburg: University of Tilburg.

Graafland, J.J. (2002a) "Modelling the trade-off between profits and principles," *De Economist*, 150: 129–54.

Graafland, J.J (2002b) "Sourcing ethics in the textile sector: the case of C&A," *Business Ethics: A European Review*, 11: 282–94.

Graafland, J.J. (2002c) "Profits and principles: Four perspectives," *Journal of Business Ethics*, 35: 293–305.

Graafland, J.J. (2003) "Distribution of responsibility, ability and competition," *Journal of Business Ethics*, 35: 293–305.

Graafland, J.J. (2004) "Cosmetische chirurgie, nut en vrijheid," in J. Graafland and F. van Peperstraten (eds.), *De omheining doorbroken. Economie en filosofie in beweging*, Budel: Damon.

Graafland, J.J. (2006) "IHC Caland in Burma: Een analyse," in W. Dubbink and H. van Luijk (eds.), *Bedrijfsgevallen. Morele beslissingen van ondernemingen*, Assen: Van Gorkum.

Graafland, J.J. (2007a) *Economics, ethics and the market: Introduction and applications*, London: Routledge.

Graafland, J.J. (2007b) *Het oog van de naald. Over de markt, geluk en solidariteit*, Kampen: Ten Have.

Graafland, J.J. (2008) "Christian perspectives on the market," *Zeitschrift für Wirtschafs- und Unternehmensethik*, 9: 41–57.

Graafland, J.J. and Smid, H. (2004) "Reputation, corporate social responsibility and market regulation," *Tijdschrift voor Economie en Management*, XLIX: 269–306.

Graafland, J.J. and Mazereeuw van der Duijn Schouten, C. (2005) "Levensovertuiging en dilemma's binnen organisaties," in T. Jardjono and H. Klamer (eds.), *Breng spirit in je werk*, Zoetermeer: Meinema.

Graafland, J., Kaptein, M., and Mazereeuw van der Duijn Schouten, C. (2006) "Business dilemmas and religious belief: An explorative study among Dutch executives," *Journal of Business Ethics*, 66: 53–70.

Graafland, J.J., de Mooy, R.A., Nibbelink, A.G.H., and Nieuwenhuis, A. (2001) *MIMIC-ing tax policies and the labor market*, Amsterdam: North Holland.

Grant, R. and Visconti, M. (2006) "The strategic background to corporate accounting scandals," *Long Range Planning*, 39: 361–83.

Gutiérrez, G. (1972) *Theologie van de bevrijding*, Baarn: Ten Have.

Haan, J. de and Sturm, J.E. (2000) "On the relationship between economic freedom and economic growth," *European Journal of Political Economy*, 16: 215–41.

Haan, R. (1985) *Economie van de eerbied, kanttekeningen bij het bijbelse spreken over geld en goed*, Delft: Meinema.

Hall, B. and Liebman, J. (1998) "Are CEOs really paid like bureaucrats?," *Quarterly Journal of Economics*, 113: 653–91.

Harrison, J.S. and Fiet, J.O. (1999) "New CEOs pursue their own self-interests by sacrificing stakeholder value," *Journal of Business Ethics*, 19: 301–8.

Hausman, D.M. (1992) *The inexact and separate science of economics*, Cambridge: Cambridge University Press.

Hausman, D.M. and McPherson, M.S. (1996) *Economic analysis and moral philosophy*, Cambridge: Cambridge University Press.

Henley, A. (2003) "Review: Happiness – has social science a clue?," *Christian Economists Journal*, 32: 37–8.

Henrich, J., Boyd, R., Bowles, S., Camerer, C., Gintis, H., and McElreath, R. (2001) "Cooperation, reciprocity and punishment in fifteen small scale societies," *American Economic Review*, 91: 73–8.

Hess, D. (2007) "Social reporting and new governance regulation: The prospects of achieving corporate accountability through transparency," *Business Ethics Quarterly*, 17: 453–76.

Hill, P.J. (1994) "Information, values and government action," in H. Schlossberg, V. Samuel and R.J. Sider (eds.), *Christianity and economics in the post-cold war era. The Oxford Declaration and beyond*, Grand Rapids, Mich.: William B. Eerdmans.

Hirsch, F. (1977) *Social limits to growth*, London: Routledge and Kegan Paul.

Hirschman, A.O. (1982) "Rival interpretations of market society: Civilizing, destructive or feeble?," *Journal of Economic Literature*, XX: 1463–84.

Hoeven, R. van de (2009) "Income distribution," in J. Peil and I. Van Staveren (eds.), *Handbook of Economic Ethics*, Cheltenham: Edward Elgar.

Höffner, J.C. (1983) *Christian social teaching*, Ordo Socialis, Bratislava: LUC.

Huntington, S.P. (1997) *The clash of civilizations and the remaking of world order*, London/New York: Touchstone Books.

Inglehart, R. (2000) "Globalization and postmodern values," *The Washington Quarterly*, 23: 215–28.

Iyengar, S.S. and Lepper, M.R. (2000) "When choice is demotivating: Can one desire too much of a good thing?," *Journal of Personality and Social Psychology*, 79: 995–1006.

Jacobs, B., de Mooij, R.A., and Folmer, C. (2006) "Vlaktaks en arbeidsparticipatie," in C.A. de Kam and A.P. Ros (eds.), *De vlaktaks. Naar een inkomstenbelasting met een uniform tarief?*, Willem Drees Stichting voor Openbare Financiën, The Hague: Van Deventer.

Jongeneel, R.A. (1996) *Economie van de barmhartigheid, een Christelijk-normatieve visie op de economie*, Kampen: Kok.

Jospe, R. (1997) "Sabbath, sabbatical and Jubilee: Jewish ethical perspectives," in H. Ucko (ed.), *The Jubilee challenge. Utopia or possibility? Jewish and Christian insights*, Geneva: World Council of Churches.

Kam, C.A. de and Pen, J. (2006) "Fiscale vervlakking is goed voor de rijken," in C.A. de Kam and A.P. Ros (eds.), *De vlaktaks. Naar een inkomstenbelasting met een uniform tarief?*, Willem Drees Stichting voor Openbare Financiën, The Hague: Van Deventer.

Kam, C.A. de and Ros, A.P. (2006a) "Een vlak tarief voor de polder?," in C.A. de Kam and A.P. Ros (eds.), *De vlaktaks. Naar een inkomstenbelasting met een uniform tarief?*, Willem Drees Stichting voor Openbare Financiën, The Hague: Van Deventer.

Kam, CA. de and Ros, A.P. (2006b) "Vlaktaks: lessen voor politici," in C.A. de Kam and A.P. Ros (eds.), *De vlaktaks. Naar een inkomstenbelasting met een uniform tarief?*, Willem Drees Stichting voor Openbare Financiën, The Hague: Van Deventer.

Kant, I. (1997) *Grundlegung zur metaphysik der sitten*, trans. T. Mertens, Amsterdam: Boom.

Keil, S.K., Reibstein, D., and Wittink, D.R. (2001) "The impact of business objectives and the time horizon of performance evaluation on pricing behavior," *International Journal of Research in Marketing*, 18: 67–81.

Kellenberger, J. (1980) "Religious faith and Prometheus," *Philosophy*, 55: 497–507.

Kenny, C. (1999) "Does growth cause happiness, or does happiness cause growth?," *Kyklos*, 52: 3–26.

Keynes, J.M. [1930] (1960) *Essays in persuasion*, London: Macmillan.

Klein, N. (2002) *No logo*, Rotterdam: Lemniscaat.

Klenicki, L. (1997) "Jewish understandings of sabbatical year and jubilee," in H. Ucko (ed.), *The Jubilee challenge. Utopia or possibility? Jewish and Christian insights*, Geneva: World Council of Churches.

Klundert, T. van de (2005) *Vormen van kapitalisme. markten, instituties en macht*, Utrecht: Lemma.

Knack, S. and Keefer, P. (1997) "Does social capital have an economic payoff? A cross-country investigation," *The Quarterly Journal of Economics*, 112: 1251–88.

Knight, F.H. (1923) "The ethics of competition," *Quarterly Journal of Economics*, 37: 579–624.

Knight, F.H. (1925) "Economic psychology and the value problem," *Quarterly Journal of Economics*, 34: 372–409.

Koehn, D. (1995) "A role for virtue ethics in the analysis of business practice," *Business Ethics Quarterly*, 5: 533–9.

Kreps, D.M. (1997) "The interaction between norms and economic incentives. Intrinsic motivation and extrinsic incentives," *American Economic Review*, 87: 359–64.

Kruijf, G.G. de (1999) *Christelijke ethiek. Een inleiding met sleutelteksten*, Zoetermeer: Meinema.

Kuyper, A. (1880) *Soevereiniteit in eigen kring*, Amsterdam: Kruyt.

Kynge, J. (2006) *China zet de wereld op z'n kop*, Amsterdam/Tielt: Nieuw Amsterdam/ Lannoo.

Landes, D.S. (1998) *The wealth and poverty of nations: Why some are so rich and some so poor*, translated by A. Abeling and P. Verhagen, Utrecht: Het Spectrum.

Laverty, K.J. (1996) "Economic 'short-termism': The debate, the unresolved issues, and the implications for management practice and research," *Academy of Management Review*, 21: 825–60.

Layard, R. (2003) "Happiness – has social science a clue?," Lionel Robbins Memorial Lectures 2002/3, Centre for Economic Performance, London School of Economics and Political Science, London.

Layard, R. (2005) *Happiness: Lessons from a new science*, New York: Penguin.

Leeuwen, A.Th. van (1984) *De Nacht van het Kapitaal. Door het oerwoud van de economie naar de bronnen van de burgerlijke religie*, Nijmegen: SUN.

Leeuwen, C. van (1956) *Sociaal besef in Israël*, Baarn: Bosch and Keuning.

Leeuwen, C. van (1975) "Het dier in de bijbelse wetten," Uitgave van de Werkgroep Kerk en Dierenbescherming, The Hague.

Lewis, C.S. (1974) *De grote scheiding*, Baarn: Ten Have.

Lindbeck, A. (1995) "Welfare state disincentives with endogenous habits and norms," OcfEB, Research Memorandum 9505.

Lindijer, C.H. (1981) *De armen en de rijken bij Lucas*, The Hague: Boekencentrum.

Loonstra, B. (2000) *Zo goed en zo kwaad: naar een ethiek van de Christelijke gemeente*, Zoetermeer: Boekencentrum.

Lucas, R.E. Jr. (2000) "Some macroeconomics for the 21st century," *Journal of Economic Perspectives*, 14: 159–68.

Luijk, H. van (1993) *Om redelijk gewin. Oefeningen in bedrijfsethiek*, Amsterdam: Boom.

McCloskey, D.N. (2006) *Bourgeois virtues: Ethics for an age of commerce*, Chicago: The University of Chicago Press.

MacIntyre, A. (1985) *After virtue. A study in moral theory*, London: Duckworth.

MacIntyre, A. (1995) *Marxism and Christianity*, London: Duckworth.

McKerlie, D. (2003) "Understanding egalitarianism," *Economics and Philosophy*, 19: 45–60.

Macneil, I. (1986) "Exchange revisited: Individual utility and social solidarity," *Ethics*, 96: 567–93.

McPherson, M., Smith-Lovin, L., and Brashears, M.E. (2006) "Social isolation in America: Changes in core discussion networks over two decades," *American Sociological Review*, 71: 353–75.

Maitland, I. (1997), "Virtuous markets. The market as school of virtues," *Business Ethics Quarterly*, 7: 17–33.

Major, V.S., Klein, K.J., and Ehrhart, M.G. (2002) "Work time, work interference with family and psychological distress," *Journal of Applied Psychology*, 87: 427–36.

Mandeville, B. (1714) *The fable of the bees: or, private vices, publick benefits*, www. xs4all.nl/~maartens/philosophy/mandeville/fable_of_bees.html.

Manenschijn, G. (1982) *Eigenbelang en christelijke ethiek. Rechtvaardigheid in een door belangen bepaalde samenleving*, Baarn: Ten Have.

Manenschijn, G. (1988) *Geplunderde aarde, getergde hemel. Ontwerp voor een christelijke milieu-ethiek*, Baarn: Ten Have.

Meeks, M.D. (1989) *God and the economist: The doctrine of God and political economy*, Minneapolis: Fortress Press.

Mian, A. and Sufi, A. (2008) "The consequences of mortgage credit expansion: evidence from the 2007 mortgage default crisis," NBER Working Paper.

Mick, D.G., Broniarczyk, S.M., and Haidt, J. (2004) "Choose, choose, choose, choose, choose, choose: Emerging and prospective research on the deleterious effects of living in consumer hyper choice," *Journal of Business Ethics*, 52: 207–11.

Milanovic, B. (2005) *Worlds apart: Measuring interregional and global inequality*, Princeton, NJ: Princeton University Press.

Mill, J.S. (1871) *Utilitarianism*, Oxford: Oxford University Press.

Monsma, G.N. (1999) "What is economic justice? A Christian economist's view," presentation at the Theological Symposium on Justice, April 22–23, 1999.

Moore, G. (2005) "Humanizing business: A modern virtue ethics approach," *Business Ethics Quarterly*, 15: 237–55.

Mott, S.C. (1994) "The partiality of biblical justice: A response to Calvin Beisner," in H. Schlossberg, V. Samuel, and R.J. Sider (eds.), *Christianity and economics in the post-cold war era. The Oxford declaration and beyond*, Grand Rapids, Mich.: William B. Eerdmans.

Murphy, L.B. (1998) "Institutions and the demands of justice," *Philosophy and Public Affairs*, 27: 251–91.

Musiolek, B. (1999) *Gezähmte Modemultis. Verhaltenskodizes: ein Modell zur Durchsetzung von Arbeitsrechten? Eine kritische Bilanz*, Frankfurt am Main: Brandes & Apsel/Südwind.

Noordegraaf, A., Kwakkel, G. Paas, S. Peels, H.G.L., and Zwiep, A.W. (2005) *Woordenboek voor bijbellezers*, Zoetermeer: Boekencentrum.

Norberg, J. (2002) *Till världskapitalismens försvar*, translated by B. de Koster, Antwerp/Amsterdam: Houtekiet.

Novak, M. (1982) *The spirit of democratic capitalism*, New York: Simon & Schuster.

Nozick, R. (1974) *Anarchy, state and utopia*, New York: Basic Books.

Opdebeeck, H. (1986) *Schumacher is beautiful. Het onmogelijke toch mogelijk?*, Kapellen/Kampen: Pelckmans/Kok Agora.

Orlitzky, M., Schmidt, F.L., and Rynes, S.L. (2003) "Corporate social and financial performance: A meta-analysis," *Organization Studies*, 24: 403–41.

Ovaska, T. and Takashima, R. (2006) "Economic policy and the level of self-perceived well-being: An international comparison," *Journal of Socio-Economics*, 35: 308–25.

Parfit, D. (1998) "Equality and priority," in A. Mason (ed.), *Ideals of equality*, Oxford: Blackwell.

Parijs, P. van (2003) "Difference principles," in S. Freeman (ed.), *The Cambridge companion to Rawls*, Cambridge: Cambridge University Press.

Peil, J. (1995) *Adam Smith en de economische wetenschap. Een methodologische herinterpretatie*, Tilburg: Tilburg University Press.

Persson, T. and Tabellini, G. (1994) "Is inequality harmful for growth?," *American Economic Review*, 84: 600–21.

Pew Research Center (2006) "Labor Day 2006," http://pewresearch.org.

Plato (1998) *Politeia*, Amsterdam: Athenaeum – Polak & Van Gennip.

Pogge, T. (2001) "Priorities of global justice," in T. Pogge (ed.), *Global justice*, Oxford: Blackwell Publishers.

Prahalad, C.K. (2006) *The fortune at the bottom of the pyramid. Eradicating poverty through profits*, Upper Saddle River, NJ: Wharton School Publishing.

Putman, R. (2000) *Bowling alone: The collapse and revival of American community*, New York: Simon & Schuster.

Rabin, M. (1998) "Psychology and economics," *Journal of Economic Literature*, XXXVI: 11–46.

Randers, J. and Meadows, D. (1971) "The carrying capacity of our global environment – a look at the ethical alternatives," in G. Chryssides and J.H. Kaler (1993) *An introduction to business ethics*, London: Chapman & Hall.

Ranis, G. and Stewart, F. (2005) "Dynamic links between the economy and human development," DESA Working Paper 8, United Nations, www.un.org/esa/desa/papers.

Rappaport, A. (2005) "The economics of short-term performance obsession," *Financial Analyst Journal*, 61: 65–79.

Rawls, J. (1999a) *A theory of justice (revised edition)*, Boston, Mass.: Harvard University Press.

Rawls, J. (1999b) *The law of peoples: With "The idea of public reason revisited,"* Boston, Mass.: Harvard University Press.

Rezaee, Z. (2005) "Causes, consequences, and deterrence of financial statements fraud," *Critical Perspectives on Accounting*, 16: 277–98.

Richardson, V.J. and Waegelein, J.F. (2002) "The influence of long-term performance plans on earnings management and firm performance," *Review of Quantitative Finance and Accounting*, 18: 161–83.

Robins, N. and Humphrey, L. (2000) *Sustaining the rag trade*, London: International Institute for Environment and Development.

Rodrik, D. (2002) "Feasible globalizations," NBER Working Paper 9129.

Rodrik, D., Subramanian, A., and Trebbi, F. (2002) "Institutional rule: The primacy of institutions over geography and integration in economic development," CEPR Discussion Paper series 3643.

Safranski, R. (1997) *Das Böse oder Das Drama der Freiheit*, Munich/Wenen: Calr Hanser Verlag.

Sahoo, A. (2008) "Essays on the Indian economy: Competitive pressure, productivity and performance," dissertation, Tilburg: Tilburg University.

Sala-i-Martin, X. (2006) "The world distribution of income: Falling poverty and convergence period," *The Quarterly Journal of Economics*, 121: 351–98.

Santa Ana, J. de (1977) *Good news to the poor: The challenge of the poor in the history of the church*, Geneva: World Council of Churches.

Scheffler, S. (1994) *The rejection of consequentialism*, revised edition, Oxford: Clarendon Press.

Schlossberg, H., Samuel, V., and Sider, R.J. (1994) *Christianity and economics in the post-cold war era. The Oxford declaration and beyond*, Grand Rapids, Mich.: William B. Eerdmans.

Schor, J.B. (1997) *Beyond an economy of work and spend*, Tilburg: Tilburg University Press.

Schumpeter, J.A. (1976) *Capitalism, socialism and democracy*, fifth edition, London/Boston: George Allen & Unwin.

Schwartz, B. (2004) *The paradox of choice*, New York: HarperCollins.

Scully, G.W. (2002) "Economic freedom, government policy and the trade-off between equity and economic growth," *Public Choice*, 113: 77–96.

Segelod, E. (2000) "A comparison of managers' perceptions of short-termism in Sweden and the U.S.," *International Journal of Production Economics*, 63: 243–54.

Seligman, M.E.P. (2002) *Authentic happiness: Using the new positive psychology to realize your potential for lasting fulfillment*, New York: Free Press.

Sen, A. (1977) "Rational fools: A critique on the behavioral foundations of economic theory," *Philosophy and Public Affairs*, 6: 317–44.

Sen, A. (1981) "Ethical issues in income distribution: national and international," in S. Grassman and E. Lundberg (eds.), *The world economic order: Past and prospects*, London: Macmillan.

Sen, A.K. (1984) *Resources, values and development*, Oxford: Blackwell.

Sen, A. (1987) *On ethics and economics*, Oxford: Blackwell.

Sennet, R. (1998) *The corrosion of character,: The personal consequences in the new capitalism*, New York: Norton.

Shaw, P. (1992) "Rawls, the lexical difference principle and equality," *The Philosophical Quarterly*, 42: 71–7.

Shleifer, A. (2004) "Does competition destroy ethical behavior?," *The American Economic Review*, 94: 414–18.

Shue, H. (1996) *Basic rights. Subsistence, affluence and U.S. foreign policy*, second edition, Princeton, NJ: Princeton University Press.

Sider, R.J. (1977) *Rich Christians in an age of hunger*, translated by W. Offers, Hoornaar: Gideon.

Sider, R.J. (1997) "Evaluating the triumph of the market," in H. Ucko (ed.), *The Jubilee challenge. Utopia or possibility? Jewish and Christian Insights*, Geneva: World Council of Churches.

Singer, P. (1972) "Famine, affluence and morality," *Philosophy and Public Affairs*, 3: 229–43.

Skillen, J.W. (1998) *Caring for creation. Responsible stewardship of God's handiwork*, Grand Rapids, Mich.: Baker Books.

Skreta, V. and Veldkam, L. (2009) "Ratings shopping and asset complexity: A theory of ratings inflation," New York University, Stern School of Business, February.

Slaughter, M.J. (1997) "Per capita income convergence and the role of international trade," *American Economic Review*, 87: 194–200.

Smith, Adam (1759) *The theory of moral sentiments*, New York: Prometheus Books.

Smith, Adam (1776) *Inquiry into the nature and causes of the wealth of nations*, New York: Prometheus Books.

Soggin, J.A. (1993) *An introduction to the history of Israel and Judah*, London: SCM Press.

Solnick, S.J. and Hemenway, D. (1998) "Is more always better? A survey on positional concerns," *Journal of Economic Behavior & Organization*, 37: 373–83.

Solomon, N. (1997) "Economics of the Jubilee," in H. Ucko (ed.), *The Jubilee challenge. Utopia or possibility? Jewish and Christian insights*, Geneva: World Council of Churches.

Solomon, R.C. (1992) "Corporate roles, personal virtues: An Aristotelean approach to business ethics," *Business Ethics Quarterly*, 2: 317–39.

Stackhouse, M.L., McCann, D.P., Roels, S.J., and Williams, P.N. (eds.) (1995) *On moral business. Classical and contemporary resources for ethics in economic life*, Grand Rapids, Mich.: Eerdmans.

Stevenson, B. and Wolfers, J. (2008) "Economic growth and subjective well being. Reassessing the Easterlin paradox," NBER Working Paper 14282.

Stiglitz, J. (2002) *Globalization and its discontents*, New York: Norton.

Storkey, A. (2006) "Consumeren is meer dan verbruiken: Interview door R. Jongeneel," *Beweging*, 70: 24–9.

Stott, J. (1990) *Issues facing Christians today*, Londen: Marshall Morgan and Scott.

Sturm, J.E. and Haan, J. de (2001) "How robust is the relationship between economic freedom and economic growth?," *Applied Economics*, 33: 839–44.

Südwind (Südwind Institute für Okonomie und Okumene) (2000) *Das Kreuz mit dem Faden*, 11, Siegberg.

Titmuss, R. (1970) *The gift relationship. From human blood to social policy*, London: Allen & Unwin.

Trevino, L.K. and Nelson, K.A. (2004) *Managing business ethics. Straight talk about how to do it right*, Hoboken: John Wiley & Sons.

Tungodden, B. (2003) "The value of equality," *Economics and Philosophy*, 19: 1–44.

UN (United Nations) (2005) "Investing in development. A practical plan to achieve the millennium development goals, overview," www.unmilleniumproject.org.

UN (United Nations) (2006) *World economic and social survey*, www.un.org/esa/policy/wess/index.html.

UN (United Nations) (2007) The millennium development goals report 2007, New York.

Uslaner, E.M. (2002) *The moral foundations of trust*, Cambridge: Cambridge University Press.

Vallentyne, P. (2002) "Brute luck, option luck, and equality of initial opportunities," *Ethics*, 112: 529–57.

Vaux, R. de (1989) *Hoe het oude Israel leefde*, Part I, fifth edition, The Hague: Boeken-centrum.

Velasquez, M.G. (1998) *Business ethics. Concepts and cases*, fourth edition, Upper Saddle River, NJ: Prentice Hall.

Ven, B.W. van de and Jeurissen, R.M.J. (2005) "Competing responsibility," *Business Ethics Quarterly*, 15: 299–318.

Ven, J. van de (2003) *Psychological sentiments and economic behaviour*, Tilburg: CentER/Tilburg University.

Verbrugge, A. (2004) *Tijd van onbehagen. Filosofische essays over een cultuur op drift*, Amsterdam: Sun.

Verstraeten, J. (2005) "Solidariteit in de Katholieke traditie," in E. de Jong and M. Buijsen (eds.), *Solidariteit onder druk? Over de grens tussen individuele en collectieve verantwoordelijkheid*, Nijmegen: Valkhof Pers.

Vogel, Th.J. and Lobo, G.J. (2002) "Impact of adoption of long-term performance plans on financial analysts' long-term forecasts," *Review of Quantitative Finance and Accounting*, 19: 291–306.

Wade, J.B., O'Reilly, C.A., and Pollock, T.G. (2006) "Overpaid CEO's and underpaid managers: Fairness and executive compensation," *Organization Science*, 17: 527–44.

Waide, J. (1987) "The making of self and world in advertising," *Journal of Business Ethics*, 6: 73–9.

Wall, S. (2003) "Just savings and the difference principle," *Philosophical Studies*, 116: 79–102.

Wallis, C. (2005) "The new science of happiness," *Time*, January 17.

Winters, L.A., McCulloch, N., and McKay, A. (2004) "Trade policy and poverty: The evidence so far," *Journal of Economic Literature*, XLII: 72–115.

Wogaman, J.P. (1993) *Christian ethics, a historical introduction*, London: SPCK.

Wolterstorff, N. (1987) "The bible and economics: The hermeneutical issues," *Transformation*, 4: 11–19.

World Bank (2006) *World Development Report 2006*, Washington DC: World Bank.

World Commission on Environment and Development (1987) *Our common future*, Oxford: Oxford University Press.

Wright, C.J.H. (1983) *Living as the people of God, the relevance of Old Testament ethics*, Leicester: Inter-Varsity Press.

Zak, P.J. and Knack, S. (2001) "Trust and growth," *Economic Journal*, 111: 295–321.

Register of Bible texts

Gen. 1:26–30 66, 81
Gen. 2:15–17 25
Gen. 3:17–19 20
Gen. 9: 8–12 2, 158n3
Gen. 15:3 67
Gen. 23:4 79
Gen. 24:34–5 22
Exod. 2: 22 79
Exod. 12:43–49 67
Exod. 16:13–18 161n7, 72, 78
Exod. 20:10 67, 69, 79
Exod. 20:15 *70*
Exod. 20:17 101
Exod. 21:2 66
Exod. 21:16 66
Exod. 21:20–21 67
Exod. 22:1 18
Exod. 22:4–7 69, 81
Exod. 22:21–27 66, 67, 72, 79
Exod. 23:3,6 68, *70*
Exod. 23:9 66, 67, 79
Exod. 23:10–12 67, 71, 79, 80
Exod. 31:2 162n10
Lev. 5:14–16 69
Lev. 6:1–5 69
Lev. 17:10–17 81
Lev. 19:9–11 69, *70*, 71, 79
Lev. 19:13 72
Lev. 19:15 68, *70*

Lev. 19:33–4–5–6 67, *70, 79*
Lev. 22:14 69
Lev. 22:28 81
Lev. 23:22 79
Lev. 24:22 79
Lev. 25:8–22 73
Lev. 25:6 79
Lev. 25:10 66
Lev. 25:35–37 72
Lev. 25:38–46 66, 67, 79, 67
Lev. 25:53vv 67
Lev. 27:30 71
Num. 5:5–8 69
Num. 6:24 25
Num. 18:21 71
Num. 35:15 79
Deut. 1:16 79
Deut. 4:40 20
Deut. 5:13–15 67, 79, 81
Deut. 5:16 20
Deut. 8:11–18 23
Deut. 10:17–19 79, 71
Deut. 12:6 71
Deut. 12:12,19 67
Deut. 14:22–29 71, 79
Deut. 15:3–4 21, 80
Deut. 15:7–11 71
Deut. 15:13–14 72
Deut. 15:15 67
Deut. 15:18 67
Deut. 16:11 72

Deut. 16:19 68
Deut. 19:11–13 18
Deut. 20:19 80
Deut. 22:4–7
Deut. 23:19–20 72, 80, 161n6
Deut. 23:24 vv. 71
Deut. 24:6–7 73, 66
Deut. 24:10–13
Deut. 24:14–15 72, 79
Deut. 24:16–22 66, 71, 79
Deut. 25:4–10 81
Deut. 26:12–16 69, *70*, 71, 79
Deut. 27:19 79
Deut. 30:19 2
1 Kings 5:13 69
1 Kings 18:1
Job 3:19 66
Job 13:10 68
Job 24:2 69, *70*
Job 31:13–15 66
Ps. 22:17 159n4
Ps. 24:1–2 2, 25
Ps. 35:10 69, *70*
Ps. 72:4 69
Ps. 72:12–13 72
Ps. 74:21 69
Ps. 82:3 69
Ps. 109:31 69
Ps. 127:2 162n5
Ps. 146:7–9 68, 71

Index

eBooks – at www.eBookstore.tandf.co.uk

A library at your fingertips!

eBooks are electronic versions of printed books. You can store them on your PC/laptop or browse them online.

They have advantages for anyone needing rapid access to a wide variety of published, copyright information.

eBooks can help your research by enabling you to bookmark chapters, annotate text and use instant searches to find specific words or phrases. Several eBook files would fit on even a small laptop or PDA.

NEW: Save money by eSubscribing: cheap, online access to any eBook for as long as you need it.

Annual subscription packages

We now offer special low-cost bulk subscriptions to packages of eBooks in certain subject areas. These are available to libraries or to individuals.

For more information please contact webmaster.ebooks@tandf.co.uk

We're continually developing the eBook concept, so keep up to date by visiting the website.

www.eBookstore.tandf.co.uk